Ethnic Party Bans in Africa

In Sub-Saharan Africa, the spread of democracy since the 1990s has been accompanied by the proliferation of bans on ethnic political parties. A majority of constitutions in the region explicitly prohibit political parties to organize on the basis of race, ethnicity, religion, region and other socio-cultural attributes. More than a hundred political parties have been dissolved, suspended or denied registration on these grounds. This book documents the experience with ethnic party bans in Africa, traces its origins, examines its record, and answers the question whether ethnic party bans are an effective and legitimate instrument in the prevention of ethnic conflict.

This book was published as a special issue of *Democratization*.

Matthijs Bogaards is professor of Political Science at Jacobs University, Bremen, Germany. In 2001 he was awarded the Frank Cass prize for the best article in volume 7 of *Democratization* (2000) and has published an article entitled 'Where to Draw the Line? From Degree to Dichotomy in Measures of Democracy' in the same journal (2012). His primary research interests include democratization, electoral systems and divided societies.

Matthias Basedau is head of the research programme at the GIGA German Institute of Global and Area Studies and deputy of the director at the GIGA Institute of African Affairs, Hamburg, Germany. He has published numerous articles related to African politics, including 'Do Religious Factors impact armed conflict? Evidence from Sub-Saharan Africa', in *Terrorism and Political Violence* (2011, with Georg Strüver, Johannes Vüllers and Tim Wegenast).

Christof Hartmann is professor of Political Science at University Duisburg-Essen, Germany. His key research areas include reform of political institutions, democratization, and regional integration in Sub-Saharan Africa. He has also advised on behalf of various political foundations and electoral commissions.

Ethnic Party Bans in Africa

Edited by
Matthijs Bogaards, Matthias Basedau and Christof Hartmann

Routledge
Taylor & Francis Group
LONDON AND NEW YORK

First published 2013
by Routledge
2 Park Square, Milton Park, Abingdon, Oxfordshire OX14 4RN

Simultaneously published in the USA and Canada
by Routledge
711 Third Avenue, New York, NY 10017

First issued in paperback 2015

Routledge is an imprint of the Taylor & Francis Group, an informa business

© 2013 Taylor & Francis

This book is a reproduction of *Democratization*, vol. 17, issue 4. The Publisher requests to those authors who may be citing this book to state, also, the bibliographical details of the special issue on which the book was based.

Trademark notice: Product or corporate names may be trademarks or registered trademarks, and are used only for identification and explanation without intent to infringe.

British Library Cataloguing in Publication Data
A catalogue record for this book is available from the British Library

ISBN 13: 978-1-138-94649-1 (pbk)
ISBN 13: 978-0-415-62363-6 (hbk)

Typeset in Times New Roman
by Taylor & Francis Books

Publisher's Note
The publisher would like to make readers aware that the chapters in this book may be referred to as articles as they are identical to the articles published in the special issue. The publisher accepts responsibility for any inconsistencies that may have arisen in the course of preparing this volume for print.

Contents

Citation Information

The chapters in this book were originally published in *Democratization*, volume 17, issue 4 (August 2010). When citing this material, please use the original page numbering for each article, as follows:

Chapter 1
Ethnic party bans in Africa: an introduction
Matthijs Bogaards, Matthias Basedau and Christof Hartmann
Democratization, volume 17, issue 4 (August 2010) pp. 599-617

Chapter 2
Party bans in Africa – an empirical overview
Anika Moroff
Democratization, volume 17, issue 4 (August 2010) pp. 618-641

Chapter 3
Understanding variations in party bans in Africa
Christof Hartmann and Jörg Kemmerzell
Democratization, volume 17, issue 4 (August 2010) pp. 642-665

Chapter 4
An effective measure of institutional engineering? Ethnic party bans in Africa
Anika Moroff and Matthias Basedau
Democratization, volume 17, issue 4 (August 2010) pp. 666-686

Chapter 5
Why there is no party ban in the South African constitution
Jörg Kemmerzell
Democratization, volume 17, issue 4 (August 2010) pp. 687-708

Chapter 6
Political party bans in Rwanda 1994–2003: three narratives of justification
Peter Niesen
Democratization, volume 17, issue 4 (August 2010) pp. 709-729

Ethnic party bans in Africa: an introduction

Matthijs Bogaards[a], Matthias Basedau[b] and Christof Hartmann[c]

[a]School of Humanities and Social Sciences, Jacobs University, Bremen, Germany; [b]GIGA Institute of African Affairs, Hamburg, Germany; [c]Institute of Political Science, University of Duisburg-Essen, Duisburg, Germany

During the 1990s the number of African states allowing multiparty elections increased dramatically. Paradoxically, this has been accompanied in the majority of countries by legal bans on ethnic and other particularistic parties. The main official reason has been the aim of preventing the politicization of ethnicity as this is feared to lead to ethnic conflict and political instability. Despite the resurgent interest in institutional engineering, this phenomenon has received little scholarly attention. This contribution outlines the main research questions and preliminary answers of a collaborative research project which combines large and small N comparisons and case studies. Bans are relatively rarely enforced and the decision actually to ban parties is best explained by the interaction of an experience of ethnic violence in the past and hybrid regimes using these measures to restrict political party competition. Positive effects on democracy and conflict management seem generally limited and are context dependent.

During the 1990s the number of African states[1] holding multiparty elections increased dramatically. Paradoxically, the spread of democracy and the extension of political rights in sub-Saharan Africa has been accompanied in the majority of countries by legal bans on, among others, religious, ethnic, regional, and linguistic parties. The main official reason for such party bans has been the aim of preventing the politicization of ethnicity as this is feared to lead to ethnic conflict and political instability. In Africa, parties are not allowed to organize on the basis of a wide variety of socio-cultural differences, including, in alphabetical order, brotherhood, clan, community, ethnicity, gender, language, race, region, religion, sect, social condition, social or economic status, and tribe. For example, the Constitution of Burkina Faso of 1997 outlaws parties or any 'political organization' which are 'tribalist, regionalist, religious, or racist' (article 13). The Political Parties Act in Kenya, adopted in 2007, denies registration to any party 'founded on an ethnic, age, tribal, racial, gender, regional, linguistic, corporatistic, professional or religious basis or which seeks to engage in propaganda based on any of these matters' (Art. 14). Already, in 1979, the Nigerian constitution had stipulated that political parties had to reflect the 'federal character' of this highly diverse country. As these party bans embrace more than ethnic groups in a narrow sense, we either have to employ a broad notion of 'ethnic party' in which ethnicity refers to any perceptible inherited social characteristic[2] or use the generic term of 'particularistic parties'. This term was first employed by Coleman to designate parties 'having an ethnic, racial or tribal basis'.[3]

Ethnic party bans can be found in a country's constitution, electoral law, law on political parties, or law on voluntary associations, and they can be administered by administrative decree and/or review by a judicial process.[4] The aim is invariably the same: to keep ethnicity out of (party) politics. A particularly good example can be found in the Constitution of Sierra Leone from 1991. Article 35(5) denies registration as a political party on the following grounds. First, when 'membership or leadership of the party is restricted to members of any particular tribal or ethnic groups or religious faith'. Second, in case 'the name, symbol, colour or motto of the party has exclusive or particular significance or connotation to members of any particular tribal or ethnic group or religious faith'. Third, when 'the party is formed for the sole purpose of securing or advancing the interests and welfare of a particular tribal or ethnic group, community, geographical area or religious faith'. Fourth, in case 'the party does not have a registered office in each of the Provincial Headquarter towns and the Western Area'.[5]

Surprisingly, the unprecedented scale of ethnic party bans in Africa has received little attention from international organizations, donors, non-governmental organizations, and scholars. This can be partly explained by a more general lack of interest in party bans, even in established Western democracies.[6] To our knowledge, to date there has been no research on party bans in Africa, their origin, their implementation, their effects on party competition and their success in preventing ethnic conflict. Nor has the place of ethnic party bans in democratic theory been scrutinized.

In light of the history of ethnic conflict in Africa the leading question of this special issue is: Are party bans an effective instrument in preventing and managing ethnic conflict in Africa and at what cost to democracy? This main question translates into four sub-questions:

(1) Which empirical phenomena might be defined as party bans and which main types of party bans do exist? How many countries have introduced legal provisions to ban parties and how many have actually enforced them?

(2) Why have so many new democratic regimes in Africa adopted party bans? And which variables explain that other countries did not? Why have some countries made use of these legal provisions while others have not?

(3) What are the effects of formal bans? To what extent are formal and actual bans on ethnic parties an effective instrument in ethnic conflict management and the promotion of democracy?

(4) Given that party bans pose limits to political liberty, how can their existence be squared with the democratic aspirations of new or consolidated constitutional regimes? What are the strategies used and legitimations adduced in order to integrate party bans with the democratic self-understanding of the respective polities?

This special issue on 'Ethnic Party Bans in Africa' is a first attempt to provide answers to these questions. The contributions collected here come out of a collaborative research project, 'Managing Ethnic Conflict Through Institutional Engineering: Ethnic Party Bans in Africa'.[7] The various contributions by the project members present original data on legal-constitutional party bans in the new multiparty electoral regimes of sub-Saharan Africa, creating the first-ever inventory of party bans and their implementation in Africa. The research questions formulated above are addressed at both a comparative level with regard to all sub-Saharan countries, and through five in-depth case studies.

Background

The wave of democratization that has engulfed African countries since the early 1990s has been characterized by the establishment of or return to multiparty politics. This mostly happened in political systems with a long history of *de facto* and *de jure* constraints on the ability of political parties to function effectively. While few countries continue to deny the principle and legitimacy of a pluralistic organization of political associations and parties, many political parties still face insurmountable obstacles in creating a level playing field and have to cope with legal and administrative provisions that severely restrict their free operation.

In recent years many aspects of these phenomena have been theoretically and empirically analysed by students and practitioners, especially the role of political parties during elections and electoral campaigns and aspects of party organization and finance. Quite surprisingly, the more basic problem of banning specific categories of political parties has been neglected in previous research although a preliminary overview of provisions in African countries shows how widespread these practices are: In a large number of African states, ethnic, religious and regional parties are illegal. A Christian democratic party like the German Christian Democratic Union (CDU) or a Christian and regional party like the Bavarian Christian Social Union (CSU) would not be allowed to register as a party and compete in elections in many African democracies today. While democratization is normally equated with multiparty politics, in Africa an explicit exception is made frequently for parties based on clan, community, ethnicity, faith, gender, language, region, race, sect and tribe.

In light of the prevalence of party bans in contemporary Africa, it is surprising how little attention has been paid to this phenomenon. To our knowledge, there exists no research on party bans in Africa, their origins, practice or effects. No attempt has been made to explain the adoption of party bans by so many new democracies in the region. Nor has the question been raised whether party bans are compatible with democracy and whether the *a priori* prohibition of political organization of meaningful socio-cultural differences does not undermine the democratic legitimacy of the new party systems. Ethnic and religious party bans are not an exclusively sub-Saharan African phenomenon, of course. They have been imposed in several countries in post-communist Eastern Europe,[8] have been inserted into the new constitutions of Middle Eastern countries and Afghanistan, and have been enforced with far-reaching consequences in Mediterranean countries such as Turkey and Algeria. However, the African continent is unique in the widespread use of party bans.

The main research problem of gaining a better understanding of ethnic party bans can be divided into the four distinct questions outlined above that guided our research program.

There is first an urgent need to get a proper understanding of the concept of party ban, to make sense of the empirical variety of legal bases, the extent of bans, their target, and to elaborate a typology that is necessary for further investigation. This special issue focuses on direct legal-constitutional party bans. In addition, it looks at indirect tools of party regulation such as registration requirements. We have also to understand the actual implementation of party bans. To what extent are rules about party bans enforced? Do they serve mainly ceremonial or symbolic purposes? In other words, how many parties have been banned under this type of legislation? What kind of parties have been banned and under what circumstances? And what happened next? Did these parties disband, reform, or join other political forces? Was the party ban accepted or contested? In case the matter went to court, is there jurisprudence?

Secondly, there can also be various reasons behind the introduction of party bans or the change of relevant provisions over time. How can we explain that so many new democracies introduce party bans or specific types of party bans while others allow for the free articulation and political representation of all social interests? Are there certain systematic patterns which can be discovered, such as previous experience with ethnic parties, or a history of ethnic conflict? And how did previous rules concerning party regulation shape the current provisions? Do we identify path-dependent development as previous experience with multiparty politics has shaped the institutions of party regulation and the expectations of various actors? Is it true that 'the most extensive bans on parties can be found in the least democratic countries'?[9]

A third major research question refers to the impact of both the legal provisions and the actually implemented party bans. To what extent are ethnic party bans having any impact on political and social outcomes? Do they promote inter-ethnic/religious harmony, political stability and the consolidation of fragile new

democratic dispensations? Or is ethnicity more powerfully regulated by other institutions (such as electoral or governmental systems) and variables? Whether party
bans do serve socially optimal outcomes is, however, a question which can be
empirically tested. There is little doubt that in some cases party bans are used as
one element on the 'menu of manipulation' in the hands of self-serving elites.[10]
Clearly, much depends on how countries implement ethnic party bans.

Finally, we need a more thorough understanding of the normative aspects of
party regulation. What kind of normative resources does the institutionalization
of party bans in Africa draw on? What are the arguments put forward in the drafting process of new constitutions? What are the rationales put forward by the
elites? More specifically, to what extent do those resources and arguments
appear compatible with basic tenets of democratic theory? Do political actors
notice a conflict between the ideals of democratic self-government and full political liberty on the one hand and the notion of a party ban on the other? And,
which recommendations can be derived from the contemporary experience of
emerging African democracies? Which should be the normative criteria upon
which any institutional engineering of party regulation in African countries
should be based?

Ethnicity, party politics, and institutional engineering

For decades, both scholars and practitioners have been concerned with the risks of
multiparty politics in the mostly multi-ethnic societies of Africa. Already around
the time of decolonization, it was noted how 'in the electoral struggle candidates
find it advantageous, if not necessary, to manipulate local issues in order to establish the most secure political base possible, which is normally their tribal, communal, or religious group of origin'.[11] In this view democratization and multiparty
politics together spell the politicization of ethnicity, yet there is little systematic
empirical account of ethnic parties since the re-emergence of pluralist party politics
in the 48 sub-Saharan African countries since the early 1990s. Gunther and
Diamond write about 'ethnicity-based parties' distinguished by their political
and electoral logics: 'the principal goal of the ethnic party is not any universalistic
program or platform, but rather to secure material, cultural, and political benefits
and protections for the ethnic group in its competition with other groups'.[12] The
electoral logic of an ethnic party is 'to harden and mobilize its ethnic base with
exclusive, often polarizing appeals to ethnic group opportunity and threat ...
electoral mobilization is not intended to attract additional sectors of society to
support it'.[13] There has so far been little theoretical and empirical research
trying to apply these concepts to sub-Saharan Africa and to understand the
logics behind the emergence of such ethnic parties, or the specific consequences
for the dynamics of the party systems.[14] However, several recent studies, mostly
drawing on representative survey polls, have questioned the idea that almost all
African parties are primarily ethnic.[15] Apparently, ethnicity as a base of party preference is less strong and frequent than assumed, suggesting that other social

determinants such as education and urban residence as well as rational choice elements (e.g. satisfaction with the government) are important.

Trends towards the political organization of ethnicity were and are still seen by many scholars and practitioners as undesirable, for several reasons.[16] First, in case of a majority ethnic group, ethnic politics is likely to lead to the political, social, cultural and economic suppression and exclusion of minorities. Second, to counter a majoritarian tendency of a dominant ethnic majority or majority coalition, ethnic minorities may resort to non-democratic and even violent means to protect their interests. Ultimately, this may lead to the minority establishing its own repressive, non-democratic regime against the majority. Third, irrespective of the particular constellation of ethnic groups in a society, ethnic politics is likely to raise the stakes of the political game, fanning emotions and increasing the likelihood of disturbances of public order, witness the experience with communal riots. Fourth, ethnic political parties entrench societal divisions and serve to keep people apart in their own groups instead of bringing people together in pursuit of the common good. In sum, the politicization of ethnicity in Africa is associated with ethnic conflict; ethnic violence in the form of human rights violations, repression, civil war, and even genocide; political instability; democratic erosion; and the establishment of non-democratic regimes.[17] Unfortunately, there are many instances in the more recent African political history to demonstrate the perils of ethnic politics: witness how ethnic violence followed democratization attempts in Burundi and Rwanda.[18]

Institutional engineering is one answer to these risks. Institutional engineering denotes the design of (formal) institutions such as electoral systems, party laws or to prevent state institutions conflict or promote democracy. The central question is: 'Can constitutions of divided or plural societies be engineered to help bring about inter-communal accommodation and strengthened democracy?'[19] Post-independence Africa has a long history of such 'institutional engineering' and experimentation with institutional design. Many students of African politics question the relevance of formal rules and institutions and stress the extent to which the dynamics of the political process and the behaviour of actors are effectively shaped by informal institutions.[20] Constitution-makers and political engineers have nevertheless persisted in their attempt to revise and manipulate formal institutions and the international scholarship has contributed recommendations about the design of alternatives as well as empirical evidence about their likely consequences.[21] Scholars interested more specifically in the management of ethnic conflict have analysed the role of selected institutions such as electoral systems,[22] federalism,[23] and decentralization.[24] The significance of party regulation, and party bans in particular has, however, so far attracted little interest within this debate.[25]

Ethnic party bans are best understood and analysed as part of a broader repertoire of institutional choices that can be classified on the basis of the answer to the following question: What role should the party system play as an intermediary between society and politics? In a divided society, three functions of the party system can be distinguished: blocking, aggregation, and translation. The party system can *block* the political organization of socio-cultural cleavages, it can *aggregate* socio-cultural divisions into broader formations, or it can *translate* societal differences into political cleavages.[26] Depending on the kind of party system a polity deems desirable, it can use the electoral system and party regulation to create incentives for blocking, most prominently through ethnic party bans, for aggregation, through electoral systems such as the alternative vote and through spatial distribution requirements, or for translation, through an electoral system like proportional representation. It is going too far to say that 'the most overt marker of a coercively assimilationist state is the illegalization of minority nationalist, ethnic and communal parties'.[27] The rationale for ethnic party bans in Africa is to keep ethnicity out of politics (blocking), not assimilation into a dominant culture. This is what we call a 'negative ethnic party ban'. And where spatial distribution requirements are adopted that require parties to be nationally active and representative, what we call a 'positive ethnic party ban' the aim clearly is integration or aggregation. Whereas negative party bans seek to remove ethnicity from politics, positive party bans provide parties with an incentive to organize across communal boundaries.

Party bans and democracy: normative aspects

Traditionally, research into bans on political associations within constitutional and normative political theory has been conducted against the backdrop of the European experience with two versions of totalitarianism. The concept of militant democracy was coined to cover fascism and communism as the two main challenges to democratic rule.[28] Militant democracy refers to a form of constitutional democracy authorized to protect civil and political freedom by pre-emptively restricting its exercise, via for instance banning extremist parties that threaten the survival of democracy. In its most ambitious constitutional constructions, militant democracy was symmetrically directed against political totalitarianism from the right and the left. It is characteristic for the anti-totalitarian understanding of party bans that it does not depend on violent behaviour nor its advocacy on the part of political actors, but is directed against the threat of a 'legal' anti-democratic takeover of the state apparatus.[29] This is why, although most commentators state that party bans within democracies constitute a lasting 'dilemma', 'paradox', or 'antinomy', constitutional theory has found restrictions on anti-system parties on the whole to be compatible with democratic government.[30] Still, the overall compatibility with democratic rule and the rule of law requires that stringent justifications be given for any infringement of political liberty. In today's established democracies, where neither neo-fascist nor neo-communist parties pose credible threats of a takeover of the political system, party bans have faced much criticism for their lack of effectiveness, their lack of democratic legitimacy[31] and their lack of political wisdom.[32]

Obviously, the traditional European perspective on party bans, that of anti-fascist and anti-communist militant democracy, will be of only limited help if applied to the major developments in Africa's context. However, recent developments and research on European party bans have increasingly broadened and/or corrected our understanding of militant democracy's standard anti-totalitarian rationale. Although bans on ethnic parties have not been central to these developments, some major trends in the recent history of (research on) party bans can be identified which should contribute to a more helpful heuristic for the African context.[33] These concern the fight against Islamist extremism, against regionalism/secessionism, or against the supporters of terrorism. They reflect an awareness of the symbolic role that party bans play within a politics of memory and, more generally, the political identity of a democratic collective.

Outline of this special issue

The contributions to this special issue on ethnic party bans in sub-Saharan Africa are grouped into two clusters, one with general and comparative contributions, and the other with case studies.

Laying the descriptive foundations for the special issue, Anika Moroff's contribution gives a systematic empirical overview of ethnic and other party bans in Africa. The article draws on and presents a newly compiled, extensive and unique data inventory on party bans in sub-Saharan Africa.[34] This database includes information on both prevalence and actual implementation of party bans. The first part deals with the legal and written sources of party bans, and finds that only few countries – mostly Anglophone African countries with longstanding multiparty systems – do not have such provisions. Altogether, nearly 40 out of sub-Saharan Africa's 48 countries have the legal option to ban 'particularistic' parties. Regarding the legally possible reasons for 'particularistic' party bans, the respective provisions mostly ban religion (90% of legal sources), ethnicity/tribe (83%), and region (88%) as identity bases of political parties. Particularistic party bans do not only generally outlaw identity based political parties but often mention particular features of bans such as the organization, the programme, the membership, party symbol, and electoral campaigns. Looking at the general mode of party bans – with reference to the distinction between aggregation, blocking and translation – a combination of blocking and aggregation is the most popular option. While only six countries allow 'translation' and abstain from banning parties (e.g. Botswana, Comoros, Mauritius, South Africa, Zambia and Zimbabwe), 15 rely on the purely 'negative' prohibition. Twenty-five out of 46 countries with multiparty systems combine the principal 'negative' ban with the 'aggregative' provision that political parties have to prove a national character.

While it is common to have party bans on the statutes throughout Africa, implementation is not. Since 1990, overall 12 countries have banned 138 particularistic parties. There were 112 denials of registration, 25 dissolutions, and one suspension. Most bans were enforced in Angola, Nigeria, and Tanzania; Mauritania and Rwanda also banned several parties. Some results about implementation procedures of party bans in Africa seem particularly noteworthy. First, in 23 out of 43 countries a party ban was implemented, and 12 out of 41 countries banned particularistic parties. While these numbers might seem low, they are nevertheless much higher than expected given the low regulatory capacity of many African states. Second, only some of the possible reasons to ban a party have been invoked with a clear bias on regionalism (121 cases), ethnicity (9) and religion (7). While one party was banned for its racist character, no party based on language, or colour has ever been banned as far as we know. Most parties were banned because they could not prove their national character. However, compared to the number of countries that require national representation, only few parties were banned for lack of national character.

In a second step we move to an analysis of the introduction and enforcement of party bans. The contribution by Christof Hartmann and Jörg Kemmerzell is thus less interested in the effects of party bans than in their origins and the reasons for their variation. The main questions in their contribution are why so few countries did not introduce legal provisions to ban parties and why only few of the many African countries with legal provisions actually implemented party bans. According to the authors a set of structural conditions can best explain these patterns. The authors use Qualitative Comparative Analysis to compare the introduction of party bans and the likelihood of implementation across all sub-Saharan countries. Their analysis shows that the few African countries which did not introduce legal provisions to ban political parties combine a British colonial background and a stronger tradition of multiparty democracy. The decision to actually use these provisions is best explained by the interaction of two other conditions. In the context of an experience of ethnically motivated violence in the past hybrid regimes rely on such measures to restrict political party competition. Among the 12 'implementing countries' Namibia is the only country to be rated 'free' by Freedom House. Regime type seems thus to matter a lot for the likelihood that a government will actually ban particularistic parties.

In their contribution on the effects of ethnic party bans in Africa, Anika Moroff and Matthias Basedau raise the question whether ethnic party bans in Africa are an effective measure of institutional engineering. The first part of the contribution engages in a theoretical discussion about how particularistic party bans may affect democracy and inter-communal conflict, showing that numerous hypotheses can be developed. Such hypotheses refer to general contextual conditions and the exact technical elements but are also partly mirroring the debate between consociationalists and integrationists. 'Integrationist' scholars expect that the politicization of ethnicity will be harmful to both democracy and peace. Accordingly, institutional incentives that block or aggregate ethnicity should be an effective measure to manage ethnic conflict and promote democracy. In contrast, 'consociationalists' argue that ethnicity should not be blocked but accepted and systematically accommodated through translation.[35]

The main section engages in a preliminary test of the central hypotheses of strong positive or negative effects on (a) peace and (b) democracy. For both dependent variables the impact of the more general regulation type (aggregation, blocking and translation) and actual bans are tested. Applying macro-qualitative comparison, bivariate statistics, and qualitative case studies, the results question the effectiveness of party bans as a tool of managing ethnic conflict and promoting democracy. Generally, hypotheses of strong positive or negative effects are rejected for both the legal possibility and for actually implemented bans.

With regard to conflict, countries which introduced the legal option to ban particularistic parties were not significantly more or less conflict-prone than countries without such an option. Only in a few individual cases, implemented bans might have had a stabilizing impact. For example, in Rwanda, two extremist parties that were involved in the genocide were banned. In most cases they have proven ineffective, and in one case – Kenya in 1992 – the ban even led to violent protest against this measure. Moreover, countries with an ethnic party ban were slightly less democratic in 2008 than countries without such a provision. While provisions for party bans often emerge during a period of political transition, the implementation of bans is more widespread in less democratic countries, and bans often seem to be used as one means to suppress the political representation of interests and grievances.

The second cluster of contributions, amounting to five articles, explores the relevance of party bans in different contexts. While all five articles are based on our common research project, share a common terminology, and rely on the same set of data, the main emphasis shifts towards understanding the particularities of specific bans and country contexts. The case studies also represent different settings in the sense that we analyse countries without any party ban provisions (South Africa), those with such provisions and a propensity to actually implement bans (Nigeria, Rwanda, Tanzania, Uganda), and countries that introduced formal provisions but apparently ignored them in practice (Senegal). One contribution also deals with Kenya, a country that banned parties without having any legal base for doing so.

Jörg Kemmerzell analyses the case of South Africa. He reviews the constitutional debate leading to the establishment of an unrestricted right of political association, and a lack of any legal means to dissolve extremist or particularistic parties. The South African constitution allows the banning of political associations only if the organization resorts to massive violence. Kemmerzell discusses three main factors which explain this outcome. It is first argued that party bans were rejected due to the experience with bans on parties and other political organizations under apartheid rule; unrestricted competition has thus been considered a core element of an open democratic process. The second reason for the lack of party ban provisions refers to the mode of political transition. Transition from apartheid towards liberal democracy was characterized by inclusiveness and a broad participation of all political forces. A general clause restricting political competition was thus an unlikely outcome. The third main factor discussed by Kemmerzell is the lack of serious threats against the liberal democratic order and the dominance of the African National Congress (ANC)-led government after 1994. The potential cost of undermining the liberal ethos of the constitution through party bans was considered disproportionate compared to the cost of accepting a continuous presence of otherwise marginalized extremist political actors.

If there is one African country associated in public consciousness with the horrors of ethnic conflict, it is probably Rwanda after the genocide of 1994. Peter Niesen's contribution discusses the public justifications brought forward for three waves of bans on political parties in Rwanda after Tutsi rebels conquered Kigali and restored peace in the country. While the standard narrative of protecting democracy from its enemies ('militant democracy') was not invoked, two alternative narratives carried the burden of justification. The first is that of banning what Niesen calls 'strongly particularistic parties', i.e. parties that discriminate or incite hatred and violence along ethnic or similar lines. The second is that of banning the former ruling party, responsible for mass atrocities, and its successor organizations. While both justification narratives have strong initial plausibility against Rwanda's history of ethnic conflict and genocide, and mirror analogous justifications for banning parties elsewhere, a detailed discussion of the evidence suggests that Rwanda's bans mainly served the purpose of repressing political opposition – at least in 2001 and 2003. The justifications brought forward in the later waves of bans remain unconvincing and cannot claim political legitimacy.

The contribution of Matthijs Bogaards deals with the case of Nigeria, the African country that has implemented ethnic party bans most systematically. At four points in time, a total of at least 64 parties have been denied registration. In each case, the stumbling block was a failure to demonstrate national presence. Concretely, the electoral commission was not convinced that these parties had offices and officers in no less than two-thirds of the states of the Nigerian federation. Nigeria is also among the African countries with the longest record in institutional engineering. Ethnic party bans are only one instrument, and probably not even the most important one, in a broader repertoire of incentives for the creation of national parties that transcend the various socio-cultural differences in this very diverse country. Bogaards' contribution analyses the experience with ethnic party bans in relation to other instances of institutional design, highlighting the aims – sometimes conflicting, mostly reinforcing – and outcomes. The case of Nigeria brings to the fore two features that also figure prominently in the other analyses of ethnic party bans in Africa. First, there is the crucial role of implementation. Until a Supreme Court ruling of 2002, the guidelines for party registration enforced by the electoral commission were stricter than the provisions of the constitution. Second, there is the nature of the regime. Most parties were banned by military rulers in the process of a carefully managed transition to multiparty democracy. The case of Nigeria shows that the concern of successive (military) regimes involved in institutional engineering was not simply to outlaw (mono-)ethnic parties, but to stimulate the building of multi-ethnic parties. In this respect, some success can be noted.

Anika Moroff's second contribution to this special issue focuses on Kenya, Tanzania, and Uganda as three east African countries which opted for different ways of dealing with particularistic parties ranging from President Yoweri

Museveni's movement system in Uganda and Tanzania's early introduction of particularistic party bans, with spatial distribution requirements to Kenya which had no party law at all until 2008. The main focus is however less on the reasons for these diverging paths, but on the impact of these differing provisions for the party systems. The contribution starts from the assumption that party bans and spatial distribution requirements initially target the party programme, organization, and membership structure, but ultimately, if successful, they indeed promote parties with a national electorate. Moroff's empirical analysis shows that in all three countries the party-ban provisions have actually been enforced, i.e. particularistic parties have been banned. These bans have, however, only marginally influenced the character of the political parties in the three countries. A comparison of regional voting patterns suggests that bans on particularistic parties have not ensured the emergence of political parties with a national following in Tanzania and Uganda. Moreover, in Kenya, where such a ban was absent until 2008, the so-called party nationalization scores, which measure the territorial spread of party-support, are comparable.

Senegal, finally, is an interesting case, because it has a long history of multiparty rule and since the 1970s the various regimes have used formal party regulation to restrict and structure the political competition. Party bans were first introduced at the end of the 1970s. Christof Hartmann's contribution analyses party bans as one instrument within a broader repertoire of party regulation, particularly the electoral system. Both the changing character of Senegal's political system, especially with the strengthening of presidential power since the accession of Abdoulaye Wade to the presidency in 2000, and the trend towards stronger fragmentation in the party system have modified the role of party bans. While party bans were efficient in strengthening the two larger parties throughout the 1980s and 1990s and limiting the politicization of ethnicity within the party system, the strongly presidentialist turn of the political system in recent years has diminished both the overall relevance of political parties (and greatly increased their number to over 150 in 2009) and the need to regulate their activities effectively. There are, however, in recent years a growing number of religious parties which are allowed to operate because their electoral support has been minimal but whose existence is nevertheless a violation of the core principles of the Senegalese Constitution. We see thus the emergence of particularistic parties which are not ethnic, in the narrow sense, but still confront the regime with the same political and normative dilemmas. The Senegalese case is a scenario where extensive legal regulation is hardly matched by institutional capacities, and legal provisions might be misused in isolated instances when it suits the interests of the President of the Republic or the ruling party.

Conclusion and challenges for future research

The outline of the individual contributions has provided (preliminary) answers to the more detailed research questions (1–4) outlined at the beginning of this introduction to the special issue. With regard to our primary research question, the contributions reveal that the effectiveness of party bans for managing ethnic conflict is generally limited and context-dependent, and that the main cost to democracy is that party bans are sometimes misused by rather authoritarian regimes. In the following we will elaborate in more detail on major results and their implications for future research.

One of the main findings of the contributions collected in this special issue is that almost all countries have the legal provisions to ban particularistic parties but only a minority actually make use of them. We have some evidence both from the comparative analysis and some country contributions that while almost all countries share the fear that multiparty politics may turn ethnic diversity into ethnic conflict, it is the group of less democratic regimes that actually ban political parties, at least partially as a strategy to control the opposition. Or, in countries which have witnessed an alternation of authoritarian and (more) democratic periods, such as Nigeria, we find that ethnic party bans are implemented by outgoing military regimes and much less so in the new democratic dispensations.

The effectiveness of ethnic party bans cannot be measured by the implementation record alone. In other words, it is not sufficient to look only at actual instances of denied registrations, suspensions, or dissolutions. If institutions are supposed to guide political behaviour, we should not discard the possibility that party bans are self-enforcing and political leaders refrain from creating particularistic parties through the law of anticipated reactions. The case of Senegal is quite telling in this regard, but it also leaves us with the research problem of how to attribute the outcome of a relatively non-ethnicized party system to the effects of the formal rules of party regulation.

A second conclusion we can draw regarding the contributions to this special issue is that party bans are generally not very effective measures of institutional engineering in order to strengthen democracy and create peaceful inter-communal relations. There are a number of plausible explanations. Obviously, context matters, and this holds true in at least two aspects: Firstly, party bans have to be understood as just one element in an array of possible measures of party regulation and just one option in the menu of institutional engineering, as demonstrated *inter alia* by the chapters on Nigeria and Senegal. Future studies should take a more holistic approach in this regard and investigate both the relative weight of party bans or other institutional measures and the impact of measures in conjunction.[36] There is also a need to give a stronger emphasis on informal institutions and their role in strengthening or thwarting the effects of party bans. Second, it is not only the institutional context but also the wider environment of the country that matters for the actual relevance of party bans. Specific institutional traditions, a record of interethnic problems, the socio-economic context, and the specific ethno-demographic 'landscape' may decisively impact on the link between ethnic diversity, party system, and peace and democracy.[37]

Generally, the causal chain that links ethnic party bans to peace and democracy, runs principally through (and in this order) (a) ethnic diversity → (b) party regulation (party ban) → (c) ethnicization of (party) politics → (d) peace and/or democracy. However, we have little information on the ethnicization of political parties, governments or other important institutions. There has been progress in this regard in recent databases such as the Ethnic Power Relations data set,[38] but if we want to engage in a context-sensitive process tracing of the causal chain, we need systematically to collect data on the ethnicization of politics. Ideally, we would wish to have a database of ethnic parties in Africa that would allow us to check whether ethnic parties are less common in countries that have or implement ethnic party bans. Unfortunately no such database exists. Generally, two questions need to be answered: Under what circumstances does ethnic diversity lead to the politicization of ethnicity? And, under what conditions will the politicization of ethnicity result in violence or other threats to democracy?

In normative terms, particularistic party bans prove to be a double-edged sword. On the one hand, their introduction is understandable and shows a context-sensitive adaptation of multipartyism to the structural conditions of the African continent. In principle, it is the idea of militant democracy partially to restrict political freedoms, in particular the freedom of association, in order to make a competitive party system work and contribute to the survival of democracy. On the other hand, party bans can and have obviously been misused to weaken political opposition or suppress grievances. Thus, the legitimacy of a party ban seems to be directly connected to the overall legitimacy of the regime in place. Policymakers and development organizations should thus be cautious in advocating for the introduction of party bans in countries which are in the process of liberalizing their polities. This recommendation is in line with Randall's conclusion that party regulations 'should probably be applied with a light touch'.[39]

Finally, in light of the complexity of the phenomenon under investigation in this special issue, we hope to have raised interest for more comprehensive research projects and strategies. Further research might investigate the whole 'menu' of party regulation or even institutional engineering (including electoral systems, power-sharing agreements, decentralization and federalism) and should be geographically extended. Beyond Africa, it is particularly the Middle East, with its many religious and ethnic parties, that constitutes a promising empirical field of research. We also need a continued effort to collect data systematically on the precise types of institutional measures designed to manage ethnic conflict and, particularly, the ethnicization of political parties and politics in general. This may facilitate systematic comparative, even statistical analysis. In the end, therefore, we will probably have to rely on a methodological pluralism that employs large N studies, case studies, and small N comparisons in combination, as does this special issue.

Generally, future research has to deal with a number of challenges. Given the undeniable ongoing salience of ethnic conflict in contemporary Africa we need to learn more about party bans and other institutional measures designed to manage ethnic conflict. A successful therapy requires a correct diagnosis. The findings of this special issue may form a first step in this direction.

Notes

1. If not indicated otherwise, we refer to sub-Saharan Africa (e.g. without North Africa) when using the term 'Africa'.
2. Cf. Jackson, 'Ethnicity'; Young, 'Nationalism, Ethnicity and Class'.
3. Almond and Coleman, *Politics of Developing Areas*, 556.
4. What we call in this special issue 'ethnic party bans' or 'particularistic party bans', Karvonen, 'Legislation on Political Parties', refers to as 'comprehensive party bans'.
5. The Constitution is quoted here from: www.sierra-leone.org/Laws/constitution1991. pdf.
6. For exceptions, see Finn, 'Electoral Regimes'; Fox and Nolte, 'Intolerant Democracies'; and Rosenblum, 'Banning Parties'.
7. The project was funded from 2006 to 2008 by the Fritz Thyssen Foundation. It was a collaboration of the Jacobs University Bremen (Matthijs Bogaards), the Technical University of Darmstadt (Peter Niesen), the University of Duisburg-Essen (Christof Hartmann) and the GIGA Institute of African Affairs (Matthias Basedau).
8. Bogaards, 'Electoral Systems and Management of Ethnic Conflict'.
9. Karvonen, 'Legislation on Political Parties', 448.
10. Schedler, 'The Menu of Manipulation'.
11. Almond and Coleman, *Politics of Developing Areas*, 554–5.
12. Gunther and Diamond, 'Types and Functions', 23.
13. Ibid.
14. Cf. Kuenzi and Lambright, 'Party System Institutionalization'; Randall and Svåsand, 'Contribution of Parties'; Van Cranenburgh, 'Power and Competition'; Erdmann, 'Party Research'.
15. Cheeseman and Ford, *Ethnicity as Political Cleavage*; Erdmann, *Ethnicity, Voter Alignment and Political Party Affiliation*; Basedau and Stroh, *Ethnicity and Party Systems*; Elischer, *Ethnic Parties in Africa*.
16. Cf. Horowitz, *Ethnic Groups in Conflict* and *A Democratic South Africa*; McMahon, 'Catching the Third Wave'.
17. Scarritt, McMillan and Mozaffar, 'Interaction between Democracy and Protest'.
18. Snyder, *From Voting to Violence*, 296–306
19. Belmont, Mainwaring, and Reynolds, 'Introduction', 2.
20. The first major study was Bayart, *L'Etat en Afrique*.
21. Harris and Reilly, *Democracy and Deep-Rooted Conflict*.
22. Sisk and Reynolds, *Elections and Conflict Management*; Reynolds, *Electoral Systems and Democratization*; Reilly and Reynolds, *Electoral Systems and Conflict in Divided Societies*; Bogaards, 'Crafting Competitive Party Systems' and 'Electoral Choices for Divided Societies'; Hartmann, 'Paths of Electoral Reform'.
23. De Villiers, *Local and Provincial Intergovernmental Relations*; Osaghae, 'Democracy and National Cohesion'; Levy and Tapscott, *Intergovernmental Relations*.
24. Crawford and Hartmann, 'Introduction'.
25. Bogaards, 'Comparative Strategies'.
26. Bogaards, 'Electoral Systems and Management of Ethnic Conflict' and 'Electoral Systems, Party Systems'.
27. McGarry, O'Leary, and Simeon, 'Integration or Accommodation?', 43.
28. Loewenstein, 'Militant Democracy'.
29. Bundesverfassungsgericht, *Entscheidungen*, Vol. 2, 12.
30. Morlok, 'Parteiverbot'.
31. Leggewie and Meier, *Republikschutz* and *Verbot der NPD*.
32. Preuss, 'Empfindsame Demokratie'.
33. See also Niesen, 'Anti-Extremism, Negative Republicanism, Civic Society'.

34. The data were collected during the common research project mentioned in note 7. For more details on the database please refer to Moroff, 'Party Bans in Africa', in this special issue.
35. See Choudhry, 'Bridging Comparative Politics' on integration and consociation.
36. Of particular interest may be the distinction between penalties and incentives in order to promote national parties. As McMenamin, 'Challenges for Future Research', 228 notes, 'virtually all cases of party regulation seem to rely on command and control: the regulations stipulate standards that parties must meet.' Failure to meet these standards will result in penalties. A more promising strategy may be to provide parties with positive incentives, for example, in the form of state subventions.
37. For example, McMenamin, 'Challenges for Future Research', hypothesizes that the impact of party regulation depends crucially on the social distance of social groups.
38. Cederman, Min, and Wimmer, *Ethnic Power Relations Data Set.*
39. Randall, 'More Dangers than Opportunities?', 258.

Notes on contributors

Matthijs Bogaards is Professor of Political Science in the School of Humanities and Social Sciences, Jacobs University Bremen

Matthias Basedau, PhD, Heidelberg University, is Head of Research Programme at the German Institute of Global and Area Studies, Hamburg. He is also a Senior Research Fellow at the GIGA Institute of African Affairs in Hamburg. Research interests include political parties, ethnic and religious conflict as well natural resources and conflict.

Christof Hartmann is Professor of Political Science at the University of Duisburg-Essen (Germany). His research focuses on democratization, democratic institutions and institutional change, with particular emphasis on sub-Saharan Africa.

Bibliography

Almond, Gabriel, and James Coleman, eds. *The Politics of the Developing Areas.* Princeton: Princeton University Press, 1960.
Basedau, Matthias, and Alexander Stroh. *Ethnicity and Party Systems in Francophone Sub-Saharan Africa.* Hamburg, GIGA Working Papers 100, 2009.
Bayart, Jean-François. *La Politique du Ventre, L'État en Afrique.* Paris: Fayard, 1989.
Belmont, Katharine, Scott Mainwaring, and Andrew Reynolds. 'Introduction: Institutional Design, Conflict Management, and Democracy'. In *The Architecture of Democracy: Constitutional Design, Conflict Management, and Democracy,* ed. Andrew Reynolds, 1–11. Oxford: Oxford University Press, 2002.
Bogaards, Matthijs. 'Crafting Competitive Party Systems: Electoral Laws and the Opposition in Africa'. *Democratization* 7, no. 4 (2000): 163–90.
Bogaards, Matthijs. 'Electoral Choices for Divided Societies: Multi-Ethnic Parties and Constituency Pooling in Africa'. *Commonwealth and Comparative Politics* 41, no. 3 (2003): 59–80.
Bogaards, Matthijs. 'Electoral Systems and the Management of Ethnic Conflict in the Balkans'. In *Understanding Postcommunist Nationalism: Lessons Learned,* ed. Alina Mungiu-Pippidi, 247–66. Budapest: CEU Press, 2004.
Bogaards, Matthijs. 'Electoral Systems, Party Systems, and Ethnic Conflict Management in Africa'. In *Votes, Money and Violence: Political Parties and Elections in Africa,* ed. Matthias Basedau, Gero Erdmann, and Andreas Mehler, 168–93. Uppsala: Nordiska Afrikainstitutet, 2007.

Bogaards, Matthijs. 'Comparative Strategies of Political Party Regulation'. In *Political Party Regulation in Conflict-Prone Societies*, ed. Ben Reilly, Edward Newman, and Per Nordlund, 48–66. Tokyo: United Nations University Press, 2008.

Bundesverfassungsgericht (German Constitutional Court). *Entscheidungen des Bundesverfassungsgerichts* Vol. 2. Tübingen: Mohr, 1953.

Cederman, Lars-Erik, Brian Min, and Andreas Wimmer, 2009-05-01, 'Ethnic Power Relations Dataset'. hdl:1902.1/11796 UNF:5:k4xxXC2ASI204QZ4jqvUrQ= (accessed 20 January 2010).

Cheeseman, Nic, and Robert Ford. *Ethnicity as a Political Cleavage. Afrobarometer Paper* 83. www.afrobarometer.org/papers/AfropaperNo83.pdf, 2007.

Choudhry, Sujit. 'Bridging Comparative Politics and Comparative Constitutional Law: Constitutional Design in Divided Societies'. In *Constitutional Design for Divided Societies: Integration or Accommodation?* ed. Sujit Choudhry, 3–40. Oxford: Oxford University Press, 2008.

Crawford, Gordon, and Christof Hartmann. 'Introduction: Decentralisation as a Pathway out of Poverty and Conflict?'. In *Decentralisation in Africa: A Pathway out of Poverty and Conflict?*, ed. Gordon Crawford and Christof Hartmann, 7–32. Amsterdam: Amsterdam University Press, 2008.

De Villiers, Bertus. *Local And Provincial Intergovernmental Relations: A Comparative Analysis*. Johannesburg: Konrad-Adenauer Foundation, 1997.

Elischer, Sebastian. *Ethnic Parties in Africa: A Comparative Study of Kenya, Namibia, and Ghana*. Unpublished PhD thesis, Jacobs University Bremen, 2010.

Erdmann, Gero. 'Party Research: Western Bias and the "African Labyrinth"'. *Democratization* 11, no. 3 (2004): 63–87.

Erdmann, Gero. *Ethnicity, Voter Alignment and Political Party Affiliation – An African Case: Zambia*. Hamburg, GIGA Working Papers 45. 2007.

Finn, John. 'Electoral Regimes and the Proscription of Anti-Democratic Parties'. In *The Democratic Experience and Political Violence*, ed. David Rapoport and Leonard Weinberg, 51–77. London: Frank Cass, 2001.

Fox, Gregory, and Georg Nolte. 'Intolerant Democracies'. *Harvard International Law Journal* 36, no. 1 (1995): 1–70.

Gunther, Richard, and Larry Diamond. 'Types and Functions of Parties'. In *Political Parties and Democracy*, ed. Larry Diamond and Richard Gunther, 3–40. Baltimore: Johns Hopkins University Press, 2001.

Harris, Peter, and Ben Reilly, eds. *Democracy and Deep-Rooted Conflict: Options for Negotiators*, Stockholm: IDEA, 1998.

Hartmann, Christof. 'Paths of Electoral Reform in Africa'. In *Votes, Money and Violence: Political Parties and Elections in Africa*, ed. Matthias Basedau, Gero Erdmann, and Andreas Mehler, 144–67. Uppsala: Nordiska Afrikainstitutet, 2007.

Horowitz, Donald. *A Democratic South Africa? Constitutional Engineering in a Divided Society*. Berkeley: University of California Press, 1991.

Horowitz, Donald. *Ethnic Groups in Conflict*. Berkeley: University of California Press, 1985.

Jackson, Robert. 'Ethnicity'. In *Social Science Concepts: A Systematic Analysis*, ed. Giovanni Sartori, 205–33. Sage: Beverly Hills, 1984.

Karvonen, Lauri. 'Legislation on Political Parties: A Global Comparison'. *Party Politics* 13 (2007): 437–55.

Kuenzi, Michelle, and Gina Lambright. 'Party System Institutionalization in 30 African Countries'. *Party Politics* 7, no. 4 (2001): 437–68.

Leggewie, Claus, and Horst Meier. *Republikschutz. Maßstäbe für die Verteidigung der Demokratie*. Reinbek: Rowohlt, 1995.

Leggewie, Claus, and Horst Meier, eds. *Verbot der NPD oder Mit Rechtsradikalen Leben?* Frankfurt: Suhrkamp, 2002.

Levy, Norman, and Chris Tapscott. *Intergovernmental Relations in South Africa: The Challenges of Co-operative Government.* Cape Town: Juta, 2001.

Loewenstein, Karl. 'Militant Democracy and Fundamental Rights I and II'. *American Political Science Review* 31, no. 3/4 (1937): 417–432, 638–658.

McGarry, John, Brendan O'Leary, and Richard Simeon. 'Integration or Accommodation? The Enduring Debate in Conflict Regulation'. In *Constitutional Design for Divided Societies: Integration or Accommodation?*, ed. Sujit Choudhry, 41–88. Oxford: Oxford University Press, 2008.

McMenamin, I. 'Party Regulation and Democratization: Challenges for Further Research'. In *Political Parties in Conflict-Prone Societies: Regulation, Engineering and Democratic Development*, ed. Ben Reilly and Per Nordlund, 223–241. Tokyo: United Nations University Press, 2008.

McMahon, Edward R. 'Catching the "Third Wave" of Democratization? Debating Political Party Effectiveness in Africa since 1980'. *African and Asian Studies* 4, no. 3/4 (2004): 295–320.

Morlok, Martin. 'Parteiverbot als Verfassungsschutz – Ein Unauflöslicher Widerspruch?'. *Neue Juristische Wochenschrift* 54, no. 40 (2001): 2931–42.

Moroff, Anika. 'Party Bans in Africa – An Empirical Overview'. *Democratization* 17, no. 4 (2010): 618–41.

Niesen, Peter. 'Anti-extremism, Negative Republicanism, Civic Society: Three Paradigms for Banning Political Parties'. In *Europe's Century of Discontent: The Legacies of Fascism, Nazism and Communism*, ed. Shlomo Avineri and Zeev Sternhell, 249–86. Jerusalem: Hebrew University Press, 2003.

Osaghae, Eghosa. 'Democracy and National Cohesion in Multiethnic African States: South Africa and Nigeria Compared'. *Nations and Nationalism* 5 (1999): 259–80.

Preuss, Ulrich. 'Die empfindsame Demokratie'. In *Verbot der NPD oder Mit Rechtsradikalen leben?*, ed. Claus Leggewie and Horst Meier, 104–19. Frankfurt: Suhrkamp, 2002.

Randall, V. 'Party Regulation in Conflict-Prone Societies: More Dangers than Opportunities?'. In *Political Party Regulation in Conflict-Prone Societies*, ed. Ben Reilly and Per Nordlund, 242–60. Tokyo: United Nations University Press, 2008.

Randall, Vicky, and Lars Svåsand, eds. 'The Contribution of Parties to Democracy and Democratic Consolidation'. In *Democratization* 9, no. 3, 2002, special issue.

Reilly, Ben, and Andrew Reynolds. *Electoral Systems and Conflict in Divided Societies.* Washington: National Academy Press, 1999.

Reynolds, Andrew. *Electoral Systems and Democratization in Southern Africa.* Oxford: Oxford University Press, 1999.

Rosenblum, Nancy. 'Banning Parties: Religious and Ethnic Partisanship in Multicultural Democracies'. *Law & Ethics of Human Rights* 1 (2007): 1–59.

Scarritt, James, Susan McMillan, and Shaheen Mozaffar. 'The Interaction between Democracy and Ethnopolitical Protest and Rebellion in Africa'. *Comparative Political Studies* 34, no. 7 (2001): 800–27.

Schedler, Andreas. 'The Menu of Manipulation'. *Journal of Democracy* 13, no. 2 (2002): 36–50.

Sisk, Timothy, and Andrew Reynolds, eds. *Elections and Conflict Management in Africa.* Washington, DC: United States Institute of Peace Press, 1998.

Snyder, Jack. *From Voting to Violence: Democratization and Nationalist Conflict.* New York: W.W. Norton, 2000.

Van Cranenburgh, Oda. 'Power and Competition: The Institutional Context of African Multi-Party Politics'. In *African Political Parties: Evolution, Institutionalisation, and Governance*, ed. M.A. Salih, 188–207. London: Pluto Press, 2003.

Young, Crawford. 'Nationalism, Ethnicity, and Class in Africa. A Retrospective'. *Cahiers d'Etudes Africaines* 26, no. 103 (1986): 421–95.

Party bans in Africa – an empirical overview

Anika Moroff

GIGA Institute of African Affairs, Hamburg, Germany

With the re-introduction of multiparty politics at the beginning of the 1990s most African countries started to regulate political parties extensively, especially ethnic and other particularistic parties. This article presents a new database on particularistic and other party bans in sub-Saharan Africa, drawing on a comprehensive collection of African party regulations and records of their implementation since 1990. After demonstrating the magnitude and complexity of party bans in Africa the article deals in depth with enforcement institutions and legal procedures. It shows that party bans are especially pervasive in less democratic countries and have often targeted politically relevant parties.

Introduction

Democracy today is generally understood as representative, party-based democracy.[1] Over the years, the legal regulation of political parties has greatly increased and is now particularly widespread in new democracies and democratising countries.[2] Party regulation today is an institutional engineering tool among other, long established instruments such as the electoral system, the regime type, or federal arrangements.[3]

While the tendency of greater party regulation can be observed over the last few decades, academic interest in the topic has developed rather slowly. Only recently have political scientists started to think about the origins and potential impacts of party regulation.[4] Studies on party regulation in new democracies are even rarer.

This special issue aims at filling this gap. While the regulation of political parties can deal with various issues such as funding, campaigns, or organization, the contributions focus on party bans and concentrate on sub-Saharan Africa – a region where legislation on political parties is particularly widespread. Most sub-Saharan countries allow for party bans and introduced bans on ethnic, regional and other identity-based parties in the 1990s in order to prevent the creation of such particularistic parties, which were deemed to foster ethnic conflict.[5]

While the special issue deals with the broader question of whether particularistic party bans in Africa are an effective way of preventing and managing violent conflict and at what costs to democracy, this contribution presents a unique and original database, which includes information on the prevalence and implementation of party bans in Africa since 1990. The article tackles four central questions: (1) Where can party bans be found, in which countries and legal codes? (2) For what reasons are parties banned? (3) Who may ban a party? (4) And how are the laws implemented?

Where can party bans be found?

Party legislation can be found in constitutions, election laws, party laws, opposition laws (where existing), and in some cases association laws.[6] While there are some comprehensive databases for constitutions worldwide, and some institutions that collect election laws, political party laws are hard to find.[7] Nevertheless, we managed to get an almost complete compilation of African constitutions, election laws, and party laws since 1990 and were also able to crosscheck most of the pre-1990 constitutions.[8]

A first look at party regulation in Africa shows how widespread legislation is. In 2010 political parties are mentioned in nearly all African constitutions; only Rwanda is using the expression 'political organization' while Eritrea and Swaziland do not have a multiparty-system. Thirty-five countries have a political party law, eight countries regulate political parties in their election law, while Zimbabwe has a 'Political Parties (Finance) Act'. Only Botswana does not have a specific party legislation at all; it treats parties like other associations.[9] Democracy in Africa seems to be understood clearly as party democracy.

This degree of regulation differs significantly from the independence era in the 1960s, when most African countries created their first multiparty constitutions. At that time, only 17 – almost exclusively francophone – countries referred to political parties in their constitutions (out of 32 constitutions that could be found, see Table 1). No Anglophone constitution mentioned parties.[10] Thus, the degree of explicit legislation on political parties has significantly increased with the new wave of democratization and expanded to Anglophone countries.

The same tendency can be observed if we focus on party bans: while the banning of particularistic parties clearly has a long tradition in Africa, today's magnitude is a new phenomenon. The first countries to introduce particularistic party bans were Ghana in 1957 with the 'Avoidance of Discrimination Act' and Somalia, which outlawed 'tribal parties' in its first constitution of 1960. Other African countries demanded parties not to act against territorial integrity (six countries) or against national unity (one country).[11] Eleven countries outlawed 'ethnic', 'racist' or 'regionalist' propaganda without referring in this prohibition explicitly to political parties. We can easily see a pattern between countries with

Table 1. Constitutions and parties in the 1960s.

Constitutions mentioning parties	Constitutions regulating campaigns	Constitutions not mentioning parties	Σ
Benin (Dahomey), Cameroon, Central African Republic, Chad, Congo-Br. (République du Congo), Democratic Republic of Congo (DRC), Côte d'Ivoire, Gabon, Guinea, Madagascar, Mali, Mauritania, Niger, Rwanda, Senegal, Somalia, Togo	Benin (Dahomey), Chad, Congo-Br. (République du Congo), Côte d'Ivoire, Gabon, Guinea, Mali, Mauritania, Niger, Senegal, Togo	Burkina Faso (Haute Volta), Burundi, Ethiopia (1955), Ghana, Kenya, Liberia, Malawi, Mauritius, Nigeria, Sierra Leone, Tanzania, Uganda, Zambia	32
17	11	13	

Source: Author's compilation.

different colonial backgrounds here: none of the former British colonies regulated political campaigns in this way.[12]

The 1960s constitutions did not last long and in most countries a one-party state or a military regime was soon established. The arguments to end multiparty politics were very similar to the ones for introducing party bans and focused on the need to foster national unity and integration as well as on the potentially conflictive and divisive effects of political parties.[13] Over the years, some of the countries that experimented with a multiparty system introduced bans on particularistic parties in their constitutions: Ghana did so in its 1969 constitution, Senegal followed in 1978, while Nigeria introduced such legislation in 1979. Finally, Liberia integrated a party ban into its 1986 constitution.

While the regulation of particularistic parties and campaigns has a long tradition in Africa, the big wave of party bans occurred with renewed democratization in the 1990s: 39 of 45 countries opted for banning particularistic parties. Today, only five anglophone countries do not ban particularistic parties (see Table 2).[14] Also, there is no single party law in sub-Saharan Africa that does not include a ban on particularistic parties. More generally, only two countries do not ban any parties at all.

On what grounds can a party be banned?

A party ban can take different legal forms: The term 'ban' may include (1) the dissolution of an already existing party; (2) a temporary suspension of a party; or (3) the denial of registration to a group that wants to transform itself into a political party. General reasons to ban parties exist in 43 African countries; they vary widely and include whether parties are judged to have an undemocratic character, be intolerant or practice fanaticism, use violence, employ already existing party

Table 2. Party bans in Africa since 1990.

	Only in the constitution	Only in the party law	Only in the election law	In party law and constitution	In election law and constitution	Total/percent
Particularistic party ban possible	Somalia (since 2004) Uganda (until 2002) 1	Benin, Cameroon, Chad, Central African Republic (until 2004), Congo-Br. (until 2002), Côte d'Ivoire (until 2000), DRC, Ethiopia, Kenya (since 2008), Malawi, Mauritania, Mali, Rwanda (until 2003), São Tomé e Príncipe, Seychelles, Sudan (until 2005) 11	Lesotho Namibia 2	Angola, Burkina Faso, Burundi, Cape Verde, Central African Republic (since 2004) Congo-Br. (since 2002), Côte d'Ivoire (since 2000), Djibouti, Equatorial Guinea, Gabon, Ghana, Guinea, Guinea-Bissau, Liberia, Madagascar, Mozambique, Niger, Rwanda (since 2003), Senegal, Sierra Leone, Sudan (since 2005), Tanzania, Togo, Uganda (since 2002) 24	Gambia, Nigeria (since 1979 in constitution, 1996-99 also in party law, 1999-2002 only in constitution, since 2002 additionally in election law) 2	40 / 89%
Only general ban possible		Botswana* 1			South Africa, Zambia 2	3 / 7%
No ban possible	Mauritius Zimbabwe 1					2 / 4%
Total of ban countries		12	2	24	4	45

Source: Author's compilation.
Note: As of March 2010. Information on the Comoros missing. * Botswana: Societies Act.

names, fail to select party leaders democratically or to account for the use and origin of funds. In addition, several countries, including Botswana and Zambia, also ban parties if they are judged to be against peace, welfare, and good order or to have unlawful purposes.

Particularistic party bans are defined here as a highly restrictive official legal sanction that aims to prohibit the existence or activity of a political party that is composed of, seeks the support of, and acts on behalf or in the interest of a specific ethnic or particularistic identity group. We developed a two-dimensional framework of particularistic party bans that asks (1) on which identity base a party can be outlawed or denied registration (for example, ethnic group, tribe, religion, race, colour, or language).[15] (2) It also asks which aspects of the party are not permitted to be particularistic. We distinguish between the general party character (for example, 'ethnic parties are prohibited'), the party programme (for example, 'the party shall not have an ethnic programme'), its organization and membership structure, name or symbol, and party campaign/propaganda.

The categories are developed on the empirical bases of what we found in the relevant laws. However, in order to prevent the creation of a particularistic party it is not only possible to *prohibit* something but the law might also *prescribe* requirements a party must fulfil. Regulations that require parties to prove their national character through party offices nationwide or by membership in all regions of the country (representation requirements) aim – amongst other possible goals – at the prevention of regionally based parties.[16] We therefore included this type of regulation as a type of party ban.

Figure 1 shows that a broad range of identities is outlawed as a mobilization base for political parties (for more detailed information see Appendix A). Out of 40 countries in Africa that ban particularistic parties, 36 outlaw parties based on religion or sects. Thirty-three countries prohibit ethnic or tribal parties while 35 countries do not allow regional parties:[17] in 33 countries the creation of regional

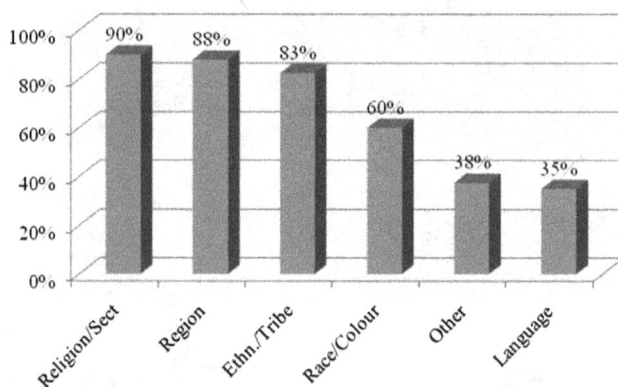

Figure 1. Outlawed identity bases.
Source: Author's compilation.

parties is prohibited, 23 of these countries additionally introduced representation requirements which are designed to prevent regional parties; Gabon and Sudan rely exclusively on prescriptive regulations. However, the number hides quite a broad variance. While Benin, for example, asks for 10 founding members per department (*département*), Ghana requires (1) one member from each region on the national executive committee, (2) party branches in all regions and organized in at least two-thirds of the districts in each region, and (3) one founding member in each district.[18] Ethiopia distinguishes between 'nation-wide' and 'regional' parties, which have to fulfil different registration requirements.[19]

Finally, parties based on race or colour are outlawed in 24 countries. Additionally, 14 outlaw parties based on language and 15 include additional reasons for banning parties, such as divisionism, segregation, family, brotherhood or 'other sectional divisions'. The presented data shows that most countries outlaw more than one party type.

As Figure 2 shows, almost all countries that ban particularistic parties regulate them in a general way (such as, 'ethnic parties are prohibited'; for more details see Appendix B).[20] Twenty-eight countries regulate party organization and 21 the party programme: if the organization or the party programme does not fulfil the criteria formulated in the law (such as including members from all regions in the national executive committee or not having an ethnic program), the party will not be registered or might be dissolved. Parties that restrict their membership to specific groups can be banned in 18 countries. Particularistic symbols may lead to a party ban in 16 countries, as may a particularistic electoral campaign in 14 countries.[21] However, particularistic campaigns are prohibited in an additional five countries, while general incitation of hatred or violence is outlawed in 14 African countries (see Appendix B).

Finally, as presented in the introduction, we distinguish three main aims of party regulation. Parties might be allowed or even encouraged to translate social and political cleavages into the party system (translation). Otherwise, the

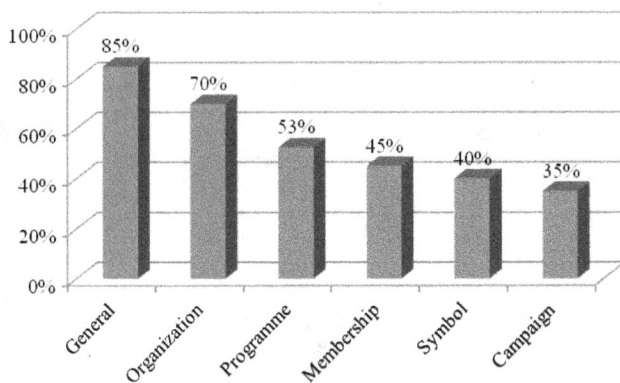

Figure 2. Regulation of party features.
Source: Author's compilation.

regulations might aim – through representation requirements – at the aggregation of cleavages by political parties (for example through multiethnic parties). Finally, regulations might also block the expression of social cleavages within the party system by a purely proscriptive party ban.[22] As shown in Table 3, 25 African countries have introduced representation requirements to create aggregative parties. None of them, however, relies on aggregation alone; in addition, they all prohibit particularistic parties. It is clear, therefore, that blocking is the preferred option of dealing with particularistic parties in Africa. This result is particularly interesting if we consider that it runs against the principles of consociational democracy, as developed by Lijphart, that are often considered appropriate for heterogeneous and divided societies.[23]

Who may ban a party?

The question of who is responsible for the enforcement of party bans is highly important: the degree of independence as well as the level of resources and capacities of the enforcement institutions can potentially influence strongly the fairness and neutrality of the procedures and decisions as well as the chances of the law to be implemented at all. Empirically we might distinguish between the state institutions being responsible for the registration of political parties, their suspension, and their dissolution. These tasks are assigned to courts, electoral commissions, registrars of political parties, and ministries or cabinets. Their degree of independence correlates with the extent of political freedom and rule of law in the country but also depends on regulations on appointment or tenure of

Table 3. Three types of party regulation.

Type of regulation	Translation	Aggregation + blocking	Blocking
Party ban	No party ban or encouragement of particularistic parties	Representation requirement and proscriptive party ban	Proscriptive party ban only
Countries	Botswana, Comoros, Mauritius, South Africa, Zambia, Zimbabwe	Angola, Benin, Burundi, Cape Verde, Congo-Br., DRC, Djibouti, Equatorial Guinea, Ethiopia, Gabon, Ghana, Guinea, Guinea Bissau, Kenya, Liberia, Madagascar, Mozambique, Niger, Nigeria, Rwanda, Sierra Leone, Sudan, Tanzania, Togo, Uganda	Burkina Faso, Cameroon, Central African Republic, Chad, Côte d'Ivoire, Gambia, Lesotho, Malawi, Mali, Mauritania, Namibia, São Tomé e príncipe, Senegal, Seychelles, Somalia
Σ	6	25	15

Source: Author's compilation.

office. Broadly speaking, ministries and cabinets can be assumed to be most likely politically biased.

Looking at Table 4, we discover different patterns:[24] all anglophone countries opted for the electoral commission or a registrar of political parties that are most often responsible for registering and dissolving political parties. However, in Sierra Leone and Uganda only a court may cancel a party's registration, whereas in Ghana the electoral commission may cancel the registration of a party only during the first 90 days. Afterwards, the high court may order the commission to do so if a party is convicted of an infringement. In Tanzania, the registrar must consult the minister of interior affairs before dissolving a party.

In four lusophone countries, courts are responsible for the registration of parties, while in all remaining – including all francophone – countries a ministry has the decision-making power (in 13 countries it is the ministry of internal affairs, in five the ministry of territorial administration and in three other ministries). While in eight countries the ministry or the cabinet may also decide to dissolve a party, the decision by a court is more common. The laws do not always specify who may summon the court; where it is done, we see that most often it is a ministry or the electoral commission that may plead for a party's deregistration. Most often, the responsible court is the high court or the supreme court.

The suspension of a party is mentioned in the laws of 13 countries. While in Rwanda and Guinea-Bissau a court is responsible for the suspension of a party, in Ethiopia the electoral commission and in Côte d'Ivoire the *conseil des ministres* may suspend a party. In all other countries the ministry that registers parties is also the one who may suspend them.

Once a party has been denied registration, 31 countries allow for an appeal against the decision (all except Madagascar, Mali, Mauritania, São Tomé, Senegal, Togo and Sudan). After a dissolution an appeal is generally possibly where an electoral commission, a registrar, or a ministry is responsible (except for Nigeria, Madagascar, Senegal and Sudan. In Tanzania an appeal is impossible, only a judicial review is possible).

Finally, not only the degree of independence of the responsible institution matters but also its capacities and resources. This is most obvious if we think of countries with a prescriptive regulation: the responsible institution (see Table 4) needs not only personnel to go to each region, to verify party members or party offices, but also vehicles and fuel for the vehicles. If party members are required to be registered voters, the controlling institution needs access to lists of registered voters. If it wants to follow and observe the behaviour of a party once the party is registered, it needs reliable sources (for example the media or observers) not only in the capital but countrywide.

Implementation of party bans

This last section tackles the following questions: In which countries have party bans been implemented? Which parties have been banned and on which

Table 4. Responsible institutions.

	Registration	Σ	Suspension	Σ	Dissolution	Σ
Court	Angola, Cape Verde, Guinea Bissau, São Tomé e Príncipe	4	Guinea Bissau, Rwanda	2	Angola, Benin, Burundi, Cape Verde, Central African Republic, Chad, Congo-Br, Côte d'Ivoire, Djibouti, DRC, Ethiopia*, Ghana, Guinea Bissau, Mali, Mozambique, Niger, Rwanda, São Tomé e Príncipe, Sierra Leone, Togo, Uganda,	20
Electoral commission	Ethiopia, Gambia, Ghana, Lesotho, Liberia, Namibia, Nigeria, Seychelles, Uganda, Zambia	10	Ethiopia	1	Gambia, Lesotho, Liberia, Namibia, Nigeria, Seychelles, Zambia	7
Registrar of political parties	Kenya, Malawi, Sierra Leone, Sudan**, Tanzania	5			Kenya, Malawi, Sudan, Tanzania (with Minister)	4
Ministry/ Cabinet	Benin, Burkina Faso, Burundi, Cameroon, Central African Republic, Chad, Congo-Br, Côte d'Ivoire, Djibouti, DRC, Equatorial Guinea, Gabon, Guinea, Madagascar, Mali, Mauritania, Mozambique, Niger, Rwanda, Senegal, Togo	21	Benin, Burkina Faso, Burundi, Central African Republic, Chad, Congo-Br., Côte d'Ivoire, Djibouti, Mauritania, Niger	10	Burkina Faso, Cameroon, Equatorial Guinea, Gabon, Guinea, Madagascar, Mauritania, Senegal	8
Total		40		13		40

Source: Author's compilation.
Note: As of March 2010. * Parties can be dissolved by a court and by the Election Board. ** Parties are registered by the Political Parties Affairs Council.

grounds? Did the procedure follow the rules? What happened after the decision? Was there a court appeal and if yes, was it successful? Did the party try to re-register under a new name? While some information about general party bans is included, the focus is on particularistic party bans.[25] We do not present information about other forms of restricting party activity, such as harassment or criminal proceedings against party officials.

Since 1990, 12 African countries have banned particularistic parties. These countries are: Angola, Burundi, the Central African Republic (CAR), Equatorial Guinea, Kenya, Mauritania, Namibia, Nigeria, Rwanda, Tanzania, Uganda, and Zambia. All in all, they enforced 138 bans of which 112 were denials of registration, 25 dissolutions, and one suspension (see Figure 3). Denials of registration are thus by far the most widespread practice. If we include party bans for other reasons, such as the use of violence, double names or technical problems, the number of countries that banned a party increases to 23 and the number of banned parties to 757.[26]

The high number of affected parties is, however, mainly linked to a small number of countries. Looking only at particularistic party bans, we see that Angola de-registered 25 small parties in 2007, while Nigeria denied registration to 51 and Tanzania to 50 (see Table 5). The high number of dissolved parties for other reasons is caused by the Democratic Republic of Congo, which dissolved all existing parties in 1999 (around 400) with the introduction of a new party law. All parties had to register anew.[27]

Reasons for implemented party bans

Among general party bans the dissolution of previous parties after a regime change (in Angola, Democratic Republic of Congo (DRC), Ethiopia, Gambia, Mali and

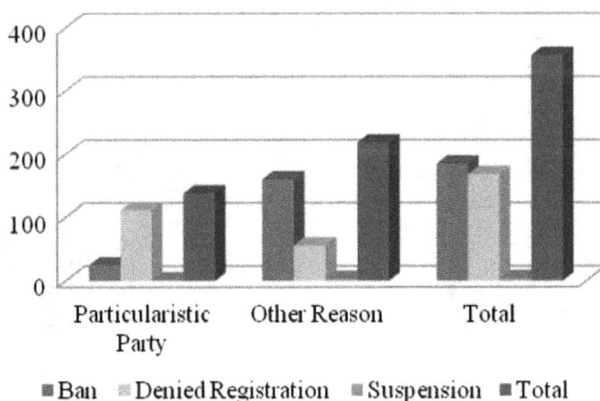

Figure 3. Implemented party bans.
Source: Author's compilation.
Note: Without Congo 1999.

Table 5. Implemented particularistic party bans.

	Region	Ethnicity	Religion	Race	Total
Denial of registration	107	5	6		112
	Nigeria* (13 1996; 17 1998; 21 2002) Tanzania (50 1993–2000, 2002–2005)	Burundi (Palipehutu 1992) Equatorial Guinea (MAIB 1994) Mauritania (CC 2002) Rwanda (PDR-Ubuyanja 2001) Uganda (KY 2004)	Kenya (IPK 1992) Mauritania (IUP 1991; PCD 2004, 2005) Uganda (UIRP 1993) Zambia (1 1993)		
Suspension		1			1
		Central African Republic (NDUCAP 1998)			
Dissolution	20	3	1	1	25
	Angola (19 2007) Namibia (UDP 2006)	Rwanda (MRND, CDR 1994; MDR 2003)	Central African Republic (1 1995)	Mauritania (AC 2002)	
Total	121	9	7	1	138

Source: Author's compilation.
Note: AC: Action pour le Changement; CC: Convention pour le Changement; CDR: Coalition pour la Défense de la République; DP: Democratic Party; IPK: Islamic Party of Kenya; IUP: Islamic Umma Party; KY: Kabaka Yekka; MAIB: Movimiento para la Autodeterminacion de la Isla de Bioco; MDR: Mouvement Démocratique Républicain; MRND: Mouvement Républicain National pour la Démocratie et le Développement; NDUCAP: National Democratic Union for Central African People; Palipehutu: Parti pour la Liberation du People Hutu; PCD: Parti pour la Convergence Démocratique; PDR-Ubunyanja: Parti Démocratique du Renouveau; UDP: United Democratic Party; UIRP: Uganda Islamic Revolutionary Party. *No party bans before 1990 are included.

Nigeria) and of parties judged to constitute a security threat (in Burundi, CAR, Chad, Equatorial Guinea, Mauritania and Sudan) are most common. Other reasons include a royalist program (Burundi), name resemblances (Malawi) and various formal reasons, such as failure to elect party leaders or to account for funding (DRC, Liberia, Rwanda, Tanzania, Zambia).[28] However, as case studies of Kenya, Senegal, Tanzania and Uganda have shown, these last-mentioned regulations are seldom enforced.[29] The lack of democratic internal leadership elections and accounting, for example, is often so widespread that responsible institutions did not outlaw any parties on these grounds.[30]

Considering particularistic party bans, most of the parties were banned due to their regional character (see Table 5).[31] Only one party was banned for its allegedly secessionist tendency, the United Democratic Party (UDP) in Namibia, while all other parties did not fulfil representation requirements. In Nigeria, party registration occurred in waves linked to regime changes and elections; parties that were unable to prove their 'federal character' through nationwide offices and leadership from at least two-thirds of the states were denied registration. Fifty Tanzanian parties were not able to recruit the mandatory 2000 party members from 10 different regions and were not registered either. In Angola, where a national membership base is also required, the high court de-registered existing parties when it reviewed the party member lists and discovered large numbers of faked names on them.

All in all, nine parties were banned for their alleged ethnic character. 'Ethnicity' here covers somewhat different reasons for bans: in 1994, the Mouvement Républicain National pour la Démocratie et le Développement (MRND) and the Coalition pour la Défense de la République (CDR) in Rwanda were not included in the transitional government because of their central role in the 1994 genocide and were, therefore, outlawed. An attempt by ex-president Bizimungu to found the Parti Démocratique du Renouveau (PDR-Ubunyanja) in 2001 was prevented with reference to the alleged divisive character of the party and to the general interdiction to found new parties during the transition period.[32] The Mouvement Démocratique Républicain (MDR) was also outlawed for its allegedly 'divisive' character, while the Movimiento para la Autodeterminacion de la Isla de Bioco (MAIB) in Equatorial Guinea was not only judged to be an ethnic party but was additionally accused of following a secessionist programme. In Burundi, the Parti pour la Liberation du People Hutu (Palipehutu) was denied registration for its ethnic character; it had acted as a Hutu rebel group before the start of the democratization process and its military wing continued to do so up to 2006.[33] The Kabaka Yekka (KY) in Uganda was not allowed to register because the registrar judged its name to be ethnic and to lead to divisive misunderstandings given that the Bugandan Kabaka (the traditional king of Buganda) is not allowed to participate in politics.[34] The National Democratic Union for Central African People (NDUCAP) was suspended for tribalism and sectarianism for three months.[35]

Most of the seven parties banned as religious represented very small splinter groups; for two of them it was not possible even to obtain their names (Central African Republic and Zambia). Finally, one Mauritanian party, the Action pour le Changement (AC), was deregistered because the government judged it to be racist.[36]

Procedures of implementation

When it comes to the implementation of party bans, most institutions responsible for the implementation seem to follow a mixture of formal and informal procedures. Interviews conducted by the author in April 2008 in Uganda, Kenya and Tanzania, for example, have shown that parties who applied for registration with incomplete or faulty documents were given a chance to revise their mistake instead of being denied registration right away.

Generally, party bans are much more common in autocratic countries and countries with some autocratic tendencies (rated as not or partly free by Freedom House) than in more liberal and democratic countries. Focusing on particularistic parties, numerous parties have been outlawed even before an official demand of registration by the parties was made. For example, it seems that the MAIB did not officially ask for registration but was immediately declared illegal by the Equatoguinean government after the announcement of its creation. The same is true for the Uganda Islamic Revolutionary Party (UIRP). When it was founded in 1993, President Yoweri Museveni quickly declared that an Islamic party would be against the principles of the 'movement system' and therefore illegal.[37] Another example is the already mentioned PDR-Ubuyanja, where the Rwandan government declared the attempt to form a party illegal and put Bizimungu into prison. The attempts to create both UIRP and PDR thus occurred in a strongly and formally restricted multiparty environment.

Kenya and Zambia, on the other hand, did not possess an official law prohibiting the creation of particularistic parties when they outlawed allegedly religious parties in the 1990s. The 'Society Acts' of both countries – passed in 1952 and 1958 respectively – outlawed associations with unlawful purposes, or associations that were prejudicial to or incompatible with peace, welfare or good order without mentioning religious parties. While we were unable to find more background information about the decision in Zambia, the Kenyan example is highly instructive. The Islamic Party of Kenya (IPK) was founded in early 1992 and declined registration in June.[38] President Daniel arap Moi had argued during a public rally that an Islamic party should not be legalized even before the IPK had officially asked for registration. When the party complained, the attorney-general agreed with the registrar's decision, referring to the constitution of Kenya. However, no article of the constitution explicitly prohibits religious parties and the attorney-general himself did not quote any article of the constitution but was rather vague in his arguments. Opposition parties and other critics of the government, therefore, argued that the decision lacked any judicial base.[39] The IPK went to court, but the government used delaying tactics and refused to reverse its decision.[40]

In Namibia, the UDP was outlawed without being an officially registered party. Founded in 1985, the UDP was part of the Democratic Turnhalle Alliance (DTA).

When its party leader, Misheke Muyongo, was excluded from the DTA because he supported the independence of the Caprivi, the UDP split from the DTA but never formally registered as a political party. After a short-lived rebellion in Caprivi in 1998 and 1999 when the alleged military wing of the UDP, the Caprivi Liberation Army, tried to bring about the region's independence, Muyongo and his allies left the country and the UDP remained largely inactive for several years. In 2006, a revival of the party was announced with the aim to fight peacefully for the independence of Caprivi. The Namibian government immediately declared the party illegal for two reasons: firstly, the party was claimed to be pursuing illegal aims (secession) and, second, it was not officially registered (and would not be, given its political aims).[41]

Finally, in Rwanda, none of the bans took place according to a party law. As already described, the MRND and the CDR were not included in the transitional government and thus outlawed. The same restriction of party politics applied to the PDR. All bans were, however, also justified by referring to ethnic divisionism as a central threat to Rwandan political stability.[42] The MDR was never officially banned in a strict sense. A parliamentary commission recommended the dissolution of the MDR in a detailed report.[43] The MDR did not apply for registration when, shortly afterwards, the new constitution and party law went into effect, demanding a new registration of all political parties.[44]

After the bans

If a party is denied registration or outlawed, it has several options: it may dissolve, appeal against the decision, try to register again (maybe under another name) or be active clandestinely. While most of the banned parties seemed to dissolve, examples of all strategies can be found. Several parties went to court against a decision (for example, the Democratic Party (DP) in Tanzania, the AC in Mauritania, the KY in Uganda, and the IPK in Kenya). Yet, only once was such a complaint successful: in Nigeria, in 2002, several parties that saw themselves denied registration appealed to the Supreme Court, which finally ruled that the electoral commission was too strict. The commission then registered 24 new parties. Only one party, the MAIB in Equatorial Guinea, is known to operate clandestinely, like many other parties that are not legally registered in the highly authoritarian state. The party is part of the exiled opposition group Demócratas por el Cambio and is also in close contact with an exile government in Spain.

Many party leaders try to register a party several times. However, while several parties that were banned for other reasons managed to re-register under a new party name (examples include Burundi, Malawi, Mali, Mauritania, and Zambia), particularistic parties were usually not allowed to do so. In Mauritania, for example, the leader of the AC, Ould Boulkheir, whose party was banned for criticizing the situation of the Haratines, the former slaves, and the Black African population, tried to found another party after his judicial appeal had been denied. Despite his efforts to integrate different groups in the new party, the Convention pour le Changement

(CC), his party was denied registration on grounds of being an ethnic party. Party leaders later joined another party, the Alliance Populaire Progressiste.[45]

The moderate Islamists in Mauritania showed even more persistence. They first tried to register the Islamic Umma Party (IUP) in 1991; when registration was denied they stayed politically active despite repeated crackdowns by the government.[46] In 2004, moderate Islamists tried again to register a party, the Parti pour la Convergence Démocratique (PCD), but without success. The government referred to the constitution and the party law, which both prohibit parties that claim a monopoly over Islam, and also reproached the party for harbouring Islamists. After a successful coup in 2005, the PCD tried to register with the new military government, who also declined.[47] Only in 2006, under the newly elected president Ould Cheikh Abdallahi (deposed in the 2008 coup), the Tawassoul (Rassemblement National pour la Réforme et le Développement), a party of the PCD leader Jemil Ould Mansour, was registered. A second Islamic party, Al Fadila, was also registered in 2006 and members of both parties participated in the government for several months.[48]

Fourteen of the Tanzanian parties also tried to register several times.[49] The DP, led by Reverend Mtikila, had the most political weight of these parties. Mtikila argued strongly against the union between Tanzania mainland and the Zanzibar islands, claiming that Zanzibar should not be part of Tanzania and, therefore, opposed looking for members on the island.[50] The Tanzanian party law, however, makes it obligatory for parties to have at least 200 members in at least 10 regions, with two of the regions being in Zanzibar. Mtikila unsuccessfully appealed against the decision and finally, in 2002, changed his radical programme and got members from Zanzibar, and the DP was registered.[51]

The IPK in Kenya opted for a more radical way; its protests against the government and later clashes with the United Muslims of Africa, a government-sponsored competing Muslim organization, led to eruptions of violence in Mombasa for almost two years. However, despite repeated attempts, the IPK never managed to get registered.[52] Finally, the Palipehutu-FNL became one of the main actors in the Burundian civil wars. The wing of Agathon Rwasa that signed a peace agreement in 2006 had heated debates with the government about the name it should take in order to register as a political party. While Rwasa claimed his right to keep the movement's name, the government invoked the party law that prohibits ethnic parties. Finally, the group was registered under the name of Forces Nationales de Libération in April 2009.[53]

Summary

In sum, four results about implementation procedures of party bans in Africa are particularly noteworthy. First, 23 out of 43 countries have implemented a party ban and 12 out of 41 countries have banned particularistic parties.[54] While these numbers might seem low, they are nevertheless much higher than expected given the low regulatory capacity of many African states. Second, only some of the possible reasons to ban a party have been invoked with a clear accent on regionalism, ethnicity, and religion. While one party was banned for its alleged racist character, no party based on language or colour has ever been banned as far as we know. The largest numbers of parties were banned because they could not prove their national character, all of them in Angola, Nigeria, and Tanzania.[55] In Burundi, Kenya, Mauritania, and Rwanda, banned parties had such wide political support that they might have represented a challenge for the incumbent parties. The banned parties in the CAR, in Equatorial Guinea, Namibia, Uganda, and Zambia were rather small and focused on the concerns of smaller groups.

Third, if we exclude bans on the grounds of representation requirements, almost half of the bans were not in accordance with the law or took place in a situation where party laws were not fully in force. This makes it necessary to take a closer look at the relationship between the level of democracy, the rule of law, and the implementation of party bans. It seems that bans are not very common in democratic countries. Finally, legal protection for banned parties in the form of a possible judicial appeal rarely seems to lead to a reversal while only a few of the parties find other ways to escape the verdict. While one party was found to exist clandestinely, all of the other parties disappeared at least formally after the ban.

Conclusion

The legislation of political parties has been on the rise in Africa since 1990. Most countries ban specific types of parties, especially ethnic or other particularistic parties – such party bans have become the dominant paradigm in Africa. Based on a unique database on party legislation in Africa, this article presented an overview of African party bans with a focus on particularistic parties. While the relevance of formal legislation in African countries has often been doubted, our presentation of implemented party bans shows that bans have been used by more than half of the countries. Particularistic parties have been banned in one-third of the countries. Bans lead mostly to a disappearance of the respective party while only one party in Equatorial Guinea, the MAIB, continued to operate clandestinely and very few political groups finally managed to register in a new attempt, such as the DP in Tanzania. However, the discussion of procedures and reasons of party bans points to the risk of the use of bans in undemocratic contexts. Only one single ban has occurred in a country rated as free by Freedom House, namely Namibia. This finding raises the question of the origins and political impact of party bans, which will be discussed in the following contributions of this special issue.

Notes

1. Lipset, 'The Indispensability of Political Parties'.
2. Van Biezen, 'Party Regulation and Constitutionalization'; Karvonen, 'Legislation on Political Parties'.
3. Reilly, 'Political Engineering and Party Politics in Conflict-Prone Societies'.

4. Janda, 'Political Parties and Democracy'; Reilly and Nordlund, *Political Parties in Conflict-Prone Societies*.
5. For a discussion of party bans worldwide see Bogaards, 'Comparative Strategies of Political Party Regulation'. For an overview for sub-Saharan Africa see appendix A and B.
6. Janda, 'Political Parties and Democracy'.
7. Starting points are the database by Kenneth Janda, www.ndi.org/db, and the collection by International IDEA, www.political-parties.org.
8. The author wishes to thank the GIGA Institute of African Affairs, the Max-Planck-Institute for Comparative and International Private Law in Hamburg, EISA as well as local offices of German party foundations, which were of great help in the collection of the relevant laws.
9. No information was available for the Comoros.
10. Zimbabwe later followed this pattern, while Angola and Mozambique introduced one-party states.
11. The laws did not specify what constitutes an act against territorial integrity or national unity.
12. It is important to keep in mind that we only looked at constitutions and not at election, party or association laws.
13. Bogaards, 'Comparative Strategies of Political Party Regulation', 52.
14. The draft constitution of Zambia also includes a party ban; the constitution is however not ratified yet.
15. In order to capture the behavioural dimension of the ban ('acts on behalf of or in the interest of'), we assign respective party bans regarding, for instance, 'tribalism' to ethnic parties, 'racism' to racial parties, and 'regionalism' to regional parties.
16. For a discussion of these regulations with regard to Latin America, see for example Birnir, 'Stabilizing Party Systems'.
17. If the relevant law or constitutions outlawed secessionist parties we put this under the heading of region.
18. Loi no 2001–21 portant Charte des partis politiques; Political Parties Act 2000.
19. Political Parties Registration Proclamation 46/1993 and 573/2008.
20. We only included regulations that explicitly refer to particularistic party politics (for example, incitation of ethnic hatred is included; general incitation of hatred is not). The outlawing of discrimination is not counted as a particularistic party ban.
21. In Lesotho, parties have to register under the Societies Act as well as under the Election Act in order to participate in elections.
22. See also Bogaards, 'Comparative Strategies of Political Party Regulation'.
23. See for example Lijphart, *Democracy in Plural Societies*.
24. The following overview draws on our database of African party law. Information on country-specific resources is available upon request from the author.
25. In order to capture all implemented bans, we systematically examined pertinent sources such as various editions of the German language *Afrika-Jahrbuch* (1990–2003) and its English language successor the Africa Yearbook, Economist Intelligence Unit (EIU) country reports, Freedom House country reports, US Department of State Human Rights Country Reports, and International Institute for Democracy and Electoral Assistance (IDEA) country reports. In addition, we conducted a survey of some 100 experts on the 48 countries in sub-Saharan Africa; approximately two-thirds responded.
26. Kenya deregistered 121 parties in 2008, when the new Political Parties Act was implemented. These parties failed to fulfil the registration requirements, which include nationwide membership, district branches and a high registration fee. As we could not establish what exactly prevented them from being registered, we here

count them as 'general bans'. See Moroff, 'Comparing Ethnic Party Regulation in East Africa', this issue.

27. The parties, however, protested against these regulations. In 2001, President Joseph Kabila introduced a new law that re-legalized the existing parties and gave them six months to fulfil the remaining requirements. We therefore present the figures in the graphic without the 400 Congolese parties.

28. For a number of cases it proved impossible to find more information about the reasons.

29. See Hartmann, 'Senegal's Party System: The Limits of Formal Regulation', Kemmerzell, 'Why There Is No Party Ban in the South African Constitution', and Moroff, 'Comparing Ethnic Party Regulation', all this issue.

30. Ibid.

31. If not indicated otherwise, the following illustrations draw on the Africa Yearbook (until 2004 Afrika Jahrbuch) and the Economist Intelligence Unit (EIU) Country Reports since 1990.

32. See Niesen, 'Rwanda', this issue.

33. Institute for Security Studies, *Another Crossroad for Burundi.*

34. See Moroff, 'Comparing Ethnic Party Regulation', this issue. Traditional leaders, like the Kabaka, are not allowed to engage in party politics according to the 1995 constitution and the party law. A previous party called KY had participated in a coalition government in 1962–66.

35. US State Department, *Central African Republic: Country Report on Human Rights Practices.*

36. See Moroff and Basedau, 'An Effective Measure of Institutional Engineering?', this issue.

37. Uganda outlawed political party activities from 1986 onwards, and introduced a so-called 'movement-system' under the National Resistance Movement of President Museveni. For a discussion of its main features see for example Kasfir, 'No-Party Democracy'.

38. Oded, *Islam and Politics in Kenya.*

39. *Daily Nation*, 22 June 1992.

40. *Daily Nation*, 12 February 1993; *Daily Nation*, 23 July 1993; US State Department, *Kenya: Country Report on Human Rights Practices.*

41. *The Namibian*, 5 September 2006; Melber, 'One Namibia'.

42. See Niesen, 'Political Party Bans in Rwanda', this issue.

43. Commission Parlementaire, 'Rapport'.

44. In 2009 the Rwandan government argued that the Parti Social Ideal could not be registered because its acronym was already in use; it did not have enough female party leaders; and it lacked nationwide members. Later on, the party was registered as Parti Social-Imberakuri. *The New Times*, 9 March 2009; http://www.imberakuri.org/historique.php.

45. For a discussion of the AC, see Marty, 'Mauritania'.

46. ICG, *L'Islamisme.*

47. Ibid.

48. Economist Intelligence Unit (EIU), *Country Report Mauritania October 2007*; EIU, *Country Report Mauritania July 2008.*

49. Source: Registrar of Political Parties.

50. See Moroff, 'Comparing Ethnic Party Regulation', this issue.

51. While Mtikila lost the case in 1993, he won an appeal against the decision of the Registrar in 1996. When he applied a second time, Registrar Liundi denied the registration again. Mtikila tried to force Liundi to register his party by a second appeal, which was denied. Liundi, 'Political Parties'; *The Guardian*, 5 August 2000.

52. Oded, *Islam and Politics in Kenya.*

53. Institute for Security Studies, *Another Crossroad for Burundi*.
54. The 39 countries that allow for a ban plus Kenya (included in 2008) and Zambia.
55. We cannot conclude with absolute certainty that we detected all of these denials of registration. As they are regarded as mostly administrative, they are not always treated in the relevant country sources that were consulted here.

Notes on contributor

Anika Moroff is a PhD candidate at the Department of Political Science at the University of Duisburg-Essen and an Associate Research Fellow at the GIGA Institute of African Affairs in Hamburg. Her research interests include political parties in Africa, ethnic conflict and institutional engineering.

Bibliography

Birnir, Jóhanna Kristín. 'Stabilizing Party Systems and Excluding Segments of Society? The Effects of Formation Costs on New Party Foundation in Latin America'. *Studies in Comparative International Development* 39, no. 3 (2004): 3–27.

Bogaards, Matthijs. 'Comparative Strategies of Political Party Regulation'. In *Political Parties in Conflict-Prone Societies: Regulation, Engineering and Democratic Development*, ed. Benjamin Reilly and Per Nordlund, 48–66. Tokyo & New York: United Nations University Press, 2008.

Commission Parlementaire. 'Rapport de la Commission Parlementaire sur les problèmes du MDR'. Kigali: 2003.

Hartmann, Christof. 'Senegal's Party System: The Limits of Formal Regulation'. *Democratization* 17, no. 4 (2010): 769–86.

International Crisis Group. *L'islamisme en Afrique du Nord IV: Contestation islamiste en Mauritanie: Menace ou bouc émissaire?* 2005.

Institute for Security Studies. *Another Crossroad for Burundi. From the FNL to Peaceful Elections in 2010*, Situation Report, 2009.

Janda, Kenneth. *Political Parties and Democracy in Theoretical and Practical Experience: Adopting Party Law*. Washington, DC: National Democratic Institute, 2005.

Karvonen, Lauri. 'Legislation on Political Parties: A Global Comparison'. *Party Politics* 13, no. 4 (2007): 437–55.

Kasfir, Nelson. '"No-Party Democracy" in Uganda'. *Journal of Democracy* 9, no. 2 (1998): 49–63.

Kemmerzell, Jörg. 'Why There Is No Party Ban in the South African Constitution'. *Democratization* 17, no. 4 (2010): 687–708.

Lijphart, Arend. *Democracy in Plural Societies: A Comparative Exploration*. New Haven: Yale University Press, 1977.

Lipset, Seymour Martin. 'The Indispensability of Political Parties'. *Journal of Democracy* 11, no. 1 (2000): 48–55.

Liundi, George B. 'Political Parties in a Multiparty Democracy'. In *Fundamental Rights and Freedoms in Tanzania*, ed. Chris Maina Peter and Ibrahim H. Juma, 199–209. Dar es Salaam: Mkuki na Nyota Publishers, 1998.

Marty, Marianne. 'Mauritania: Political Parties, Neo-Patrimonialism and Democracy.' *Democratization* 9, no. 3 (2002): 92–108.

Melber, Henning. 'One Namibia, One Nation? The Caprivi as Contested Territory'. *Journal of Contemporary African Studies* 27, no. 4 (2009): 463–81.

Moroff, Anika. 'Comparing Ethnic Party Regulation in East Africa'. *Democratization* 17, no. 4 (2010): 750–68.

Moroff, Anika and Matthias Basedau. 'An Effective Measure of Institutional Engineering? Ethnic Party Bans in Africa'. *Democratization* 17, no. 4 (2010): 666–86.

Niesen, Peter. 'Political Party Bans in Rwanda 1994–2003: Three Narratives of Justification'. *Democratization* 17, no. 4 (2010): 709–29.

Oded, Arye. *Islam and Politics in Kenya.* Boulder, CO: Lynne Rienner Publishers, 2000.

Reilly, Benjamin. 'Political Engineering and Party Politics in Conflict-Prone Societies'. *Democratization* 13, no. 5 (2006): 811–27.

Reilly, Benjamin and Per Nordlund, eds. *Political Parties in Conflict-Prone Societies: Regulation, Engineering and Democratic Development.* Tokyo & New York: United Nations University Press, 2008.

US State Department. *Central African Republic: Country Report on Human Rights Practices*, 1998.

US State Department. *Kenya: Country Report on Human Rights Practices*, 2000.

van Biezen, Ingrid 'Party Regulation and Constitutionalization: A Comparative Overview'. In *Political Parties in Conflict-Prone Societies: Regulation, Engineering and Democratic Development*, ed. Benjamin Reilly and Per Nordlund, 25–47. Tokyo & New York: United Nations University Press, 2008.

APPENDIX A

Possible legal reasons for party bans in sub-Saharan Africa – identity bases (as of March 2010).

Country	Year of first introduction	Ethnicity/ Tribalism	Religion/ Sect	Region	Region - National Representation	Race/ Colour	Language	Other	Gender
Angola	1991	X	X	X	X	X	-	-	X
Burkina Faso	1991	X	X	X	-	X	X	-	X
Benin	1990	X	X	X	X	X	X	-	X
Burundi	1992	X	X	X	X	-	X	X	X
Cameroon	1990	X	X	X	-	-	-	X	-
Cape Verde	1990	-	X	X	X	X	X	X	-
CAR	1991	X	X	X	-	X	X	X	X
Chad	1991	X	X	X	-	X	X	-	X
Congo Br.	1990	X	X	X	X	X	X	-	X
Congo DR	1999	X	X	X	X	X	X	X	X
Côte d'Ivoire	1993	X	X	X	-	X	X	-	X
Djibouti	1992	X	X	X	X	X	X	-	X
Eq. Guinea	1991	X	X	X	X	-	-	-	X
Ethiopia	1993	-	X	-	X*	-	-	-	-
Gabon	1991	-	-	-	X	-	-	X	-
Gambia	1995	X	X	X	-	-	X	X	X
Ghana	1957	X	X	X	X	-	X	X	-
Guinea	1990	X	X	X	X	X	X	-	X
Guinea-Bissao	1991	X	X	X	X	X	X	-	-
Kenya	2008	X	X	X	X	X	X	X	X
Lesotho	1992	X	X	X	-	X	X	-	X
Liberia	1986	X	X	X	X	-	-	X	X
Madagascar	1990	-	-	-	X	X	-	X	-
Malawi	1996	-	X	-	-	-	-	-	-
Mali	1991	X	X	X	-	-	X	-	X

(*Continued*)

Continued.

Country	Year of first introduction	Ethnicity/ Tribalism	Religion/ Sect	Region	Region - National Representation	Race/ Colour	Language	Other	Gender
Mauritania	1991	X	X	X	-	X	-	X	X
Mozambique	1990	X	X	X	X	X	-	-	-
Namibia	1992	X	X	-	-	X	-	-	X
Niger	1991	X	X	X	X	X	X	-	X
Nigeria	1979	X	X	X	X	-	-	-	X
Rwanda	1991	X	X	X	X	X	-	X	X
Senegal	1978	X	X	X	-	X	X	-	X
Seychelles	1991	-	-	X	-	-	-	-	-
Sierra Leone	1991	X	X	X	X	-	-	X	-
Somalia	(1960) 2004	X	-	-	-	-	-	-	-
São Tomé and Principe	1990	-	X	X	-	X	-	-	X
Sudan	1998	X	X	-	X	-	-	-	-
Tanzania	1992	X	X	X	X	X	-	-	X
Togo	1991	X	X	X	X	X	-	X	-
Uganda**	1995	X	X	X	X	X	-	X	X
Σ	40	33	36	33	25	24	14	15	24

Source: Author's compilation.

Note: *Depending on the type of party. **Political parties were allowed to exist but did not have the right to be active until 2005. Other: Clan, family, brotherhood, 'other sectional divisions', secessionism, divisionism, segregationism. Countries without the explicit possibility to ban a party because of its particularistic nature: Botswana, Comoros, Mauritius, South Africa, Zambia, Zimbabwe. Countries without a multiparty system: Eritrea, Swaziland.

Appendix B

Possible legal reasons for party bans in sub-Saharan Africa – party features (as of March 2010).

Country	Year of first introduction	General	Program	Symbol	Organization	Membership	Campaign
Angola	1991	X	X	X	X	X	-
Burkina Faso	1991	X	X	-	-	X	(X)
Benin	1990	X	X	-	X	X	X
Burundi	1992	X	-	-	X	X	X
Cameroon	1990	X	-	-	-	-	-
Cape Verde	1990	X	X	X	X	X	(X)
CAR	1991	X	-	-	-	-	-
Chad	1991	X	X	X	X	-	X
Congo Br.	1990	X	X	-	X	-	-
Congo DR	1999	X	-	-	X	-	-
Côte d'Ivoire	1993	X	-	-	-	-	-
Djibouti	1992	X	-	-	X	-	-
Eq. Guinea	1991	X	X	X	X	-	X
Ethiopia	1993	X	-	X	X	-	X
Gabon	1991	X	-	-	X	-	(X)
Gambia	1995	X	X	X	X	-	-
Ghana	1969	X	-	X	X	X	X
Guinea	1990	X	-	-	X	-	X
Guinea-Bissao	1991	X	X	X	X	X	-
Kenya	2008	X	-	X	X	X	X
Lesotho	1992	-	X	X	-	X	-
Liberia	1986	X	X	X	X	X	-
Madagascar	1990	X	-	-	X	-	-
Malawi	1996	-	X	X	-	X	-
Mali	1991	X	-	-	X	-	-
Mauritania	1991	X	-	-	-	-	X

(*Continued*)

Continued.

Country	Year of first introduction	General	Program	Symbol	Organization	Membership	Campaign
Mozambique	1990	X	X	X	X	-	-
Namibia	1992	X	-	-	X	-	-
Niger	1991	X	X	-	X	X	X
Nigeria	1979	-	-	X	X	X	(X)
Rwanda	1991	X	X	-	X	-	X
Senegal	1978	X	-	-	-	-	(X)
Seychelles	1991	-	X	-	-	X	-
Sierra Leone	1991	-	X	X	X	X	-
Somalia	(1960) 2004	X	X	-	-	X	-
São Tomé and Principe	1990	X	-	X	X	X	X
Sudan	1998	X	X	-	X	X	X
Tanzania	1992	-	X	-	X	X	-
Togo	1991	X	X	-	X	-	X
Uganda**	1995	X	X	-	X	X	X
Σ	40	34	21	16	28	18	14

Source: Author's compilation.
Note: *Depending on the type of party. **Political parties were allowed to exist but did not have the right to be active until 2005. If in parenthesis: outlawed but does not lead to ban.

Understanding variations in party bans in Africa

Christof Hartmann[a] and Jörg Kemmerzell[b]

[a]Institute of Political Science, University of Duisburg-Essen, Duisburg, Germany;
[b]Institute of Political Science, Technical University Darmstadt, Darmstadt, Germany

The article is interested in the main reasons for the emergence and enforcement of party bans in sub-Saharan Africa. While the introduction of legal provisions that allow for the banning of particularistic political parties is the standard on the African continent, few countries actually use these provisions and actually deny registration or ban existing parties. We use qualitative comparative analysis to compare the introduction of party bans and the patterns of implementation across all sub-Saharan countries. Our analysis shows that structural conditions do matter. Countries that did not introduce legal provisions to ban political parties combine a British colonial background and a stronger tradition of multi-party democracy. With regard to the decision to actually use these provisions our analysis shows the interaction of two conditions to be decisive: Countries which have experienced ethnically motivated violence in the past and which are at the same time 'liberalizing' their regimes rely on party bans to restrict political party competition.

Introduction

The re-introduction of multiparty systems which occurred in most African countries in the five years between 1989 and 1994 occurred with heavy *de facto* and often also *de jure* restrictions of the activities of political parties. To re-admit political parties into the political game was certainly often as much a regime strategy to avoid full competition (by controlling the extent and the practice of competition) as a true attempt at democratization. While some incumbent presidents went so far as to artificially increasing the number of registered political parties (by directly creating several of them or by creating incentives for split-offs from existing parties) in order to weaken the authentic party opposition to their rule, political parties became easy targets of popular frustration about rent-seeking politicians and of manipulation by powerful heads of state within the strongly presidential systems of government.

The idea of regulating and controlling the number and the activities of political parties is thus a familiar feature to students of African politics. Even before the wave of liberalization various African governments (Ghana and Senegal in the 1970s, Uganda in the 1980s, Nigeria in the 1990s) went very far in engineering the party systems by legally fixing the number of parties or their ideological orientation.

Within the emerging research agenda on party politics in Africa there is an astonishing lack of consideration for formal regulation of party activities. If the topic has been tackled, the main focus has been on understanding the relevance of different rules of party regulation.[1] No study exists, on the contrary, about why party regulation was introduced in the first place and how we can account for the emergence and enforcement of different institutional arrangements. Our contribution is intended to shed some light on this new research topic by concentrating on one specific aspect of party regulation, i.e. party bans.

Since the early 1990s nearly all African states have formalized regulation by introducing constitutional or legal norms, with party bans featuring prominently among these norms. What strikes the observer of the day-to-day politics in many African states, however, is the fact that these formal rules are seldom enforced, and that there is a gap between a pervasive and nearly continent-wide trend towards extensive formal regulation and a patchy and incongruent practice of actually sanctioning the behaviour and nature of parties. This paper intends to contribute to an explanation of this institutional reform puzzle, i.e. the incongruence between the widespread legal introduction of party bans and the similar widespread lack of implementation of those bans in sub-Saharan Africa.

Our contribution compares all sub-Saharan countries, thus accounting for similarities and differences with regard to the introduction of party bans and to their implementation in a time span from 1990 to 2007.[2] We assume that these variations are not random but that some systematic patterns and causal paths account for their introduction (or not) and relative importance. We will use the method of qualitative comparative analysis (QCA) to detect these patterns and paths. Our analysis will proceed in four steps. The next two sections will give a brief overview of our methodology and discuss which theoretical conditions are selected. We will then use Multi-Value QCA (MV-QCA) in the two remaining sections to explain first the introduction, and second, the actual implementation of party bans. Our analysis shows that structural conditions do matter. Only a few African countries did not introduce legal provisions to ban parties. These countries combine a specific British colonial background and a stronger tradition of multiparty democracy. With regard to the decision to actually use these provisions two conditions are shown to be decisive: countries which have experienced ethnically motivated violence in the past and which are 'liberalizing' their regimes rely on party bans to restrict political party competition.

Methodological considerations

Party bans have received rather limited interest in comparative political science so far. The analysis of their occurrence and implementation, which concentrates generally on Europe and the OECD world,[3] has been interested in specific cases and the juridical dimension of party bans, or been mainly concerned with the legitimacy of party bans, as seen in research by Nancy Rosenblum and Peter Niesen.[4] This literature highlights some common features about the conditions under which party bans are likely being adopted. Besides their manipulative (mis)use by authoritarian or semi-authoritarian regimes, one critical element identified is the mode of political transitions as a structuring environment in which party bans become a likely institutional choice. Nancy Rosenblum has thus emphasized the role of party bans in plural societies and their relevance for the adoption of ethnic or other types of particularistic identities in democratizing polities.[5] Even though we can derive some helpful suggestions from this body of literature, there is no set of well-established variables or hypotheses to test. Our objective is thus rather to identify structural patterns of the introduction and implementation of party bans in an inductive manner, thereby contributing to theory-building on the emergence and dynamics of party regulation in sub-Saharan Africa. We are less interested in assessing the explanatory relevance of a single factor but rather in reconstructing patterns or conditional configurations of party bans. Therefore the macro qualitative method of QCA and its strength in detecting different equifinal causal paths towards similar outcomes should be a valuable approach.

The method is placed within the group of case-oriented comparisons and follows a qualitative and categorical logic. First, in QCA each case is recognized as a configuration of several theoretical conditions (i.e. independent variables) leading to an outcome (i.e. dependent variable), but the method avoids disintegrating the cases into variables which is typical for quantitative probabilistic approaches.[6] While probabilistic approaches, which rely on linear algebra, are intended to reveal 'more or less' relations, QCA, based on Boolean algebra, is concerned with deterministic 'either-or' relations. Secondly, QCA allows for a transparent and systematic presentation of complex configurations in small and medium N comparisons. The first step of our analysis covers 48 cases, the second step 37 cases. Thus, it belongs to the medium N category. Thirdly, QCA can be used to deduce logical minimal explanations by minimization (see below). Here is not the place to give a concise overview of the method[7] but we will point to specific shortcomings of classic crisp set QCA that guided our decision to adopt a specific enhancement of QCA, namely MV-QCA.[8]

The main problem of Crisp Set QCA is the necessity to construct dichotomized conditions, and the setting of reasonable thresholds for the indication as 'present' or 'absent'. This becomes even more critical if one is concerned with originally interval-scaled variables. There are at least two recent developments within QCA which address these shortcomings: Fuzzy Set QCA[9] and Multi-Value QCA

(MV-QCA).[10] We used MV-QCA for our analysis, employing the recent version of the software tool TOSMANA.[11]

We are fully aware of the criticisms raised against MV-QCA.[12] MV-QCA appears, however, to be appropriate because we deal with originally nominal multi-valued conditions. This means we are not confronted with two of the main problems of Crisp Set QCA, that is the transformation of originally interval or ordinal scaled variables by setting more or less arbitrarily thresholds and its incapacity to deal with multichotomous nominal data at all. Most of our conditions, e.g. 'former regime types', belong to this category of 'multichotomous nominal data'. MV-QCA is suggested to 'provide an elegant solution'[13] to deal with this kind of data.

But we should not underestimate the problems of a strategy which relies on multi-valued conditions. We are confronted with a proliferation of degrees of freedom which may lead quickly to an 'individualization' of cases.[14] In the application of a more complex research design, the usage of multi-valued conditions may cause more difficulties than it contributes to a good explanation. We should thus apply multi-valued variables in a rather parsimonious way and stick to a restrictive practice of operationalization.

Party bans are defined both as the banning and dissolution of already existing parties and the temporary suspension of party organization. In addition to that the denial of registration of a political party – if the legal procedure of party registration is required – should also be considered as a party ban.[15] By applying this definition to the empirical universe of African states, 42 of 48 countries have legal provisions to ban parties.[16] Between 1990 and 2007, 22 states enforced party bans including some rather doubtful cases which do not allow for an unambiguous classification. If we apply stricter selection rules and count only particularistic party bans, i.e. bans that prohibit the existence or activity of a political party which is composed of, and acts in the interest of a specific ethnic or particularistic identity group (tribe, religion, race, colour, or language), the number of countries which enforced particularistic party bans in a narrow sense is reduced to 12.[17]

Two caveats are in order: there are certainly differences in the precise format of party bans that we will have to ignore in our analysis. We will code countries as having introduced a legal particularistic ban or not, and ignore whether the ban is primarily ethnic, religious, race-based or regional. As a rule, we will also not take into account the timing of the introduction, i.e. the precise year when the clause was enacted. Nearly all countries that introduced party bans did so in the period between 1989 and 1995, with some latecomers and a few countries that already had party bans before 1989.[18]

Theoretical conditions

We assume that four conditions are decisive for the introduction of particularistic party bans: the colonial background of the country; former regime type; the mode of transition towards a multiparty regime; and previous experience with (ethnic) violence. We will briefly discuss these conditions and their coding, develop some hypotheses and explain why other potential factors (such as neo-patrimonialism) are not taken into account. For the analysis of the implementation of party bans we will use a similar set of structural conditions. There are sound reasons to assume that colonial background, former regime type and experience with ethnic violence still matter, but instead of transition mode the actual regime type at the time of implementation is added as a fourth explanatory factor in our analysis of implementation (see also the summary of our conditions in Tables 1 and 2 on pages 650 and 651).

Colonial background

The legacy of colonial rule is considered to be a major explanatory factor for the evolution of the political institutions in African states.[19] The independence constitutions of African states were often blueprints of the constitutions of the colonial rulers, or a negotiated solution with heavy input from French or British ministries or universities.[20] Equally important, many ordinary laws (such as those regulating associations) enacted by the colonial governments remained in force, or were formally re-edited but without changing the substance.[21]

The main hypothesis that we want to advance here is that different types of colonial legacies have created different institutional paths of party regulation that matter both for the introduction and the actual implementation of party bans. The French tradition was essentially centralist and universalistic, and as such was transferred to the francophone African countries. The central state was all-mighty in its ambition and highly suspicious of particularistic tendencies, whether political or cultural. In contrast, the British colonial rule was much more willing to accommodate existing local or regional authorities and practices. Before independence, British colonial authorities advocated federalism or decentralized forms of government. While few of these decentralized units survived much into independence, the political-social landscape remained much more pluralistic than in francophone countries.[22] After independence, former French colonies abolished multiparty rule much faster and more strictly than former British colonies. Belgium's, Italy's and Portugal's colonial rule certainly developed their specific features, but were, as a rule, even more centralist and repressive towards local associations or political activities.[23] The only initially surviving democratic systems, that is, Botswana, Gambia and Mauritius, were all former British protectorates or colonies. Countries with a British legacy would thus be expected to be more tolerant towards particularistic parties and less expansive in their attempt to regulate social and political affairs. In our MV-QCA, countries with a British colonial background are coded with *2*; countries with a French background are coded with *1*; and all other countries with *0*.[24]

Former regime type

A regime's or legislator's willingness to ban specific types of political parties might also be directly related to the type of political competition experienced by this country in the past.

There are several ways to distinguish political regime types in post-independence Africa.[25] The most widely used typology stems from Bratton and van de Walle's 1997 seminal study.[26] They classify regimes according to the degree of participation and competition and accordingly build five types:[27] the 'multiparty systems' with full competition and participation; the 'settler oligarchies' such as apartheid South Africa where there was limited participation, but those who participated had access to a highly competitive political system; the 'competitive' and 'plebiscitarian' one-party systems and the 'military obligarchies'. Bratton and van de Walle distinguish three other types of authoritarian regimes, the 'competitive' and 'plebiscitarian' one-party systems[28] and the 'military oligarchies'.

While some sub-Saharan African states, such as Botswana or Mauritius, have had a fairly stable regime pattern, others such as Ghana, Nigeria, Burkina Faso and Uganda have gone through various different types of regimes. Grouping these countries into one type of previous regime is thus not without problems; we follow Bratton and van de Walle in identifying the regime previous to the latest phase of democratization (regime type in 1989) as decisive type. We depart from Bratton and van de Walle's coding exercise where legal party bans were introduced *before* 1989. This is the case for Senegal, Liberia, Ghana, and Nigeria. For these countries the regime type in the period before the introduction of party bans is coded.[29]

Previous experience with multiparty competition can be linked to particularistic party bans in two ways. We hypothesize that in the course of the political liberalization a complete lack of competition in the past (i.e. in countries with plebiscitarian one-party systems or military autocracies) is less likely to lead to an unrestricted competition of political parties than in those countries that have some (limited) experience with political party competition. There is, however, a second hypothesis which concerns those countries with a discontinuous history of party competition (the group mentioned above). In nearly all these cases (Ghana, Nigeria, Uganda), previous episodes of multiparty competition were or are still perceived as periods of instability, corruption, and ethnic clientelism. A 'bad' experience with party competition could thus be a reason for strict and comprehensive legal party bans rather than the lack of experience, especially in combination with ethnic violence. In these cases, we would also expect a reliance on the actual banning of parties, because in the light of 'bad' experiences with 'ethnicized' parties, governments could claim a stronger legitimacy for such strict policy measures.

We opted here for a multi-valued condition. All countries that had a continuous competitive party system before 1990 are coded with *0*. This includes both the liberal democracies and the settler oligarchies (or 'exclusive democracies' according to Wolfgang Merkel).[30] Countries with a limited degree of party competition are coded with *1*, while countries without any previous competition are coded with *2*.

Transition mode

Most party bans were introduced following the transition of an authoritarian regime towards democracy, because it is during this interval when parties are allowed to operate (and apparently a need for regulation emerges).[31] Transition studies have typically distinguished modes of transition according to a number of criteria such as the actor constellation (elite-based or 'from above', mass-based or 'from below') or the decision mode (pacted or managed).[32] We opt here for a distinction between those countries with a coordinated or pacted transition and a residual category with all transitions without substantial compromises. This latter category then covers the 'managed transitions' with incumbent leaders remaining in full control, the regime breakdowns (through a victory of opposition movements in free elections such as Zambia in 1991 or through the so-called National Conferences in the Francophone countries which paved the way for transitional governments) and the blocked transitions where the political reforms were rolled back (such as Togo in 1991).

Our main hypothesis is that the more consensual modes of transition should inhibit the introduction of party bans because more parties are involved in the transition itself and are stakeholders that cannot be excluded through legal *fiat*. The victory of one 'party', whether a popular opposition movement, a revolutionary military force, or a clever former authoritarian leader, should, in contrast, facilitate the use of party bans, as these bans could become one instrument to formalize the victory and to systematically exclude the opponents from further competition (the prime case being Uganda's 'Movement' system in post-1986).

We do not assume, on the contrary, that the mode of transition is relevant for the actual banning of parties, as the banning exercise might take place years after the transition has been completed, and is thus no longer relevant for guiding the behaviour of the political actors.

The coding is thus *0* for countries that were democratic before 1989 (without transition); *1* for countries with a co-ordinated transition; and *2* for the remaining transition modes.

Ethnic violence

The final theoretical condition that we consider potentially relevant for the explanation of the introduction and implementation of party bans is previous experience with identity-based violent conflicts. Party bans might be introduced in a pre-cautionary or pre-emptive way, i.e. to protect the regime from the growing politicization of ethnic or religious cleavages within society or from spilling over across border of problems of inter-communal conflict experienced in neighbouring countries. Party bans might, however, also be introduced in a backward-looking or reactive way, as a reaction to violent conflict promoted or not by ethnic entrepreneurs and irresponsible political party leaders.[33] The experience of such large-scale conflicts in the past is likely to trigger a politicization of ethnic or other particularistic identities and a much stronger fear that unrestricted competition might increase this politicization and the return to ethnic violence.

We thus distinguish between countries with such relevant experience (coded with *1*) and those without (coded with *0*). We refer to every reported incident of ethnic violence or warfare in the database on 'Major Episodes of Armed Conflict in Sub-Saharan Africa' as a relevant experience of ethnic violence.[34]

Regime type

The introduction of party bans as legal instruments is a matter of constitutional choice or legislative decision-making. There is strong empirical evidence (even without any systematic test) that party bans in Africa were introduced in the wake of political transitions and not as a reaction of political convenience by the rulers of the day.

It might be different with regard to the decision of a government to deny registration or to actually dissolve a specific political party.[35] Even if we were not able to accommodate situational factors and short-term actors' interests within our methodological framework, we tried to consider at least the actual regime type at the time of the party ban.

Our main hypothesis is that neither autocratic nor democratic regimes resort to the ban of a particularistic party: autocratic regimes deny political parties the possibility to operate freely anyway, and democratic regimes shy away from restricting political competition. Various types of hybrid regimes, on the contrary, are more likely to use party bans as part of the 'menu of manipulation',[36] because democratic rules are not institutionalized, and rulers might have started to liberalize their regimes only due to international pressure but with little commitment to create a fair level playing field.[37]

For the purpose of operationalizing regime types within MV-QCA we distinguished three overall regime types based on Freedom House scores for the whole period between 1990 and 2008: stable authoritarian regimes, coded with 2, are all those regimes which have been classified as 'not free' over the entire period. Democratizing and democratic regimes, coded with 0, are those which have been classified by Freedom House as free for the entire period or which have moved towards 'free' and maintained this category since then. The residual category 'liberalizing/blocked transitions', coded with 1, covers a more heterogeneous group of countries most of which have moved from 'not free' to 'partly free' over the period 1990–2008.

Neo-patrimonialism

It is, of course, important to keep in mind that there are other potential factors that could be analysed when explaining the existence of party bans. According to neo-patrimonial explanations of African politics, formal institutions are a mere façade built up to please the international community and to assure the ongoing flow of resources while hiding the 'real politics' of largely personal relationships and informal norms which dominate political processes and guide actor behaviour. There are various strands of this approach which tend to attribute more or less autonomy to formal institutions vis-à-vis these informal networks,[38] but all would concur in

51

seeing the widespread introduction of formal party regulation both as an important step in building up a superficially efficient political system and as an equally useless way of effectively regulating the behaviour of political actors, in this case, political parties. According to these approaches the explanation for the scarce occurrence of actual bans is thus to be located in the effective informal regulation of political actors through personal networks and self-enforcing informal institutions.

Neo-patrimonial explanations of the legal introduction and application of party bans has several flaws. The quite comprehensive list of justifications for party bans[39] is a departure from international practice and thus no simple exercise of copying formal institutions to create the 'show' of a state.[40] At first glance, there is something peculiarly African to this broad regulation which does not fit into the standard explanation of a mismatch between 'Western formal institutions' and a truly indigenous world of informal norms and networks.

Neo-patrimonial approaches are certainly better equipped to make sense of broader developments in African politics than to account for the differences between the dynamic political developments of sub-Saharan countries. We still lack valid measurements of the varying relevance of neo-patrimonialism, which is a major obstacle for the comparative empirical assessment of neo-patrimonialism as a theoretical condition.

We also did not consider in our empirical analysis a final potential explanation. Given the extraordinary leverage of external actors over policy-making in some African states, one might assume that changing international norms concerning party regulation and the role of foreign governments or international non-governmental organizations matter for the introduction of party bans. This varying exposure to international pressure should indeed be explored when comparing Africa with other world regions where party bans are indeed less frequently adopted and applied.[41]

Table 1. Introduction of party bans: overview of conditions.

	Condition	Value: 2	Value: 1	Value: 0
1	Colonial Tradition (C)	British	French	Other
2	Former Regime Type Competition (F)	No Competition	Limited Competition	Multi Party Competition
3	Mode of Transition (T)	Managed transition/ Regime Breakdown	Pacted Transition	Democracy before 1990
4	Ethnic Violence (V)	–	Yes	No
Out	Party Ban (PB)	–	Yes	No

Sources: *Outcome: Ethnic Party Bans in Africa Database* (please see contribution by Moroff, 'Party Bans in Africa', in this volume); Condition 1: own classification; Condition 2: Bratton and van de Walle, *Democratic Experiments in Africa*; Condition 3: Bratton and van de Walle, *Democratic Experiments in Africa*; Condition 4: Marshall, 'Major Episodes of Armed Conflict in Sub-Saharan Africa'.

Table 2. Implementation of party bans: overview of conditions.

	Condition	Value: 2	Value: 1	Value: 0
1	Colonial Tradition (C)	British	French	Other
2	Former Regime Type Competition (F)	No Competition	Limited Competition	Multi Party Competition
3	Regime type (R)	Stable Authoritarian	Liberalizing/ Blocked	Democratic/ Democratizing
4	Ethnic Violence (V)	–	Yes	No
Out	Party Ban (PBI)	–	Yes	No

Sources: see Table 1; Condition 3: own classification on the basis of Freedom House scores, http://www.freedomhouse.org/template.cfm?page=439.

Explaining the introduction of party bans

We will now explain the introduction of party bans as legal instruments. The analysis covers all 48 countries of sub-Saharan Africa. The first systematic step of a qualitative comparative analysis shows data as a truth table (Table 3).[42] A truth table lists the different combinations of values of the conditions and the value of the outcome for each case or for the cases belonging to each combination. Before applying MV-QCA we will display the cases as configurations in such a truth table; the coding of the values for the single cases becomes thus transparent.[43]

The empirical cases represent 23 of 54 possible configurations. Three configurations covering four cases are unambiguous in an outcome 0 (that means no provisions for party bans, cf. Table 1); 19 configurations covering 28 cases result in an outcome 1 (provisions for party bans are present). There is one contradictory configuration covering four cases with two cases among them having party ban provisions.

The absence of party ban provisions is thus rather an exception. Therefore MV-QCA is supposed to be applied first to these configurations. The minimal expression that indicates the formula for the explanation of the absence of party ban provisions covers two thirds of the countries with an outcome of 0:

$$PB\{0\} = C\{0\}^*T\{0\} + F\{0\}^*V\{1\}$$

The first term indicates longstanding multiparty systems which are former British colonies. It covers the cases of Botswana, Mauritius, and Zimbabwe.[44] The second term covers just one case, South Africa. Despite a history of violent ethnic conflict South African constitutional law does not provide party bans. The South African case is characterized by democratic experience before 1990 (even though as an 'exclusive democracy') and a coordinated transition to democracy which will be analysed in detail in a separate article of this issue.[45] The two other cases where party ban provisions are absent belong to a contradictory configuration, lacking a well-defined outcome.

Table 3. Party bans as legal provisions.

Country	Out	C	F	T	V	No. of cases
Angola	1	0	2	1	1	1
Benin, Niger	1	1	2	1	0	2
Burkina Faso, Chad, Comoros, Djibouti, Gabon, Guinea, Mauritania	1	1	2	2	0	7
Burundi, Congo D.R., Ethiopia	1	0	2	2	1	3
CAR, Cameroon, Cote d'Ivoire, Togo	1	1	1	2	0	4
Cape Verde, Equatorial Guinea, Eritrea, Guinea-Bissau, Liberia, Somalia	1	0	2	2	0	6
Congo	1	1	2	1	1	1
Gambia	1	2	0	2	0	1
Lesotho, Ghana, Swaziland	1	2	2	2	0	3
Madagascar	1	1	1	1	0	1
Malawi	1	2	1	1	0	1
Mali	1	1	1	1	1	1
Mozambique	1	0	2	1	0	1
Namibia	1	2	0	1	0	1
Rwanda	1	0	1	2	1	1
Sudan, Uganda	1	2	2	2	1	2
Senegal	1	1	0	0	0	1
Sierra Leone	1	2	1	2	0	1
Botswana, Mauritius	0	0	0	0	0	2
South Africa	0	0	0	1	1	1
Zimbabwe	0	0	0	0	1	1
Kenya (0), Nigeria (1), Tanzania (1), Zambia (0)*	C*	2	1	2	1	4
Sao Tome & Principe, Seychelles	1	0	1	2	0	2

Notes: *Numbers in parentheses indicate the outcome of the single cases of the contradictory expression; C: Colonial tradition; F: Former Regime Type/Political competition; T: Mode of transition; V: Ethnic Violence; Out: Party ban (legal provision). In order to avoid confusion with the theoretical condition C, contradictory configurations are denoted C*.

The formula for the presence of party ban provisions is:

$$PB\{1\} = T\{0, 1\} + C\{2\} + T\{1, 2\}^*V\{0\}$$

The formula contains two clear results. A non-British colonial background and a complete lack of party competition before 1990 each serve as a sufficient condition for the introduction of party bans. A British background, on the contrary, serves as a necessary condition for the abandonment of party bans. This confirms our initially formulated hypotheses. The remaining formula produced by MV-QCA may be interpreted as follows: in countries without democratic legacy and an experience of ethnic violence, the introduction of multiparty politics is supposed to restrict mobilization along ethnic cleavage.

An important feature of QCA is the identification of contradictory configurations. In our analysis one contradictory configuration emerged covering a total of four cases. For the dissolution of contradictions several measures can be applied simultaneously. The related single cases must be put under further investigation, the 'contradictory condition' may be specified or so far neglected intervening factors should be identified.

In this case, the contradiction can rather easily be resolved. The configuration brings together four African countries with a British colonial background: Nigeria, Tanzania, Zambia, and Kenya, with the latter two lacking the legal provisions for party bans. Kenya eventually introduced party bans in 2008 (outside the empirical scope of our database), and thus confirms our hypothesis that this combination of structural conditions (limited competition, history of ethnic violence, no pacted transition) leads to the introduction of legal provisions. Kenya and Zambia are also the only two African countries which actually banned political parties in reality even when lacking the legal provisions for doing so. The only remaining puzzle would be then, why Zambia did restrain from introducing a legal provision when both the structural conditions and the actual practice made this very likely.

Explaining the actual banning of parties

In the second part of the analysis we will turn to the factors which account for the actual banning of parties. As mentioned before, there exists a rather peculiar gap between the trend towards the introduction of party ban provisions and the practice of banning parties. Less than a third of the countries which have legal provisions for banning parties have implemented a ban effectively (and as previously outlined, this includes also the cases of non-registration).[46]

In this step of the analysis the universe of cases has thus to be reduced to those countries with legal party ban provisions and the two countries which banned parties without having specific legal means at their disposal (e.g. party laws or pertinent constitutional provisions). The new sample covers 37 countries. In addition to those five countries which do not have party ban provisions and did not implement party bans, we dropped the following cases: D.R. Congo and Somalia due to the absence of an effective central government; Sudan, Swaziland and Eritrea because of the absence of any minimal development towards a democratic transition; and Comoros and Djibouti due to unreliable data on the implementation of particularistic bans.

The outcome alters to the effect that now cases covering effective particularistic party bans are coded with *1* and cases without effective particularistic party bans are coded with *0*. Data will again first be presented in a truth table (see Table 4). Please note that this sample is reduced to 37 cases.

The empirical cases represent 21 of 54 possible configurations. Twelve configurations covering 18 cases result unambiguously in an outcome *0* (that means no party bans were implemented), six configurations covering nine cases are resulting in an outcome *1* (party bans were implemented). Three contradictory configurations covering 10 cases remain. Three of these 10 cases belong to the ban and

Table 4. Implementation of party bans.

Country	Out	C	F	R	V	No. of cases
Angola	1	0	2	2	1	1
Equatorial Guinea	1	0	2	2	0	1
Kenya, Nigeria, Tanzania, Zambia	1	2	1	1	1	4
Namibia	1	2	0	0	0	1
Rwanda	1	0	1	2	1	1
Uganda	1	2	2	1	1	1
Cameroon, Togo	0	1	1	2	0	2
Chad, Guinea	0	1	2	2	0	2
Guinea-Bissau, Liberia, Mozambique	0	0	2	1	0	3
Malawi, Sierra Leone	0	2	1	1	0	2
Benin	0	1	2	0	0	1
Cape Verde	0	0	2	0	0	1
Gambia	0	2	0	1	0	1
Ghana, Lesotho	0	2	2	0	0	2
Mali	0	1	1	0	0	1
Sao Tome & Principe	0	0	1	0	0	1
Senegal	0	1	0	0	0	1
Seychelles	0	0	1	1	0	1
Burkina Faso (0), Congo (0), Gabon (0), Mauritania (1), Niger (0)	C*	1	2	1	0	5
Burundi (1), Ethiopia (0)	C*	0	2	1	1	2
CAR (1), Cote d'Ivoire(0), Madagascar (0)	C*	1	1	1	0	3

Note: C: Colonial Tradition; F: Former Regime Type/Political Competition; R: Current Regime Type; V: Ethnic Violence; Outcome: Party Ban (implementation). In order to avoid confusion with the theoretical condition C, contradictory configurations are denoted C*.

seven to the no-ban outcome. As in the examination of party ban provisions also this analysis rests on the use of logical remainders.

The formula for the **presence of implemented party bans** appears comparatively clear-cut. It covers 75 per cent of the countries with an outcome of 1:

$$PBI\{1\} = C\{0\}^*R\{2\} + C\{2\}^*V\{1\} + C\{2\}^*F\{0\}^*R\{0\}$$

This solution covers two major groups of countries which implemented party bans. Three countries belong to the first term: Angola, Equatorial Guinea, and Rwanda. None of them have a French or a British colonial background, and all are characterized by the absence of a democratizing or even liberalizing trend during our period of investigation. They all feature a history of regime-prohibited or blocked democratic transition. In the cases of Equatorial Guinea and Rwanda party bans might be interpreted as instruments of stabilizing authoritarian rule. The Rwandan government justified its proceedings against the Parti démocratique du renouveau (PDR-Ubunynja) in 2001 and particularly against the Mouvement démocratique républicain (MDR) in 2003 as suppression of 'political divisionism' and its often deadly consequences.[47] But to many observers it appeared rather as a means of strengthening the de facto one-party regime of the Front patriotique rwandais (FPR), also against the country's majority Hutu population.[48] By contrast, the banning of the Movimento para la Autodeterminacion de la Isla Bioco (MAIB) in Equatorial Guinea in 1994 was targeted at a minority ethnic group which required better representation at the central governmental level. In fact the banning of MAIB must be seen in the broader context of regimes' attempts to repress the organization of effective opposition at all, which affects non-ethnic parties as well.[49] It seems remarkable, especially in view of the Rwandan case, that the record of ethnic violence, which has been particularly upheld for the justification of the various party bans, plays no decisive role as a structural condition explaining the implementation of party bans.

The second term of the formula belongs to five countries with a British colonial tradition. Actual regime type is not part of the minimal solution reported above, but it might be worthwhile emphasizing that all cases belong to the category of 'liberalizing' countries. That means that they fall short of becoming fully democratic, while making significant steps towards democracy. All these countries have experienced ethnic conflicts or ethnic warfare, which is most obvious in Nigeria (Biafra War, 1967–70; ethnic violence in the Niger delta and the north and the centre since the 1990s), but applies also to Uganda (ethnic violence in Buganda in the 1970s and especially between 1981–85, and in the north since 1986) or Tanzania (conflict over Zanzibar). But we should not forget to mention the obvious differences within this group of cases. Bans on ethnic parties follow a pattern in Tanzania and Nigeria, where parties that fail to establish a national presence are denied registration.[50] In the three other cases ethnic party bans appear rather singular incidents of varying political importance. While we lack reliable background information on the ban on an Islamic party in Zambia in 1993, the denial of registration for the Islamic Party of Kenya (IPK) has been clearly introduced with the aim to prevent promotion of ethnic tensions between Muslims and Christians. If we add the ban on the Uganda Islamic Revolutionary Party (UIRP) in 1993 and the non-registration of the Kabaka Yekka (KY) 2004 in Uganda we can state that this group of countries features several examples of a reactive use of banning. This refers to the experience of ethnic violence in general and the awareness of a need to prevent those incidents happening again. It is worth noting that this fairly coherent cluster of countries implemented party bans at all, and that administrations in former British colonies seem to take the enforcement of formal rules more seriously.

The third term of the solution is referring to the singular case of Namibia, which is the only democratic country in sub-Saharan Africa to have implemented a party ban. The outlawing of the United Democratic Party (UDP) in 2006 may be indeed identified as party ban,[51] but the outcome *1* itself remains ambiguous because the UDP was not registered as a party at this particular time. The UDP has been declared illegal because of its alleged affiliation with the rather obscure Caprivi Liberation Army which promotes a secession of the Caprivi region in the northeastern part of Namibia. Thus, the reason behind this incident is more typical of a pre-emptive ban that is introduced to restrict the growing politicization of ethnic (or, in this case, regional) cleavages and to protect rulers from new political competitors.

The formula for the **absence of party bans** is:

$$PBI\{0\} = C\{0, 1^*\}R\{0\} + C\{1\}^*R\{2\}^*V\{0\} + F\{1, 2\}^*R\{0\}$$
$$+ C\{0\}^*R\{1\}^*V\{0\} + C\{2\}^*R\{1\}^*V\{0\}$$

We should first consider that the bulk of countries with a French colonial background belong to the category of 'non-implementers'. The second, third, and fifth term of this formula indeed contribute to the explanation of the absence of party bans. The second term covers only countries with a French background (Cameroon, Togo, Chad, Guinea). They combine the persistence of authoritarian rule with an absence of ethnically motivated violence before 1990. In these cases the restriction of political competition is apparently enforced through informal mechanisms. The third term covers six countries which underwent a steady transition towards (electoral) democracy, starting from a very limited or fully lacking party competition before 1990. That allows us to conclude that democratic countries do not resort to party bans as a means for regulating political competition and that bans tend to prevail in authoritarian, liberalizing and/or instable contexts. The fifth term covers exclusively former British colonies, which differ from those of the 'implementation set' in one respect. While they belong just as well to the group of liberalizing countries, they experienced no ethnic motivated violence before 1990. In comparison to the group of 'implementers' this restates similarly the interpretation of the party bans as reactive measures.

On the whole the picture with regard to the non-implementation of party bans is much less clear, but $C\{1\}^*R\{2\}^*V\{0\}$ and $C\{2\}^*R\{1\}^*V\{0\}$ on the one hand and $F\{1,2\}^*R\{0\}$ on the other appear to be the most instructive implicants. The first pair of implicants highlights the importance of the experience of ethnic violence as a reason for the (reactive) banning of particularistic parties. The other term emphasizes the significance of the actual regime type. Party bans are obviously not a typical feature of democratizing countries.

Three of the 12 countries which implemented party bans, finally, belong to three contradictory configurations. In two of these countries, Burundi and Central African Republic, party bans were used in isolated instances, while the Mauritanian government made extensive and more or less systematic use of them.

But before taking a closer look at Mauritania we will examine the three contradictory configurations in detail. They differ on all conditions, except for the actual regime type which belongs to the category of 'liberalizing' countries. Party bans in this kind of political environment seem to be of a rather idiosyncratic nature and precautionary means of authoritarian and semi-authoritarian regimes in a 'divide et impera' strategy towards opposition, so that it becomes difficult to capture them in a rather macro-structural framework. The empirical evidence should thus be clarified with an illustration of the Mauritanian case.

In the broader context of political development during the presidency of Ould Taya (1984–2005) party bans may be understood as a means of restraining the politicization of social cleavages that were still present.[52] Party bans were imposed both on Islamist parties (like the Ummah party in 1991 and the Parti pour la Convergence Dèmocratique in 2004) and on political forces representing oppressed and underrepresented groups (dissolution of the Action pour la change-ment in 2002, representing so far excluded groups of 'black' African descent).[53] While the Islamist parties were accused of exploiting the state religion for their par-ticular aims, the AC was charged with 'racism' and 'incitement to political vio-lence'. All bans were more or less based on existing constitutional and legal norms, but their structural impact[54] was to perpetuate an authoritarian presidential regime in a context of semi-competitive elections. But what is then accounting for the differences between authoritarian ban and non-ban countries? A possible expla-nation refers to different regime strategies and capacities. One may be more related to repressive and the other to more 'cooperative' means of co-opting oppositional forces and mitigating political competition. This might be the case in a country like Gabon, where an old-style presidential system with strong financial means survived particularly by means of a policy of incorporation.[55]

The actual implementation of party bans can be best explained by the combi-nation of rather flawed transition processes and the experience of ethnic violence in the past. The colonial background is supposed to be of particular importance. All countries with a British heritage and a record of ethnic violence resorted to the banning of particularistic parties. By contrast, particularly in countries with a French heritage, all of which have introduced party ban provisions, the implemen-tation of party bans is rather uncommon. One additional result emphasizes the importance of actual regime type. Besides the (doubtful) case of Namibia, demo-cratic and democratizing countries abstained from particularistic party bans. Party bans might rather be interpreted as a strategy of strengthening autocratic rule or managing limited liberalization. There is also little evidence that party bans play a decisive role in the promotion of democracy.[56]

Conclusion

This article has looked at the variation in the occurrence and implementation of party bans in sub-Saharan Africa. The methodological path was qualitative comparative analysis and we have thus concentrated on the deeper historical and political constellations as main drivers of institutional change. QCA has been a useful instrument in detecting some patterns that explain similarities and differ-ences across our African cases.

The introduction of the institution of legal party ban has occurred on a nearly continent-wide basis. From a comparative perspective it is quite interesting to have a closer look at those few countries that did not introduce party bans. Our analysis has revealed that these countries do share some similar conditions, in particular a British legacy (for all of them, if we put South Africa into this group), and a stronger tradition of multiparty democracy (for nearly all of them). The combination seems to make regimes confident in their capacity to maintain ethnic peace and political stability without relying on formal party bans.[57] The much larger group of countries with party bans is necessarily more heterogeneous, but colonial background emerged as a sufficient condition, i.e. all former French, Portuguese, Italian, Spanish, and Belgian colonies introduced formal party bans.

It is obviously more difficult to analyse the implementation of party bans by looking at broader structural political and institutional features of the countries under investigation. The actual decision to ban a party (or to deny registration) should logically be strongly related to the interests of actors and other situational variables such as political convenience. We opted nevertheless to systematically compare countries where parties were actually banned by using the same method of QCA. We obtained a surprisingly clear result with regard to the country group of implementers. Party bans are primarily implemented in two contexts. Implementation is likely in former British colonies where 'political liberalization' is occurring having also experienced significant ethnic violence in the past; party bans are also used in the context of authoritarian or semi-authoritarian rule by incumbents as a precaution against the formation of political opposition. These results confirm our hypotheses that the implementation of party bans is more common under 'liberalizing' but not under 'democratizing' conditions and that the lack of a history of ethnic mass violence might not prevent the introduction of party bans but makes their use very unlikely.

Our analysis has concentrated on the macro-structural level, and with regard to the implementation, less on an explanation of individual party bans and more on a country's disposition of implementing party bans. Regime type is relevant to a regime's propensity to rely on bans. Countries with a strong democratic record or a sustained commitment to democratization do not need to 'misuse' party bans. It is the larger group of what we have labelled 'liberalizing countries' where the short-term interests of actors and the perceived vulnerability of rulers might matter more for the decision to ban a party.

Notes

1. International IDEA, *Funding of Political Parties and Electoral Campaigns*; Ashiagbor, *Party Finance Reform in Africa*; Salih and Nordlund, *Political Parties in Africa*.
2. The data used for this comparison are drawn from our database on ethnic party bans. The contribution by Moroff, 'Party Bans in Africa' in this special issue goes into the data and data collection in more detail.
3. As an exception see Basedau et al., 'Ethnic Party Bans in Africa'.
4. Rosenblum, 'Banning Parties'; Rosenblum, *On the Side of the Angels*; Niesen, 'Zwischen Pfadabhängigkeit und Kommensuration'; see also Fox and Nolte, 'Intolerant Democracies'; Pabel, 'Parteiverbote auf dem europäischen Prüfstand'; Capoccia, *Defending Democracy*; Navot, 'Fighting Terrorism in the Political Arena'.

5. Rosenblum, 'Banning Parties', 52–8.
6. Berg-Schlosser and de Meur, 'Conditions of Democracy in Interwar Europe'.
7. Cronqvist and Berg-Schlosser, 'Multi-Value QCA (MVQCA)'; Ragin, *The Comparative Method*; Ragin, *Fuzzy-Set Social Science*; Rihoux and de Meur, 'Crisp-Set Qualitative Comparative Analysis (CSQCA)'.
8. Two common problems of QCA are contradictions and the use of logical remainder cases for the purpose of analysis. Contradictory configurations have to be considered as a major challenge within QCA, because not any configuration of conditions coincides with a non-contradictory outcome. There are several ways to handle the problem of 'contradictions' (coded with C), some rather 'technical' and others rather 'contextual' (for an overview see Rihoux and de Meur, 'Crisp-Set Qualitative Comparative Analysis (CSQCA)', 48ff.). A contextual way of dealing with contradictions is applied below in sections 3 and 4. Therefore we attach importance to an illustrative analysis of cases which are part of the contradictory configurations. More complex comparisons like the ones conducted below, rely on the application of particular software tools. One additional feature which is facilitated much by computer analysis is the use of 'logical remainders' for minimization (Berg-Schlosser and de Meur, 'Conditions of Democracy in Interwar Europe', 255). These are hypothetical configurations which are not represented in the set of empirically existing configurations. The use of logical remainders enables the researcher to reach solutions as parsimonious as possible, even if we are urged to apply those techniques carefully. The notation for our purpose follows the MV-QCA routine, denoting a present condition with {1} and an absent condition with {0}.
9. Ragin, *Fuzzy-Set Social Science*.
10. For a concise and elaborated presentation of the approach cf. Cronqvist, 'Konfigurationelle Analyse mit Multi-Value QCA; Cronqvist and Berg-Schlosser, 'Multi-Value QCA (MVQCA)'.
11. TOSMANA: Tool for Small-N Analysis, Version 1.3.
12. Vink and van Vliet, 'Not Quite Crisp, Not Yet Fuzzy?'
13. Ibid., 287.
14. Berg-Schlosser, 'Determinants of Democratic Successes and Failures in Africa', 294.
15. It is difficult to distinguish between merely 'procedural' non-registrations and 'substantive' ones. Procedural non-registration refers to cases where registration is denied because of a lack of signatures, deposits, or the non-compliance with notification terms, while substantive non-registration refers to political reasons, such as party claims to ethnicity, tribe or religion. As do all other contributions to this volume, we thus apply an 'expansive' understanding of party ban which subsumes registration requirements under the category of ban, and which defines the denial of registration as the implementation of a party ban, cf. Moroff, 'Party Bans in Africa', this special issue.
16. Kenya has introduced recently a party ban provision. Our empirical analysis covers the period until 2007. The recent changes in Kenya are thus not included here.
17. For more details on the definition of particularistic party bans and on the data used here see, Moroff, 'Party Bans in Africa', this issue.
18. These exceptions are taken into account by the theoretical condition 'previous regime type', in so far as – in these cases – we refer not to the regime type in 1989, but to the regime type at the moment of the introduction of the party ban.
19. Chazan et al., *Politics and Society in Contemporary Africa*; Tordoff, *Government and Politics in Africa*; Young, *The African Colonial State in Comparative Perspective*.
20. Collier, *Regimes in Tropical Africa*.
21. Cooper, *Africa since 1940;* Young, *The African Colonial State in Comparative Perspective*.

22. See Widner, *Economic Change and Political Liberalization in Sub-Saharan Africa* for a similar hypothesis.
23. Historical research has shown that the differences between colonial administrations on the ground might have been less clear-cut, but the relevance of different administrative legacies is not really contested, cf. Firmin-Sellers, 'Institutions, Context, and Outcomes'; Young, *The African Colonial State in Comparative Perspective.*
24. This includes countries with Portuguese, Spanish, Belgian or Italian colonial background and those that were never formally colonized, such as Ethiopia and Liberia.
25. The general importance of former regimes for the prospects of democratic transition is discussed by Linz and Stepan, *Problems of Democratic Transition*, and Geddes, 'What Do We Know About Democratization'.
26. Bratton and van de Walle, *Democratic Experiments in Africa.*
27. Ibid., 77–82.
28. A competitive one-party system refers to parliamentary election rules where voters are allowed to choose between different candidates all running for the single party. Such a system was (temporarily) applied in Tanzania, Kenya, Zambia, Côte d'Ivoire and Cameroon.
29. The only actual difference to Bratton and van de Walle is the case of Senegal.
30. Merkel, 'Defekte Demokratien'. The reason for classifying them into this group is the fully competitive character of these systems. They were 'exclusive' democracies, because they lacked full political participation (or any political participation) by the majority of the population.
31. McMenamin, 'Party Regulation and Democratisation'.
32. Arato, 'The Occupation of Iraq and the Difficult Transition from Dictatorship'; Huntington, *The Third Wave*; Karl and Schmitter, 'Modes of Transition in Latin America, Southern and Eastern Europe'.
33. We owe this distinction to a suggestion by Peter Burnell at the conference on ethnic party bans in Africa held at Jacobs University Bremen in September 2008.
34. In addition we also coded '1' countries with incidents of civil violence and a clear particularistic tendency (e.g. Angola).
35. See Moroff and Basedau, 'An Effective Measure of Institutional Engineering?', this special issue.
36. Schedler, 'The Menu of Manipulation'.
37. Van de Walle, 'Africa's Range of Regimes'.
38. For these two variants Engel and Erdmann, 'Neopatrimonialism Reconsidered', and Chabal and Daloz, *Africa Works.*
39. See Moroff, 'Party Bans in Africa', this special issue.
40. The expression is borrowed from Cruise O'Brien, 'The Show of State in a Neo-colonial Twilight'.
41. Diffusion effects might have been at work in quickly spreading party bans over the continent, but they have been apparently limited to the areas defined by common colonial legacies.
42. Ragin, *The Comparative Method*, 87–9.
43. The appendix gives a full account of the MV-QCA solutions for all six explained outcomes (introduction of party bans: present, absent, contradictory; implementation of party bans: present, absent, contradictory).
44. We are fully aware of the regime change in Zimbabwe. What matters for our analysis is the fact that Zimbabwe was considered democratic at independence and maintained this regime type until the mid-1990s.
45. See Kemmerzell, 'Why There Is No Party Ban in the South African Constitution', this special issue.

46. If we assume that party bans are self-enforcing, i.e. parties adapt automatically to these rules, there is no peculiar gap to be explained. The case studies collected in this volume, however, show little evidence for such self-enforcement.
47. Cf. Niesen, 'Political Party Bans in Rwanda 1994–2003', this special issue.
48. Reyntiens, 'Rwanda, Ten Years On'.
49. Wood, 'Business and Politics in a Criminal State'.
50. See Bogaards, 'Ethnic Party Bans and Institutional Engineering in Nigeria', this special issue.
51. See Moroff and Basedau, 'An Effective Measure of Institutional Engineering?', this special issue.
52. N'Diaye, 'Mauritania's Stalled Democratisation'; N'Diaye, 'To "Midwife" – and Abort – a Democracy'.
53. Szajkowski, *Political Parties of the World*, 407.
54. See N'Diaye, 'Mauritania's Stalled Democratisation'; N'Diaye, 'To "Midwife" – and Abort – a Democracy'.
55. Gardinier, 'France and Gabon since 1993'.
56. See Moroff and Basedau, 'An Effective Measure of Institutional Engineering?', this special issue.
57. As mentioned before, two of these countries, however, did in the end ban parties without any legal basis.

Notes on contributors

Christof Hartmann is Professor of Political Science at the University of Duisburg-Essen (Germany). His research focuses on democratization, democratic institutions, and institutional change, with particular emphasis on sub-Saharan Africa.

Jörg Kemmerzell is Lecturer and Research Associate at the Department of Political Science, Technical University Darmstadt (Germany). His research focuses on comparative politics, particularly political parties and change and stability of political regimes.

Bibliography

Arato, Andrew. 'The Occupation of Iraq and the Difficult Transition from Dictatorship'. *Constellations* 10, no. 3 (2003): 408–24.
Ashiagbor, Sefakor. *Party Finance Reform in Africa, Lessons Learned from Four Countries: Ghana, Kenya, Senegal and South Africa*. Washington, DC: National Democratic Institute for International Affairs, 2005.
Basedau, Matthias, Matthijs Bogaards, Christof Hartmann, and Peter Niesen. 'Ethnic Party Bans in Africa: A Research Agenda'. *German Law Journal* 8, no. 6 (2007): 617–34.
Berg-Schlosser, Dirk. 'Determinants of Democratic Successes and Failures in Africa'. *European Journal of Political Research* 47, no. 2 (2008): 269–308.
Berg-Schlosser, Dirk, and Gisele de Meur. 'Conditions of Democracy in Interwar Europe. A Boolean Test of Major Hypotheses'. *Comparative Politics* 26 no. 3 (1994): 253–79.
Bogaards, Matthijs. 'Ethnic Party Bans and Institutional Engineering in Nigeria'. *Democratization* 17, no. 4 (2010): 730–49.
Bratton, Michael, and Nicolas van de Walle. *Democratic Experiments in Africa. Regime Transitions in Comparative Perspective*. Cambridge: Cambridge University Press, 1997.
Capoccia, Giovanni. *Defending Democracy: Reactions to Extremism in Interwar Europe*. Baltimore: The Johns Hopkins University Press, 2005.

Chabal, Patrick and Jean-Pascal Daloz. *Africa Works. Disorder as Political Instrument*. Oxford: James Currey, 1999.

Chazan, Naomi et al. *Politics and Society in Contemporary Africa*, 3rd ed. Boulder, CO: Lynne Rienner Publishers, 1999.

Collier, Ruth. *Regimes in Tropical Africa*. Berkeley: University of California Press, 1982.

Cooper, Frederick. *Africa Since 1940. The Past of the Present*. Cambridge: Cambridge UP.

Cronqvist, Lasse. 'Konfigurationelle Analyse mit Multi-Value QCA als Methode der Vergleichenden Politikwissenschaft mit einem Fallbeispiel aus der Vergleichenden Parteienforschung'. PhD thesis, University of Marburg, 2007.

Cronqvist, Lasse and Dirk Berg-Schlosser. 'Multi-Value QCA (MVQCA)'. In *Configurational Comparative Methods. Qualitative Comparative Analysis (QCA) and Related Techniques*, ed. Benoit Rihoux and Charles Ragin, 69–85. London: Sage, 2008.

Cruise O'Brien, Donal B. 1991. 'The Show of State in a Neo-colonial Twilight: Francophone Africa'. In *Rethinking Third World Politics*, ed. James Manor, 145–65. London: Longman 1991.

Engel, Ulf, and Gero Erdmann. 'Neopatrimonialism Reconsidered: Critical Review and Elaboration of an Elusive Concept'. *Journal of Commonwealth and Comparative Studies* 45, no. 1 (2007): 95–119.

Firmin-Sellers, Kathryn. 'Institutions, Context, and Outcomes. Explaining French and British Rule in West Africa'. *Comparative Politics* 32, no. 3 (2000): 253–72.

Fox, Gregory H., and Georg Nolte. 'Intolerant Democracies'. In *Democratic Governance and International Law*, ed. Gregory Fox and Brad R. Roth, 389–435. Cambridge: Cambridge University Press, 2000.

Gardinier, David. 'France and Gabon since 1993. The Reshaping of a Neo-Colonial Relationship'. *Journal of Contemporary African Studies* 18, no. 2 (2000): 225–42.

Geddes, Barbara. 'What Do We Know about Democratization after Twenty Years'. *Annual Review of Political Science* 2 (1999): 115–44.

Huntington, Samuel P. *The Third Wave. Democratization in the Late Twentieth Century*. Norman: University of Oklahoma Press, 1991.

International IDEA. *Funding of Political Parties and Electoral Campaigns*. Stockholm: International Institute for Democracy and Electoral Assistance, 2007.

Karl, Terry Lynn, and Philippe Schmitter. 'Modes of Transition in Latin America, Southern and Eastern Europe'. *International Social Science Journal* no. 128 (1991): 269–85.

Kemmerzell, Jörg. 'Why There Is No Party Ban in the South African Constitution'. *Democratization* 17, no. 4 (2010): 687–708.

Linz, Juan J., and Alfred Stepan. *Problems of Democratic Transition and Consolidation: South America, Southern Europe, And Post-Communist Europe*. Baltimore: Johns Hopkins University Press, 1996.

Marshall, Monty G. 'Major Episodes of Armed Conflict in Sub-Saharan Africa, 1946–2004'. Center for Systemic Peace. http://www.systemicpeace.org/africa/ACPPAnnex1a.pdf.

McMenamin, Iain. 'Party Regulation and Democratisation: Challenges for Further Research'. In *Party Regulation in Conflict-Prone Societies: Regulation, Engineering and Democratic Development*, ed. Benjamin Reilly and Per Nordlund, 223–41. Tokyo: United Nations University Press, 2008.

Merkel, Wolfgang. 'Defekte Demokratien'. In *Demokratie in Ost und West*, ed. Wolfgang Merkel and Andreas Busch, 361–81. Frankfurt am Main: Suhrkamp, 1999.

Moroff, Anika. 'Party Bans in Africa – An Empirical Overview'. *Democratization* 17, no. 4, (2010): 618–41.

Moroff, Anika, and Matthias Basedau. 'An Effective Measure of Institutional Engineering? Ethnic Party Bans in Africa'. *Democratization* 17, no. 4 (2010): 666–86.

Navot, Suzie. 'Fighting Terrorism in the Political Arena. The Banning of Political Parties'. *Party Politics* 14, no. 6 (2008): 745–62.

N'Diaye, Boubacar. 'Mauritania's Stalled Democratisation'. *Journal of Democracy* 12, no. 3 (2001): 88–95.

N'Diaye, Boubacar. 'To "Midwife" – and Abort – a Democracy: Mauritania's Transition from Military Rule, 2005–2008'. *Journal of Modern African Studies* 47, no. 1 (2009): 129–52.

Niesen, Peter. 'Zwischen Pfadabhängigkeit und Kommensuration: Verbote politischer Parteien in Europa'. In *Schmerzliche Erfahrungen' der Vergangenheit und der Prozess der Konstitutionalisierung Europas*, ed. Christian Joerges, Matthias Mahlmann and Ulrich K. Preuß, 258–73. Wiesbaden: VS-Verlag, 2008.

Niesen, Peter. 'Political Party Bans in Rwanda 1994-2003: Three Narratives of Justification'. *Democratization* 17, no. 4 (2010): 709–29.

Pabel, Katharina. 'Parteiverbote auf dem europäischen Prüfstand'. *Zeitschrift für ausländisches öffentliches Recht und Völkerrecht* 63 (2003): 921–44.

Ragin, Charles. *The Comparative Method. Moving beyond Qualitative and Quantitative Strategies*. Berkeley: University of California Press, 1987.

Ragin, Charles. *Fuzzy-Set Social Science*. Chicago; London: University of Chicago Press, 2000.

Ragin, Charles. 'Qualitative Comparative Analysis Using Fuzzy Sets (FSQCA)'. In *Configurational Comparative Methods. Qualitative Comparative Analysis (QCA) and Related Techniques*, ed. Benoit Rihoux and Charles Ragin, 87–120. London: Sage, 2008.

Reyntjens, Filip. 'Rwanda, Ten Years on: From Genocide to Dictatorship'. *African Affairs* 103, no. 411 (2004): 177–210.

Rihoux, Benoit, and Gisele de Meur. 'Crisp-Set Qualitative Comparative Analysis (CSQCA)'. In *Configurational Comparative Methods. Qualitative Comparative Analysis (QCA) and Related Techniques*, ed. Benoit Rihoux and Charles Ragin, 33–67. London: Sage, 2008.

Rosenblum, Nancy L. 'Banning Parties: Religious and Ethnic Partisanship in Multicultural Democracies'. *Journal of Law and Ethics of Human Rights* 1, no. 1 (2007): 17–75.

Rosenblum, Nancy L. *On the Side of the Angels. An Appreciation of Parties and Partisanship*. Princeton: Princeton University Press, 2008.

Salih Mohamed M.A. *African Political Parties. Evolution, Institutionalisation and Governance*. London & Sterling: Pluto Press, 2003.

Salih, Mohamed M.A., and Per Nordlund. *Political Parties in Africa: Challenges for Sustained Multiparty Democracy*. Stockholm: International Institute for Democracy and Electoral Assistance, 2007.

Schedler, Andreas. 'The Menu of Manipulation'. *Journal of Democracy* 13, no. 2 (2002): 36–50.

Szajkowski, Bogdan, ed. *Political Parties of the World*. London: John Harper Publishers, 2005.

Tordoff, William. *Government and Politics in Africa*. Bloomington: Indiana University Press, 2002.

Van de Walle, Nicolas. 'Africa's Range of Regimes. Elections without Democracy'. *Journal of Democracy* 13, no. 2 (2002): 66–80.

Vink, Marten P., and Olaf van Vliet. 'Not Quite Crisp, Not Yet Fuzzy? Assessing the Potentials and Pitfalls of Multi-Value QCA'. *Field Methods* 21, no. 3 (2009): 265–89.

Widner, Jennifer A. *Economic Change and Political Liberalization in Sub-Saharan Africa*. Baltimore: Johns Hopkins University Press, 1994.

Wood, Geoffrey. 'Business and Politics in a Criminal State: The Case of Equatorial Guinea'. *African Affairs* 103, no. 413 (2004): 547–67.

Young, Crawford. *The African Colonial State in Comparative Perspective*. New Haven: Yale University Press, 1994.

Appendix. Solution of MV-QCA, formulas for minimized outcomes

Party ban introduction: Outcome 1*

$$PB\{1\} = C\{0, 1\} + F\{2\} + T\{1, 2\}^* V\{0\}$$

(Angola + Benin, Niger + Burkina Faso, Chad, Comoros, Djibouti, Gabon, Guinea, Mauritania + Burundi, Congo D.R., Ethiopia + CAR, Cameroon, Cote d'Ivoire, Togo + Cape Verde, Equatorial Guinea, Eritrea, Guinea-Bissau, Liberia, Somalia + Congo + Madagascar + Mali + Mozambique + Rwanda + Sao Tome & Principe, Seychelles + Senegal) +
(Angola + Benin, Niger + Burkina Faso, Chad, Comoros, Djibouti, Gabon, Guinea, Mauritania + Burundi, Congo D.R., Ethiopia + Cape Verde, Equatorial Guinea, Eritrea, Guinea-Bissau, Liberia, Somalia +Congo + Ghana, Lesotho, Swaziland + Mozambique + Sudan, Uganda) +
(Benin, Niger + Burkina Faso, Chad, Comoros, Djibouti, Gabon, Guinea, Mauritania + CAR, Cameroon, Cote d'Ivoire, Togo + Cape Verde, Equatorial Guinea, Eritrea, Guinea-Bissau, Liberia, Somalia + Gambia + Ghana, Lesotho, Swaziland + Madagascar + Malawi + Mozambique + Namibia + Sao Tome & Principe, Seychelles + Sierra Leone)

Party ban introduction: Outcome 0

$$PB\{0\} = C\{2\}^* T\{0\} + F\{0\}^* V\{1\}$$

(Botswana, Mauritius + Zimbabwe) (South Africa + Zimbabwe)

Party ban introduction: Outcome C (just one configuration, no minimization possible)

$$PB\{C^*\} = C\{2\}^* F\{1\}^* T\{2\}^* V\{1\}$$

(Kenya, Nigeria, Tanzania, Zambia)

Party ban implementation: Outcome 1

$$PBI\{1\} = C\{0\}^* R\{2\} + C\{2\}^* V\{1\} + C\{2\}^* F\{0\}^* R\{0\}$$

(Angola + Equatorial Guinea +Rwanda) (Kenya, Nigeria, Tanzania, Zambia + Uganda) (Namibia)

Party ban implementation: Outcome 0

$$PBI\{0\} = C\{0, 1\}^* R\{0\} + C\{1\}^* R\{2\} + F\{1, 2\}^* R\{0\} + C\{0\}^* R\{1\}^* V\{0\}$$
$$+ C\{2\}^* R\{1\}^* V\{0\}$$

(Benin + Cape Verde + Mali + Sao Tome & Principe + Senegal) (Cameroon, Togo + Chad, Guinea)

(Benin + Cape Verde + Ghana, Lesotho + Mali + Sao Tome & Principe) (Guinea-Bissau, Liberia, Mozambique + Seychelles) (Gambia + Malawi, Sierra Leone)

Party ban implementation: Outcome C

$$PBI\{C^*\} = C\{1\}^*R\{1\} + C\{0\}^*R\{1\}^*V\{1\}$$

(Burkina Faso, Congo, Gabon, Mauritania, Niger + CAR, Cote d'Ivoire, Madagascar) (Burundi, Ethiopia)

* Please note that the *minimization* procedure depends on the principle of *implication*. This procedure may result in the description of *one* case with *several* prime implicants. To illustrate, in the formula for the introduction of party bans Benin is covered by all minimized expressions.

An effective measure of institutional engineering? Ethnic party bans in Africa

Anika Moroff and Matthias Basedau

GIGA Institute of African Affairs, Hamburg, Germany

Following the introduction of multiparty systems, almost all sub-Saharan countries have introduced wide-ranging measures of party regulation, particularly bans on ethnic or – in more general terms – particularistic parties, in order, it is claimed, to prevent intercommunal conflict and to promote democracy. While this restrictive type of party regulation has become a dominant political feature in Africa, little is known about the efficacy of such measures. This article engages in an analysis of the possible effects on democracy and peace of different types of party regulation and implemented party bans and shows that party bans are apparently less suited to alleviating conflict than has been claimed. It also finds that implemented bans seem to be negatively related to democracy as ethnic bans are frequently abused to suppress the political opposition or to silence ethnic or religious minorities.

Introduction

The widespread and strict regulations regarding political parties in sub-Saharan Africa, in particular legal provisions to ban 'particularistic' parties, are not easily reconciled with liberal democracy as party bans restrict the freedom of association. In sub-Saharan Africa, public discourse often justifies such measures by claiming that multiparty politics inevitably results in the politicization of ethnicity and other socially attributed identities, provoking intercommunal conflict and doing harm to the prospects of democracy.[1]

While such bans have become a dominant, yet widely unchallenged political practice in Africa, the impact of these bans on violent conflict and democracy has received little scholarly attention. The academic debate has focused on other measures of institutional engineering which are designed to accommodate inter-communal relations and contribute to the survival and consolidation of democracy (for example, electoral systems or decentralization), while party regulation remains an under-researched area.[2] This article contributes to filling this gap by engaging in a preliminary analysis of whether or not legal provisions on particularistic parties and their implementation really avoid violent conflict and promote democracy in sub-Saharan Africa.[3]

Following a short definition of central concepts and a theoretical discussion about how particularistic party bans may affect democracy and intercommunal conflict, we develop a number of hypotheses and outline our methodology. The main section engages in a preliminary test of the central hypotheses on the effects of party bans on (a) peace, and (b) democracy, and tests the impact of both the more general regulation type and those bans that have actually been implemented. The final section draws theoretical and methodological conclusions and highlights areas for future research.

Concept and types of ethnic and particularistic party bans

In accord with the understanding of this special issue (see Introduction), an ethnic or particularistic party ban denotes a highly restrictive official legal sanction that aims to prohibit the existence or activity of a political party which is composed of, seeks the support of, and acts on behalf or in the interest of a specific ethnic or particularistic identity group. In a broad sense, ethnic identities and differences derive from a variable set of particular identities such as clan, community, faith (religion), language, regional provenance, race, sect or tribe, all of which are the result of self-ascription or ascription by others.[4] African party laws, however, generally rely on the narrower understanding of the concept, which is often close to the concept of 'tribe'. In order to avoid confusion, we have decided to use only the generic term 'particularistic' for the aforementioned groups and related political parties.[5]

As presented in more detail in Anika Moroff's contribution in this special issue, 'Party Bans in Africa', particularistic party bans may differ with regard to their social basis (ethnicity or tribe, religion, race and region)[6] as well as the respective legal form they take. The term 'ban' may include (1) the dissolution of an already existing party; (2) a temporary ban, that is, suspension; or (3) the denial of registration to a group that wants to transform into a political party.

Additionally, provisions can differ in terms of whether they 'negatively' prohibit such particularistic parties (thereby *blocking* particularism) or 'positively' proscribe specific requirements which are designed to ensure parties' non-particularistic nature by fostering *aggregation* (see Introduction). A 'positive' ban or 'aggregation' in this sense would be a requirement that a party is nationally represented in terms of party membership at the leader and/or the supporters' level. In contrast, a country that does not outlaw particularistic parties or even encourages the formation of particularistic parties allows the *translation* of particularisms in the party system. Finally, it makes a difference whether the party bans are just a 'legal option' or whether a ban is actually implemented. Given the low regulatory capacity of many African states and the often high degree of informal politics, we cannot take for granted that regulations are necessarily enforced and implemented. We therefore see to examine two issues: (1) legal regulation of parties, and (2) the actual implementation of party bans.

Theoretical framework: the potential impact of particularistic party bans on peace and democracy

What do existing theories predict with respect to the impact of party bans? First, we should consider that the impact may differ with regard to either peace[7] or democracy, although both are interrelated (see Table 1). Second, the answer depends strongly on assumptions about the effect of particularistic parties themselves. Ethnic heterogeneity and the political mobilization of ethnic and other particularistic identities have long been seen as obstacles to both peace and democratic stability.[8] According to this argument, if political parties organize along ethnic lines, mechanisms of ethnic outbidding threaten to deepen social and cultural divisions, fanning emotions and raising the stakes of the game. Furthermore, cultural minorities might be marginalized or permanently excluded from political power and therefore resort to violent and undemocratic means in order to counterbalance their marginalization.[9] Such developments can increase the risk of conflict, which in turn endangers democracy. Finally, ethnic parties might limit electoral choice, and politicians who 'play the ethnic card' might care less about the nation as a whole than about their specific clientele.[10]

What can party bans do about these risks? Prohibitions of particularistic parties, if effective, have the potential to prevent particularistic politics from entering party politics or to remove such politics from the party system.[11] Once accepted or effectively demonstrated, such bans may have an additional pre-emptive effect. Political parties then have to organize along other lines, seeking support from several identity groups and/or using other cleavages (class or ideas and values) as the basic source of partisan support. As a result, intercommunal conflict is less likely and the chances for sustaining democracy are higher (Hypotheses 1.1, 1.2).

However, recent studies have questioned the negative impact of particularistic parties and have argued that ethnic parties might help, or at least not necessarily hinder, peaceful democracy.[12] Contrary to the first set of hypotheses, one might therefore argue that particularistic party bans have an adverse impact on intercommunal relations and democracy (Hypotheses 2.1, 2.2). Since party bans block the representation of certain societal interests from the political system, particularistic groups may feel marginalized and seek other extra-legal or violent means of expression.[13] If abused to suppress the opposition, bans may call into question the political legitimacy of the system and hence become a source of conflict themselves.[14]

As Bieber argues, it is also possible that party bans have very little or no impact on democracy and peace (Hypotheses 3.1–3.6).[15] Democracy and conflict have numerous and interrelated determinants respectively. The classical risk factors

Table 1. Hypotheses on the impact of particularistic party bans (PPBs)*.

Direction of impact	Dependent variables	
	Conflict/Peace	Democracy
Positive	H 1.1 PPBs decrease the politicization of ethnicity and other particularistic identities. As a result, intercommunal and other violence is less likely.	H 1.2 PPBs help to create moderation in the party system because particularistic parties tend to aggravate relations between parties. Hence, party bans contribute to the functioning of democracy.
Negative	H 2.1 PPBs have a negative impact on interethnic conflicts because they exclude relevant political actors from the political scene and thus reduce the regime's legitimacy and/or force particularistic actors to resort to violent means. Party bans themselves may become a source of conflict.	H 2.2 PPBs have an adverse effect on democracy because the bans are abused (or used as pretexts) to suppress the opposition and violate fundamental rights.
Neutral	H 3.1 PPBs have no effect on conflict but are an expression of past problems.	H 3.4 PPBs have no effect on democratization but are an expression of authoritarianism.
	H 3.2 Variables or risks other than PPBs (level of development, governance, prior conflict, etc.) are superior in explaining the level of conflict.	H 3.5 Variables other than PPBs (level of development, governance, conflict, etc.) are superior in explaining the level of democracy.
	H 3.3 Ethnic party bans have no impact on interethnic conflict (a) because the main actors in conflicts are not political parties but other ethnic political groupings not affected by the party ban; (b) because, despite bans, particularistic parties find loopholes to continue to operate; or (c) because PPBs are not enforced and implemented.	H 3.6 Ethnic party bans have no impact on democracy (a) because the main actors in (democratic) politics are not political parties but other ethnic political groupings not affected by the party ban; (b) because, despite bans, particularistic parties find loopholes to continue to operate; or (c) because PPBs are not enforced and implemented.
Context dependent	H 4.1 PPBs have several types of effects. Some cases follow the pro-peace and others the anti-peace logic.	H 4.3 PPBs have several types of effects. Some cases follow the pro-democracy and others the anti-democracy logic.
	H 4.2 Negative, neutral or positive effects of PPBs on conflict depend on the context. Conditions contributing to positive effects include:	H 4.4 Negative, neutral or positive effects of PPBs on conflict depend on the context. Conditions contributing to positive effects include:
	- No cultural majorities	- No cultural majorities
	- No undemocratic regimes	- No undemocratic regimes
	- Fair legal implementation	- Fair legal implementation
	- 'Positive' bans and 'aggregation' (e.g., national representation requirements)	- 'Positive' bans and 'aggregation' (e.g., national representation requirements)
	- Positive general surrounding conditions	- Positive general surrounding conditions

Source: Authors' compilation. *Indirect effects are not included.

for democracy and peace in Africa include, for example, poverty, prior conflict, dysfunctional institutions, and the lack of responsible leadership, not to mention specific path-dependent and contingent historical developments.[16] In such a setting, party bans might have no noteworthy influence. Additionally, even if the regulations are regularly and rigidly enforced – which should not be taken for granted – particularistic parties may find 'loopholes' to escape legal sanctions. Party bans might also be more of a reaction to past problems in intercommunal relations or express the undemocratic character of the regime rather than function as an effective tool of conflict regulation.

In contrast, one may argue that the magnitude and direction of the effects of party bans vis-à-vis democracy and peace will depend on surrounding conditions (Hypotheses 4.1–4.4). Such conditions may include the political relevance of the (would-be) party in question, or the 'particularistic landscape' of the country. The banning of strong opposition parties as well as the prevention of the effective political representation of cultural minorities may be problematic for both peace and democracy.[17] Furthermore, adverse effects of party bans on conflict and democracy are more probable when the political system has found other ways to deal with diversity: if the ban thwarts other regulations, it may be more likely to have negative consequences.[18] With regard to the acceptance of implemented bans, the nature of the regime, the legal procedure, and the party system might also be of significance. When bans are put into effect in a democratic setting, with a non-dominant-party system, or by a genuinely neutral institution in a way that is transparent and consistent with the rule of law, marginalization and legitimacy, problems are less likely.[19] Finally, the type of party ban may be relevant. For instance, it has been argued that positive, aggregative measures, particularly regional distribution requirements, are more likely to promote peaceful democracy than restrictive bans.[20]

As shown in Table 1, the relationship is certainly complex and there are many possible hypotheses – not all of which can be tested here. In particular, some of the hypotheses require data on the particularistic character of parties which is unavailable. Hence, the following analysis will concentrate on hypotheses 1.1 to 2.2 on negative or positive effects on democracy and peace and whether we can observe rather *strong* effects; contextual conditions will be mainly addressed in an explorative manner.

Particularistic party bans, violent conflict and democracy

Database and methodology

The banning of particularistic parties is very widespread in sub-Saharan Africa:[21] only six countries did not have such provisions in mid-2010 (Botswana, Comoros, Mauritius, South Africa, Zambia, and Zimbabwe). While 15 countries rely exclusively on the blocking approach, 25 combine blocking with aggregative measures to regulate particularistic parties (see Table 2); that is, they outlaw particularistic parties and, additionally, require parties to have a national character.

Table 2. Type of regulation and violent ethnic conflict, 1990–2009.

	Translation	Blocking	Blocking and aggregation	N
Ethnic conflict after 1990	29% Kenya*, South Africa	27% Central African Republic*, Chad, Mali, Senegal	38% Burundi*, Congo-Brazzaville, Democratic Republic of Congo, Ethiopia, Ghana, Niger, Nigeria*, Rwanda*	14
No ethnic conflict after 1990	71% Botswana, Comoros, Mauritius, Zambia*, Zimbabwe	73% Burkina Faso, Cameroon, Côte d'Ivoire, Gambia, Lesotho, Madagascar, Malawi, Mauritania*, Namibia*, Seychelles, São Tomé	62% Angola*, Benin, Cape Verde, Djibouti, Equatorial Guinea*, Gabon, Guinea, Guinea Bissau, Liberia, Mozambique, Sierra Leone, Togo, Tanzania*	29
N	7	15	21	43

Source: Authors' compilation, based on project and MEPV data. MEPV data refers to 'ethnic violence' and 'ethnic wars'.
Notes: *Translation*: countries without a legal provision to ban particularistic parties; *blocking*: countries with a ban provision; *blocking and aggregation*: countries with a ban provision and national representation requirements. * Implemented particularistic party ban.
After relaxing enforcement in 2002, Nigeria rather belongs to the 'blocking' category. No MEPV data for Cape Verde, Seychelles, São Tomé e Principe, cases classified by the authors. Kenya is counted as a case of translation in Sample I because it only introduced a banning provision in 2008. Madagascar introduced aggregative regulations in 2009 only and is thus counted as a blocking case in Sample I. Percentages refer to the total number of countries in the respective column.

Between 1990 and early 2010, 12 African countries implemented 138 party bans (see Appendix). In order to find out if these particularistic bans have a positive or negative effect on (a) peace and (b) democracy, we decided to combine (rather simple) quantitative methods[22] with approaches that keep single cases identifiable and allow for an informed interpretation of the data and the developments in each country. Generally, a two-step approach was applied. As a first step we looked at the entire population of those African countries with a multiparty system (N = 43) between 1990 and early 2010 (Sample I). Cases should display minimal relevance of multiparty politics. We thus exclude countries which have not legally allowed multiparty politics for the greater part of the period since 1990 (Eritrea, Swaziland, Uganda) and/or have not had at least one multiparty elections since 1990 (Somalia, Sudan[23]). In order to find out whether the levels of democracy and conflict are systematically connected to the type of legal party regulation according to Bogaards – translation, blocking or aggregation – we combined macro-qualitative comparison in cross tables and bivariate statistics.

In a second step we focus on countries that implemented a party ban. Cases were coded as country years; any implementation of one (or more) particularistic party ban(s) was a case (for example, Rwanda 2003, Nigeria 1998). Thus, if in one particular year more than one party was banned, it was nevertheless counted as one case (N = 33, Sample II).[24] In order to find out whether these cases were systematically connected to our dependent variables, we used cross tables and bivariate statistics. A closer look at individual cases added anecdotal, but still systematic case study evidence and allowed an, albeit limited, test of pertinent context conditions.

Party bans and peace

Type of party regulation and peace

Does the way a country regulate particularistic parties influence the level of violent conflict in that country? As a first step towards answering this question we assessed the number of countries with the various types of regulation (translation, blocking, aggregation)[25] which, according to the Major Episodes of Political Violence data (MEPV), experienced an 'ethnic conflict' or an 'ethnic war' after 1990 (until 2008).

The results call into question a strong positive or negative impact of party regulation: countries that allow for a party ban were slightly more likely to experience an ethnic conflict or war after reintroducing multiparty politics than countries that opted for 'translation' regarding the regulation of particularistic parties (see Table 2).[26] However, this difference was not significant in bivariate statistics. In addition, the comparison does not point to a more positive effect of aggregative regulations: countries that combined blocking and aggregation regulations regarding particularistic parties were slightly more likely to experience ethnic conflict than countries relying on blocking alone, but the difference is again not significant.

These results allow for two conclusions at this stage. First, the prevention of violent conflict in culturally heterogeneous countries is possible even when particularistic parties are allowed. The cases of Mauritius, Zambia, and Zimbabwe support this argument. Second, while some authors have argued that aggregative regulations are better suited to preventing conflict than are blocking regulations, our results can so far not confirm this idea.

However, the aggregation rule's lack of effectiveness in preventing conflict might well be due to a lack of enforcement: only one of the conflict countries – Nigeria – indeed denied registration to parties because they lacked a national character. We therefore have to take a closer look at the implementation of bans.

Implemented party bans and peace

In a second step we tested the effects of implemented bans on peace or violent conflict by using actually implemented bans as cases (Sample II). Relying on MEPV conflict data we compared the level of ethnic conflict one year before and after the implementation of a ban.[27] Except for an increase in both Burundi in 1993 and in Nigeria in 1997, the level of ethnic conflict remained unchanged in all other cases, pointing to rather weak effects. However, as has been argued elsewhere,[28] it is difficult to rely exclusively on readily available conflict data when assessing a ban's impact on conflict. Indeed, the cleavage which corresponds to the party ban is not always linked to (ethnic) conflict measured through conventional conflict data, which mostly focus on high-intensity conflicts: except for those in Burundi and Rwanda, implemented bans have seldom targeted parties linked to an ongoing violent conflict in the country. In almost all the other cases, a party that represented a relatively small ethnic or religious minority was banned. In order to determine whether bans have had an impact on the level of violence in the respective cleavage, we therefore have to study the cases themselves more closely.[29]

In looking at Burundi and Rwanda, it becomes obvious that the relationship between political parties and warring factions is quite important.[30] In both countries, rebel groups linked to former parties carried out considerable violence long after the party had been dissolved. In Burundi, the Parti pour la Liberation du Peuple Hutu (Palipehutu) represented the political wing of a radical pro-Hutu rebel group. Palipehutu was not registered as a political party during the introduction of the multiparty system in 1992. This did not help to calm tensions between Hutus and Tutsis and avoid the outbreak of the civil war. Nor did it prevent the Palipehutu-Forces Nationales de Libération (FNL), which had split from the political wing in 1991, from becoming one of the main rebel forces during the civil war.[31] However, the ban did not provoke the outbreak of violence, which was actually triggered by the assassination of the Hutu president by Tutsi extremists within the military.

Rwanda banned the Mouvement Républicain National pour la Démocratie et le Développement (MRND) and the Coalition pour la Défense de la République (CDR) in 1994 as the two main parties responsible for the genocide the same year. While this decision helped to ease tensions in Rwanda, many former genocide fighters from the Interahamwe continued their fight for Hutu supremacy from the neighbouring countries. The later outlawing of the Pasteur Bizimungu's Parti Démocratique du Renouveau (PDR-Ubunyanja) and the Mouvement Démocratique Républicain (MDR) has been characterized as regime's strategy to mend the Hutu-Tutsi cleavage and to suppress all forms of 'divisionism'.[32] However, many authors and human rights organizations have seen these bans as an expression of the increasingly authoritarian character of the regime and the growing exclusion of Hutus from political life.[33]

In countries where party bans were not linked to existing conflicts – the Central African Republic (CAR), Kenya, Mauritania, Uganda, and Zambia – parties were banned due to their (allegedly) religious character. Beyond this similarity, however, we can find important differences. The religious parties in Uganda (Uganda Islamic Revolutionary Party), the CAR and Zambia (party names could not be found) were very small groups without a large following, and the decision to ban them did not have an impact on the level of violent conflict. The violent conflict in Uganda was not about Islam or Islamic groups, and Zambia had no violent conflict at all. In the CAR the violent conflict with the northern rebels, including the Union des Forces Démocratiques pour le Rassemblement (UFDR) and the Armée Populaire pour la Restauration de la Démocratie (APRD), has had religious overtones because these rebels are largely Muslim, but there is no evidence of a direct connection between the conflict and the party bans.[34]

Things were different in Kenya, where the denied registration of the Islamic Party of Kenya (IPK), founded in February 1992, helped to cause a period of violent unrest in Mombasa and several other coastal towns that lasted until 1994. The radical Shaikh Kahlid Balala, who became the spokesman of the IPK some months after its foundation, was one of the main instigators of the clashes between IPK followers, government security forces, and the government-sponsored organization United Muslims of Africa.[35] The decision not to register the IPK was seen by many Muslims as yet another sign of the discrimination carried out by a mainly Christian regime against the Muslim minority.[36] The IPK was thus able to gain a lot of support precisely because it was not allowed to register.[37] However, the growing radicalization of the group under Shaikh Balala, who for example issued fatwas against Kenyan politicians, and the enduring violent clashes in Mombasa, ultimately led to a decrease in support and a split within the IPK.[38]

In Mauritania, the government implemented various party bans and argued that the banned parties represented a threat due to their particularistic character. A closer look at the cases, however, questions this claim. Since 1990, moderate Islamists have attempted unsuccessfully to register a political party.[39] The government claimed that adherents of the Islamists were involved in terrorist activities. However, many authors have questioned this argument, pointing to the fact that Ould Taya's regime may simply have used the bans to silence members of the opposition.[40] Mauritania also banned Action pour le Changement (AC) in 2002 for alleged racism.[41] AC had campaigned against the oppression of the black Moors and non-Arabic-speaking minorities. These groups have not, however, been involved in any violent conflict since the introduction of multiparty politics.

Equatorial Guinea and Namibia have both banned secessionist parties. In Equatorial Guinea the Movimiento para la Autodetermincaion de la Isla de Bioco (MAIB) was outlawed in 1994 as an ethnic, separatist organization. The MAIB was mainly supported by the minority Bubi ethnic group, which is heavily underrepresented in the government and administration. According to the government, the MAIB was involved in an attack by some young Bubi men on several military bases in 1998. However, it is far from certain whether the MAIB was responsible for the attack. The group denied involvement and has never demonstrated the capacity to carry out such major actions, either before 1998 or afterwards.[42]

The case of the United Democratic Party (UDP) in Namibia differs in that the group was never officially registered as a party. The UDP's alleged military wing, the Caprivi Liberation Movement, was responsible for the short-lived rebellion in Caprivi in 1999. Its leaders had fled the country during a prior wave of arrests in 1998 and the UDP was not very visible in the years following the rebellion. It seems unlikely that the (outlawed) attempt to revive it in 2006 would have mobilized a large following able to carry out major violence: even at the height of the UDP's activities, the rebellion in 1999, the group does not seem to have had a strong following.[43]

Finally, it might be useful to take a closer look at the countries which have denied registration to groups that did not meet the national representation criteria. In Nigeria, large numbers of parties tried to register in 1996 under General Abacha and in 1998 under the transitional rule of General Abubakar (before the election in 1999), as well as before the 2003 elections. However, the regulations required parties to have a 'national character', and both electoral commissions proved rather strict in the implementation of these rules and denied registration to large numbers of parties.[44] The actual impact of these measures is debated though: Bogaards argues that the party laws (in combination with electoral laws) helped to discourage parties from concentrating exclusively on their regional and ethnic strongholds and that this fostered a certain level of political integration.[45] Nevertheless, political parties still have marked strongholds, and general political and economic rivalries in Nigeria continue with varying levels of conflict intensity. Other authors point out, moreover, that the conflict has simply moved to the intra-party level.[46] Intercommunal violence at the local level, for instance in Jos in late 2008 and again in early 2010, further calls into question the success of the representation requirements in Nigeria.[47]

Like Nigeria, Tanzania introduced a strict requirement that parties must demonstrate a national character when adopting multiparty politics. In order to protect the Union between the mainland and Zanzibar, the party law included inter alia the rule that parties must have members and leaders from the mainland and Zanzibar. The regulations have been implemented quite strictly and many parties have failed to meet the requirements.[48] Nevertheless, the registered parties show either a clear Zanzibar or mainland bias; only the ruling party, Chama cha Mapinduzi (CCM), is strong in both parts of the country.[49]

In sum, the (anecdotal) evidence from the case studies does not support the idea that implemented bans have had a strong impact on violent conflict. This apparently holds true irrespective of the context conditions specified in our hypotheses. We have controlled for the characteristics of the particularistic landscape of the country, political variables, the nature of the ban, and the relevance of the targeted group or party.[50] Neither the religious structure of the country, the electoral system, nor the type of party system is systematically connected to violent conflict. There is also little variance with regard to the existence of an ethnic majority. In the few countries with a clear ethnic majority, we can, however, observe a tendency of the use of bans against minorities (Equatorial Guinea, Namibia) or against (Hutu) majorities which have experienced periods of political exclusion in recent history (Burundi, Rwanda).

The type of ban implemented and the democratic quality of the regime do not yield strong results either. Even the relevance of the targeted groups seems to have no strong influence on conflict: while no change in the level of conflict occurred that could be attributed to the banning of a minor party, in most cases no change could be observed even after the banning of a larger party.[51] Finally, it is difficult to tell whether registration requirements, that is, 'positive bans', such as those in

Tanzania and Nigeria, have really had positive effects on conflict. If any, they remain limited.

Party bans and democracy

Type of party regulation and democracy

In order to assess the impact of particularistic party bans on democracy, we followed the two-step approached detailed above, starting with Sample I. However, in comparing groups of countries with different types of regulation (see Table 3), we found no significant differences with regard to these countries' level of democracy in 2009 (measured through the average of Political Rights and Civil Liberties of Freedom House).[52] While only a few countries experienced a negative trend in the democracy ratings, it turns out that the 'translation' group – that is, where legal provisions do not restrict the politicization of ethnicity in the party system – had the largest share of countries rated as 'free' in 2008 (43%), followed by the blocking group with 27% of free countries.

The relationship between the regulation of particularistic parties and the development of democracy therefore seems to be weak, at best. As already discussed, the lack of effect might be due to a lack of enforcement.

Since we lack data on the character of all or even the majority of political parties in these countries[53] – which may organize along ethnic lines despite a

Table 3. Type of regulation and changes in democracy ratings, 1990–2009.

Development of FH ratings 1990–2009	Translation	Blocking	Blocking and aggregation	N
Negative	Botswana, **Zimbabwe**	Gambia, Madagascar	**Gabon, Guinea**	6
No change	Mauritius	**Cameroon**, CAR*, **Chad, Côte d'Ivoire**, Namibia*, Senegal	**Congo-Br., Congo DR**, Djibouti, **Equatorial Guinea***, Nigeria*, **Rwanda***	13
Positive	Comoros, Kenya*, South Africa, Zambia*	Burkina Faso, Lesotho, Malawi, Mali, **Mauritania***, São Tomé, Seychelles	Angola*, Burundi*, Benin, Cape Verde, Ethiopia, Ghana, Guinea Bissau, Liberia, Mozambique, Niger, Sierra Leone, Tanzania*, Togo	24
N	7	15	21	43

Source: Authors' compilation, based on project and Freedom House (FH) data.
Notes: Changes in FH ratings of only 0.5 or below were coded as 'no change'. Numerical gains were coded as 'negative' since the highest value in Freedom House indicates the lowest level of democratic quality. Countries in *italics* were rated 'free' in 2008; countries in **bold** were rated 'not free'.
*Implemented particularistic party ban. For Kenya and Madagascar see Table 2.

general ban – we now turn to the implementation of party bans (Sample II) and try to assess the corresponding impact on the level of democracy.

Implemented party bans and democracy

Looking at the bans that were actually implemented, however, reveals little evidence that points to a straightforward connection between the implementation of particularistic party bans and democratization, at least in the short term.[54] If we look at the changes in Freedom House values (average rating of 'political rights' and 'civil liberties') one year before and one year after the implementation of such bans, no evidence for strong negative or positive effects emerges. Of 33 cases, 10 party bans were connected to stable democracy ratings; seven cases showed negative and 16 showed positive changes. These changes were very small though: only in Nigeria (1998), Rwanda (1994, both positive changes), and Zambia (1993, negative change) did the changes in the ratings exceed .5 on a scale of 1 to 7.[55]

It might additionally be questioned whether the observed variations were indeed caused by the party bans. To get an impression of the more long-lasting impact of party bans, we looked at the development of Freedom House ratings from 1990 to 2008. The only country which was rated continuously free is Namibia: the Caprivi conflict and the ban on the UDP apparently had no negative impact on Namibian democracy. FH ratings remained unchanged until 2006 and then slightly improved. The CAR, Nigeria, Uganda, Tanzania, and Zambia show a more mixed record of Freedom House ratings. It is however not very plausible that the party bans had a strong impact on these developments. Zambia's democracy ratings decreased after the party ban in 1993; yet, it seems far more convincing that this reflected the poor democratic performance by the Chiluba regime in general rather than the party ban of a very minor political party. Changes in the CAR and Uganda cannot be convincingly explained by the party bans either; rather, they appear to be the result of internal developments in the Patassé regime in the CAR and of the elections to the Constitutional Assembly in Uganda. In all three countries the banned parties were extremely small and apparently without a substantial support base.

The fairly restrictive application of registration requirements in Tanzania could be said to have weakened democracy by stabilizing Chama cha Mapinduzi's (CCM) dominant position and preventing a democratic turnover. However, such a strong impact is not convincing given that the non-registered parties were not able to mobilize even a minimal following. Other factors such as the question of party funding and issues not directly linked to party regulations may have been more important for the strong position of CCM.[56]

In Nigeria, the various electoral commissions' decisions about which parties to register always occurred before an election or after a regime change. We can suppose that they partly expressed the more or less democratic character of the regime and strengthened the respective character of the regime afterwards: the regulations applied by the military government under Abacha were extremely restrictive. The National Electoral Commission of Nigeria registered only five parties, all of which embraced Abacha as their presidential candidate in the cancelled 1998 elections. In 2002 the decision of the Independent National Electoral Commission not to register 21 new parties was one part of a larger debate about a change in the electoral law which would have assured that no new parties could participate in the 2003 elections.[57] Ultimately, the Supreme Court ruled in November 2002 that the electoral commission's registration practice was too severe and 24 new parties were registered.

Finally, Burundi, Equatorial Guinea, Kenya, Mauritania, and Rwanda have been rated fairly 'unfree' or undemocratic for the majority of the period since 1990. For Burundi, the impact of the denial of registration to Palipehutu in Burundi seems rather small. While it might be argued that the registration of the party could have strengthened a power-sharing agreement and thus would have fostered democracy, this argument is not convincing as the subsequent civil strife was caused by the rebellion of Tutsi militaries, who would not even accept a president from a more moderate Hutu party. Also, the Hutu–Tutsi cleavage has remained highly politically salient despite the ban.[58]

The remaining cases do not point to a positive effect of party bans either. In Mauritania, Ould Taya's regime's numerous party bans against particularistic and non-particularistic parties from 1991 onwards clearly did not lead to the democratization of the regime. The decision of Rwanda not to include the CDR and the MRND in the transitional government in 1994 was certainly not overly undemocratic given the parties' role in the genocide. By contrast, the later banning of the PDR-Ubunyanja and the MDR can be seen as a decision by a highly undemocratic regime to weaken the opposition.[59] A similar argument can be made for countries such as Equatorial Guinea, Kenya, and Mauritania. While the bans did not change the dynamics of democratization, they might have been an expression of the authoritarian character of the regime and thus have reinforced its repressive character by outlawing a strong opposition.

This assumption is supported by the democracy ratings of countries which have implemented party bans: only two (Namibia, Zambia) out of 33 party bans were implemented in 'free' or democratic countries. Obviously, party bans are particularly popular in non-democratic settings (see Figure 1).[60]

In sum, a closer look at the cases reveals no evidence that party bans have a positive impact on democracy: for no country it can be convincingly argued that the decision to ban a party might have strengthened democracy. In all countries, democracy ratings remained largely unchanged after such a ban; small variations can be better explained by other events such as elections (for example, Uganda in 1994, Mauritania in 2006).

However, for at least four countries – Equatorial Guinea, Rwanda, Mauritania, and Kenya – there is evidence that undemocratic regimes used bans to silence the opposition rather than to foster democracy or to prevent conflict. All four countries had highly undemocratic regimes with authoritarian-dominant (or hegemonic) parties and the banned parties can be judged to have been politically relevant.

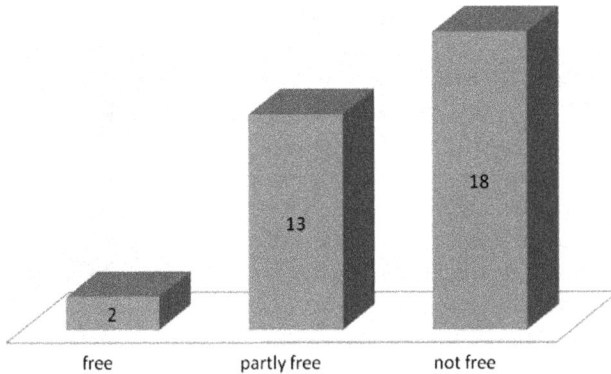

Figure 1. Levels of democracy before party-ban implementation.
Source: Authors' compilation, based on project and Freedom House data (FH one year before implementation).

All four countries harassed opposition parties more broadly in various ways (or restricted party competition altogether, as Rwanda did until 2003) and also banned various non-particularistic parties. In undemocratic regimes, particularistic party bans therefore represent an additional tool – alongside many others – for repressing the opposition. While representation requirements seem at first glance to be less prone to abuse, the evidence of a positive effect from these regulations in Tanzania and Nigeria is not convincing either.

Conclusion

Bans on particularistic parties have a long tradition in sub-Saharan Africa and represent the norm in today's practice on the continent. Applying macro-qualitative comparison, bivariate statistics and qualitative case studies, this article questions the effectiveness of party bans as a tool of managing ethnic conflict and promoting democracy. Generally, hypotheses of strong positive or negative effects (H 1.1 to H 2.2) are supported neither for the legal possibility nor for actually implemented bans. There is some evidence that party bans might have a somewhat negative impact on democracy. Evidence for stronger effects is confined to a number of individual cases.

With regard to hypothesis 1.1 and 2.1 on conflict, countries which introduced the legal option to ban particularistic parties were not significantly more or less conflict-prone than countries without such an option. Only in a few individual cases (for example, Rwanda 1994) were bans implemented that might have had a stabilizing impact. In most cases they have proven ineffective, and in one case – Kenya in 1992 – the ban may even have led to an increase in violence, supporting hypothesis 2.1.

In line with the hypothesis on negative effects on democracy (H 2.2), countries with a ban provision were slightly less democratic in 2008 than countries without such a provision. While provisions for party bans often emerge within a broader institutional process during a period of political transition, the implementation of bans is more widespread in less democratic countries in Africa, and bans often seem to be used as one means among others to suppress the political representation of interests and grievances. This phenomenon might well have destabilizing effects in the future and points to the important issue of the motive behind the ban.[61] While we have not found convincing evidence for hypothesis H 1.2 that party bans – either regulatory or actually implemented – promote democracy, in a number of cases, party bans can be interpreted as a way of stabilizing authoritarianism.[62]

Our results therefore suggest that the impact of party bans on conflict and democracy is *generally* rather weak (H 3.1-3.6.). The magnitude and direction of the impact, however, varies unsurprisingly with the context of individual country cases as our preliminary case studies have shown (H 4.1-4.4.). In order to further investigate the impact of context conditions, carefully selected comparative case studies are necessary for isolating the effects of party bans and identifying important contextual conditions – something our research design only partially allowed (and which would have been beyond the scope of this contribution). Most importantly, in order to better investigate the impact of specific regulations on political parties, data on the particularistic character of political parties remains urgently needed. This would particularly facilitate a more detailed analysis of the causal chain between regulation, parties' characters, and violent conflict and democracy.

Acknowledgements

A previous version of this article was presented at the conference on Party Regulation and Ethnic Party Bans in Africa at Jacobs University Bremen, 19 September 2008. The authors thank the participants for their helpful comments.

Notes

1. See for example The United Republic of Tanzania, *The Report and Recommendations of the Presidential Commission*.
2. For an exception, see Reilly and Nordlund, *Political Parties in Conflict-Prone Societies*.
3. The paper draws on data collected through the project 'Managing Ethnic Conflict through Institutional Engineering. Ethnic Party Bans in Africa', funded by the Fritz-Thyssen-Foundation and conducted in close cooperation with the Universities of Darmstadt and Duisburg-Essen as well as the Jacobs-University Bremen.
4. Horowitz, *Ethnic Groups in Conflict*.
5. Bogaards, 'Electoral Systems, Party Systems, and Ethnicity in Africa'.
6. In order to capture the behavioural dimension of the ban ('acts on behalf of or in the interest of'), we assign respective party bans regarding, for instance, 'tribalism' to ethnic parties, 'racism' to racial parties, and 'regionalism' to regional parties.
7. We define 'peace' as negative peace, that is, the absence of violent conflict. Violent conflict can be measured by classical databases such as Major Episodes of Political Violence (MEPV) and others.
8. Horowitz, *Ethnic Groups in Conflict*; Rabushka and Shepsle, *Politics in Plural Societies*.
9. Chandra and Boulet, 'Ethnic Cleavage Structures, Permanent Exclusion and Democratic Stability'.

10. Dowd and Driessen, 'Ethnically Dominated Party Systems and the Quality of Democracy'; Posner, 'Measuring Ethnic Fractionalization in Africa'; Sisk, *Power Sharing and International Mediation in Ethnic Conflicts.*

11. Bogaards, 'Electoral Systems, Party Systems and Ethnicity in Africa'; Özbudun, 'From Political Islam to Conservative Democracy'.

12. Birnir, *Ethnicity and Electoral Politics*; Chandra, *Why Ethnic Parties Succeed*; Ishiyama, 'Do Ethnic Parties Promote Minority Ethnic Conflict?'. See also the consociational school of Lijphart, *Democracy in Plural Societies.*

13. International Crisis Group, *Political Parties in Afghanistan.*

14. Randall, 'Party Regulation in Conflict-Prone Societies'.

15. Bieber, 'Regulating Minority Parties in Central and South-Eastern Europe'.

16. Bratton and Van de Walle, *Democratic Experiments in Africa.*

17. Birnir, 'Divergence in Diversity?'

18. McMenamin, 'Party Regulation and Democratization'.

19. Rosenblum, 'Banning Parties'.

20. Bogaards, 'Electoral Systems, Party Systems and Ethnicity in Africa'.

21. See Moroff, 'Party Bans in Africa'.

22. The low number of cases and the high degree of multicollinearity would make a more complex analysis rather problematic.

23. We could not consider the elections in Sudan in April 2010. At the time of writing results had not yet been announced.

24. This could be questioned, since there might be many differences with regard to several bans in one particular year and country. However, in almost all cases with various bans in one year, the official reason was identical. The only exception was Mauritania, which had a ban due to 'race' and a denial of registration due to 'ethnicity' in 2002.

25. No country relies on aggregation exclusively: all countries that have aggregating regulations also prohibit particularistic parties. 'Translation' here means only that countries legally allow (not necessarily encourage) particularistic parties; it does not imply that parties empirically display such characteristics.

26. In Mali, Niger, and Rwanda, the conflict started before the introduction of the party ban and continued several years afterwards.

27. We also tested other time periods (namely five years after the bans). Results remained widely unchanged.

28. Basedau and Moroff, 'Parties in Chains – Do Ethnic Party Bans in Africa Promote Peace?' Manuscript under review with *Party Politics* (as at May 2010).

29. As the ban in Angola was more recent than the others and its effects therefore difficult to assess, we decided not to include it in our analysis.

30. The following illustrations mainly draw on the (bi)monthly country reports of the Economist Intelligence Unit (EIU) and the yearly publications of the *Afrika Jahrbuch* (since 2005: *Africa Yearbook*).

31. It is only recently that the last faction of FNL – having signed a peace agreement in 2006 – has transformed into a political party.

32. Commission Parlementaire, 'Rapport de la Commission Parlementaire sur les problèmes du MDR'.

33. See Niesen, 'Political Party Bans in Rwanda', this special issue.

34. Human Rights Watch, *State of Anarchy.*

35. Oded, *Islam and Politics in Kenya.*

36. Ibid.

37. IPK rallies attracted large crowds particularly in Mombasa and in the 1992 general elections, when it allied with Ford-Kenya, its candidates performed well in

Mombasa constituencies and senior member Rashid Mzee was elected Kisauni MP. Throup and Hornsby, *Multi-party Politics in Kenya*, 501ff.

38. Oded, *Islam and Politics in Kenya*; US State Department, *Kenya: Country Report on Human Rights Practices*.

39. In 1991, Mohamed Ould Sidi Yahya tried to register the Ummah party, while in 2004 and again – after a military coup – in 2005 Mohamed Jemil Ould Mansour and other politicians attempted to register the Parti pour la Convergence Démocratique (PCD).

40. International Crisis Group, *L'islamisme en Afrique du Nord IV*; Marty, 'Les multiples usages de l'Islam dans le champ politique mauritanien'. This argument is strengthened by the fact that the regime of President Ould Cheikh Abdallahi later registered two Islamic parties.

41. Ould Boulkheir tried in the same year to register a party under a new name, Convention pour le Changement (CC); it was denied registration because of its alleged ethnic character.

42. Amnesty International, 'Equatorial Guinea'.

43. Melber, 'One Namibia'; http://www.irinnews.org/report.aspx?reportid=60892.

44. This changed with a Supreme Court ruling in 2002 that considerably relaxed the guidelines of party registration.

45. Bogaards, 'Electoral Systems, Party Systems and Ethnicity in Africa'.

46. Reilly, Nordlund, and Newman, *Political Parties in Conflict-Prone Societies*.

47. See Bogaards, 'Ethnic Party Bans', this special issue.

48. Only one party did, however, follow a clear programme against the Union: the Democratic Party (DP) of Reverend Mtikila did not recruit members from Zanzibar because it did not consider Zanzibar to be part of Tanzania.

49. See Moroff, 'Party Bans in Africa', this special issue.

50. A synopsis of the results is available from the authors. Sources: Central Intelligence Agency World Factbook (https://www.cia.gov/library/publications/the-world-factbook/), Major Episodes of Political Violence (http://www.systemicpeace.org/inscr/inscr.htm), International Institute of Democracy and Electoral Assistance (http://idea.int/), Forum of Federations (http://www.forumfed.org/en/index.php).

51. To assess the relevance, we controlled for several criteria: representation of a major cleavage of the country, connection to an armed or rebel movement, seat in parliament and strong political visibility before the registration demand for parties, and the degree of publicity of party founders for groups asking for registration.

52. Non-parametric test for the three types of regulation, the legal possibility and aggregation vs. blocking were not significant. Freedom House data are available online at http://www.freedomhouse.org/template.cfm?page=439.

53. Some studies offer data for the ethnicization of political parties, for example Cheeseman and Ford, 'Ethnicity as a Political Cleavage', and Basedau and Stroh, 'Ethnicity and Party Systems'. However, they do not cover all cases and are only at one point in time.

54. For information on Freedom House ratings in 1990 and 2009 see Appendix.

55. For Polity IV there is no change in a negative direction, 17 cases with no change, and 13 with a positive change. Namibia and Angola are missing and Burundi has a period of interregnum after the ban. Results remain widely unchanged when other time periods (five-year period) are applied.

56. Hoffmeister and Robinson, 'Tanzania's Missing Opposition'.

57. Bergstresser, 'Nigeria 2003'.

58. International Crisis Group, *Elections au Burundi*; Ndarishikanye, 'Burundi'.

59. See Niesen, 'Party Political Bans in Rwanda', this special issue.

60. According to Polity IV, in 22 cases the country showed a value below 0, and in eight cases the value was between 0 and 5. Only Namibia and Zambia showed a value of 6 in the year before the implementation.
61. See also Hartmann and Kemmerzell, 'Understanding Variations in Party Bans in Africa', this special issue.
62. Schedler, 'Electoral Authoritarianism'.

Notes on contributors

Anika Moroff is a PhD candidate at the Department of Political Science at the University of Duisburg-Essen and an Associate Research Fellow at the GIGA Institute of African Affairs in Hamburg. Her research interests include political parties in Africa, ethnic conflict and institutional engineering.

Matthias Basedau, PhD, Heidelberg University, is Head of Research Programme at the German Institute of Global and Area Studies, Hamburg. He is also a Senior Research Fellow at the GIGA Institute of African Affairs in Hamburg. Research interests include political parties, ethnic and religious conflict as well natural resources and conflict.

Bibliography

Amnesty International. 'Equatorial Guinea. A Country Subjected to Terror and Harassment', 1999.

Basedau, Matthias and Alexander Stroh. 'Ethnicity and Party-Systems in Francophone Sub-Saharan Africa'. GIGA Working Papers No. 100. Hamburg: GIGA German Institute of Global and Area Studies, 2009.

Bergstresser, Heinrich. 'Nigeria 2003'. In *Afrika Jahrbuch 2003. Politik, Wirtschaft und Gesellschaft in Afrika südlich der Sahara*, ed. Institut für Afrika-Kunde, 155–71. Wiesbaden: VS Verlag für Sozialwissenschaften, 2004.

Bieber, Florian. 'Regulating Minority Parties in Central and South-Eastern Europe'. In *Political Parties in Conflict-Prone Societies: Regulation, Engineering and Democratic Development*, ed. Benjamin Reilly and Per Nordlund, 95–125. Tokyo & New York: United Nations University Press, 2008.

Birnir, Jóhanna Kristín. 'Divergence in Diversity? The Dissimilar Effects of Cleavages on Electoral Politics in New Democracies'. *American Journal of Political Science* 51, no. 3 (2007): 602–19.

Birnir, Jóhanna Kristín. *Ethnicity and Electoral Politics*. Cambridge & New York: Cambridge University Press, 2007.

Bogaards, Matthijs. 'Electoral Systems, Party Systems, and Ethnicity in Africa'. In *Votes, Money and Violence: Political Parties and Elections in Sub-Saharan Africa*, ed. Matthias Basedau, Gero Erdmann, and Andreas Mehler, 168–93. Stockholm & Scottsville, South Africa: Nordiska Afrikainstitutet & University of KwaZulu-Natal Press, 2007.

Bogaards, Matthijs. 'Ethnic Party Bans and Institutional Engineering in Nigeria'. *Democratization* Vol. 17, no. 4 (2010): 730–49.

Bratton, Michael, and Nicolas van de Walle. *Democratic Experiments in Africa: Regime Transitions in Comparative Perspective*. Cambridge & New York: Cambridge University Press, 1997.

Chandra, Kanchan. *Why Ethnic Parties Succeed: Patronage and Ethnic Head Counts in India*. Cambridge & New York: Cambridge University Press, 2004.

Chandra, Kanchan, and Cilanne Boulet. 'Ethnic Cleavage Structures, Permanent Exclusion and Democratic Stability'. Paper presented at the Conference on Alien Rule and its discontents, University of Washington at Seattle, 3–4 June 2005.

Cheeseman, Nic, and Rob Ford. 'Ethnicity as a Political Cleavage'. Afrobarometer Working Papers No. 83, 2007.

Commission Parlementaire. 'Rapport de la Commission Parlementaire sur les problèmes du MDR'. Kigali: 2003.

Dowd, Robert A., and Michael Driessen. 'Ethnically Dominated Party Systems and the Quality of Democracy: Evidence from Sub-Saharan Africa'. Afrobarometer Working Paper No. 92, 2008.

Hartmann, Christof, and Jörg Kemmerzell. 'Understanding Variations in Party Bans in Africa'. *Democratization* 17, no. 4 (2010): 642–65.

Hoffmann, Barack, and Lindsay Robinson. 'Tanzania's Missing Opposition'. *Journal of Democracy* 20, no. 4 (2009): 123–36.

Horowitz, Donald L. *Ethnic Groups in Conflict*. Berkeley: University of California Press, 2000.

Human Rights Watch. *State of Anarchy. Rebellion and Abuses against Civilians*, 2007.

International Crisis Group. *L'islamisme en Afrique du Nord IV: Contestation islamiste en Mauritanie: Menace ou bouc émissaire?* Rapport Moyen-Orient No. 41, 2005.

International Crisis Group. *Élections au Burundi: Reconfiguration radicale du paysage politique*, Africa Briefing No. 31, 2005.

International Crisis Group. *Political Parties in Afghanistan*. Asia Briefing No. 39, 2005.

Ishiyama, John. 'Do Ethnic Parties Promote Minority Ethnic Conflict?' *Nationalism and Ethnic Politics* Vol. 15, no. 1 (2009): 56–83.

Lijphart, Arend. *Democracy in Plural Societies: A Comparative Exploration*. New Haven: Yale University Press, 1977.

Marty, Marianne. 'Les multiples usages de l'Islam dans le champ politique mauritanien'. In *L'Afrique politique, 2002: Islams d'Afrique: Entre le local et le global*, ed. CEAN, 51–68. Paris: Editions Karthala, 2002.

McMenamin, Ian. 'Party Regulation and Democratization: Challenges for Further Research'. In *Political Parties in Conflict-Prone Societies: Regulation, Engineering and Democratic Development*, ed. Benjamin Reilly and Per Nordlund, 223–41. Tokyo & New York: United Nations University Press, 2008.

Melber, Henning. 'One Namibia, One Nation? The Caprivi as Contested Territory'. *Journal of Contemporary African Studies* 27, no. 4 (2009): 463–81.

Moroff, Anika. 'Party Bans in Africa – An Empirical Overview'. *Democratization* 17, no. 4 (2010): 618–41.

Ndarishikanye, Barnabé. 'Burundi: Ethno-political Identities Forged through Violence'. *Canadian Journal of African Studies*, Vol. 33, no. 2–3 (1999): 231–91.

Niesen, Peter. 'Political Party Bans in Rwanda 1994–2003: Three Narratives of Justification'. *Democratization* 17, no. 4 (2010): 709–29.

Oded, Arye. *Islam and Politics in Kenya*. Boulder, CO: Lynne Rienner Publishers, 2000.

Özbudun, Ergun. 'From Political Islam to Conservative Democracy: The Case of the Justice and Development Party in Turkey'. *South European Society & Politics* 11, no. 3–4 (2006): 543–57.

Posner, Daniel N. 'Measuring Ethnic Fractionalization in Africa'. *American Journal of Political Science* 48, no. 4 (2004): 849–63.

Rabushka, Alvin, and Kenneth A. Shepsle. *Politics in Plural Societies: A Theory of Democratic Instability*. Columbus, OH: Merrill, 1972.

Randall, Vicky. 'Party Regulation in Conflict-Prone Societies: More Dangers Than Opportunities?' In *Political Parties in Conflict-Prone Societies: Regulation,*

Engineering and Democratic Development, ed. Benjamin Reilly and Per Nordlund, 242–60. Tokyo & New York: United Nations University Press, 2008.

Reilly, Ben, Per Nordlund, and Edward Newman. *Political Parties in Conflict-Prone Societies. Encouraging Inclusive Politics and Democratic Development*. Tokyo & New York: United Nations University Press, 2008.

Reilly, Benjamin, and Per Nordlund, eds. *Political Parties in Conflict-Prone Societies: Regulation, Engineering and Democratic Development*. Tokyo & New York: United Nations University Press, 2008.

Rosenblum, Nancy L. 'Banning Parties: Religious and Ethnic Partisanship in Multicultural Democracies'. *Law and Ethnics of Human Rights* no. 1 (2007): 17–75.

Schedler, Andreas, ed. *Electoral Authoritarianism. The Dynamics of Unfree Competition*, Boulder, CO: Lynne Rienner, 2006.

Sisk, Timothy D. *Power Sharing and International Mediation in Ethnic Conflicts*. Washington, DC: United States Institute of Peace, 1996.

The United Republic of Tanzania. *The Report and Recommendations of the Presidential Commission on Single Party or Multiparty System in Tanzania*. Dar es Salaam: Dar es Salaam University Press, 1992.

Throup, David, and Charles Hornsby. *Multi-party Politics in Kenya: The Kenyatta and Moi States and the Triumph of the System in the 1992 Election*. Athens: E.A.E.P. & Ohio University Press, 1998.

US State Department. *Kenya: Country Report on Human Rights Practices*, 2000.

Appendix: Democratic performance and party bans in multiparty systems 1990 to 2009.

Country	FH ratings 1990	FH ratings 2009	Explicit legal ban provision?	Implemented party ban?
Angola	7/7 (NF)	6/5 (NF)	Yes	Yes
Benin	6/4 (PF)	2/2 (F)	Yes	No
Botswana	1/2 (F)	3/2 (F)	No	No
Burkina Faso	6/5 (NF)	5/3 (PF)	Yes	No
Burundi	7/6 (NF)	4/5 (PF)	Yes	Yes
Cameroon	6/6 (NF)	6/6 (NF)	Yes	No
Cape Verde	5/5 (PF)	1/1 (F)	Yes	No
CAR	6/5 (NF)	5/5 (PF)	Yes	Yes
Chad	7/6 (NF)	7/6 (NF)	Yes	No
Comoros	5/5 (PF)	3/4 (PF)	No	No
Congo DR	6/6 (NF)	6/6 (NF)	Yes	No
Congo-Br.	6/6 (NF)	6/5 (NF)	Yes	No
Côte d'Ivoire	6/4 (PF)	6/5 (NF)	Yes	No
Djibouti	6/5 (NF)	5/5 (PF)	Yes	No
Equatorial Guinea	7/7 (NF)	7/7 (NF)	Yes	Yes
Ethiopia	7/7 (NF)	5/5 (PF)	Yes	No
Gabon	4/4 (PF)	6/5 (NF)	Yes	No
Gambia	2/2 (F)	5/5 (PF)	Yes	No
Ghana	6/5 (NF)	1/2 (F)	Yes	No

(Continued)

Appendix 1. Continued.

Country	FH ratings 1990	FH ratings 2009	Explicit legal ban provision?	Implemented party ban?
Guinea	6/5 (NF)	7/6 (NF)	Yes	No
Guinea Bissau	6/5 (NF)	4/4 (PF)	Yes	No
Kenya	6/6 (NF)	4/4 (PF)	No*	Yes
Lesotho	6/5 (NF)	3/3 (PF)	Yes	No
Liberia	7/7 (NF)	3/4 (PF)	Yes	No
Madagascar	4/4 (PF)	6/4 (PF)	Yes	No
Malawi	7/6 (NF)	3/4 (PF)	Yes	No
Mali	6/5 (NF)	2/3 (F)	Yes	No
Mauritania	7/6 (NF)	6/5 (NF)	Yes	Yes
Mauritius	2/2 (F)	1/2 (F)	No	No
Mozambique	6/6 (NF)	4/3 (PF)	Yes	No
Namibia	2/3 (F)	2/2 (F)	Yes	Yes
Niger	6/5 (NF)	5/4 (PF)	Yes	No
Nigeria	5/5 (PF)	5/4 (PF)	Yes	Yes
Rwanda	6/6 (NF)	6/5 (NF)	Yes	Yes
São Tomé	5/5 (PF)	2/2 (F)	Yes	No
Senegal	4/3 (PF)	3/3 (F)	Yes	No
Seychelles	6/6 (NF)	3/3 (PF)	Yes	No
Sierra Leone	6/5 (PF)	3/3 (PF)	Yes	No
South Africa	5/4 (PF)	2/2 (F)	No	Yes
Tanzania	6/5 (NF)	4/3 (PF)	Yes	Yes
Togo	6/6 (NF)	5/4 (PF)	Yes	No
Zambia	6/5 (PF)	3/4 (PF)	No	No
Zimbabwe	6/4 (PF)	6/6 (NF)	No	No

Sources: Own database and Freedom House (FH)

Notes: numbers refer to political rights and civil liberties ratings, 1 indicates a maximum, 7 a minimum of 'freedom'/democracy. Letters in brackets refer to Freedom House categories: F = 'free', PF = 'partly free', NF = 'not free'; for details on the party bans refer to Moroff, 'Party Bans in Africa', this issue, and main text.

Eritrea, Somalia, Uganda, Swaziland and Sudan are excluded because they either have not held multiparty elections since 1990 or had banned multiparty politics for the greater part of the period 1990 to 2009 (see also main text). *Kenya introduced a party ban provision in 2008.

Why there is no party ban in the South African constitution

Jörg Kemmerzell

Institute of Political Science, Technical University Darmstadt, Darmstadt, Germany

With the decision to abstain from introducing a constitutional provision for the banning of particularistic and extremist parties South Africa appears to be the exception in Africa. This article is interested in the main reasons for this particular constitutional practice. For this purpose three hypotheses will be developed. The article argues that the structures of South Africa's transition to democracy, in particular the beliefs, experiences, and interests of the main transition actors, account for this specific constitutional choice.

Introduction

South Africa is one of the few African countries which abstained from including a provision for party bans in its post-transitional constitution. This requires explanation for two reasons. First, because party bans are a common feature of other African constitutions. With the introduction of multiparty politics at the beginning of the 1990s, most African countries opted for the possibility of party bans, which typically targeted ethnic and particularistic parties. South Africa deviates from this familiar practice in that it does not even provide a constitutional clause on banning parties.[1]

Second, a number of reasons might have suggested the adoption of a militant democracy (explained further below) in South Africa. Such reasons include the history of an authoritarian regime built upon racial and ethnic discrimination, the sharp division of society along racial (between *black* and *white*) and ethnic (within the black majority) cleavages, and the presence of extremist and particularistic political forces in the course of the transition towards democracy. Yet, despite these factors South Africa has adopted a decidedly liberal constitution.

In the first section I shall briefly introduce the concept of party ban.[2] In the second section possible reasons and justifications in favour of a more restrictive conception of party regulation will be discussed, highlighting the course of South Africa's transition to democracy (1990–1994). The third section puts the applicable constitutional and public law under investigation, especially sections 18 (freedom of association), 19 (political rights) and 36 (limitation of rights) of the constitution. Then I shall develop and examine three hypotheses, which aim to explain the lack of legal provisions for party bans in South Africa. The first hypothesis refers to the specific historical experience with bans on political organizations during apartheid rule. The second hypothesis refers to the co-ordinated transition to democracy, promoting the value of inclusiveness as one of its central pillars. The third hypothesis is related to the commensurability of liberty-restricting measures against a background of threats to the rising democratic order. This main section aims at a multilayered explanation of the specific constitutional choice and is partially based on interviews with experts on South African politics and constitutional law.

The concept of party ban

According to the constitutional lawyers Gregory Fox and Georg Nolte,[3] influential authors on the theory and practice of party bans, the South African democracy could be described as a 'tolerant substantive democracy': it is 'substantive' because the constitution relies on several founding provision as well as on a bill of fundamental (and, to some extent, non-derogable) rights; and it is 'tolerant' because of its broad rights-based stand. Apart from an explicit limitation-clause on fundamental rights, the constitution does not adopt any instruments of militant democracy. The original concept of militant democracy was coined by Karl Loewenstein in 1937. In the face of the fascist threat in many European countries during the 1930s, he suggested that liberal-democratic countries take a militant stance against their internal enemies. Party bans against fascist and other extremist parties are at the core of this conception.[4]

In their article on 'intolerant democracies', Fox and Nolte point to national traditions of militant democracy as well as to norms of international law permitting substantive restrictions on an open democratic process and defining standards to which restrictions on civil and political rights must conform. They posit that democracies should not be allowed to abandon democratic rule, even if this reflects the will of the majority. Furthermore democracies should have an obligation to maintain democratic government by enacting self-protecting legislation. When they accept a body of international law (say the Universal Declaration of Human Rights or the International Covenant on Civil and Political Rights), democracies commit themselves not only to maintaining democratic rule, but also to adopting self-protective measures. In this regard the 'pre-emptive defence' of democracy by violating political rights in the short run might be justified as a means to protect 'future voting majorities'.[5]

Peter Niesen[6] labels this approach as 'anti-extremist paradigm' of party ban in that it allows associations to be targeted on the basis of their anti-constitutional ideology and activity. The problem with the anti-extremist conception of militant democracy is its reliance on the classical European idea of anti-democratic politics, along the lines of the early twentieth-century configuration of fascism and communism. But many conflicts, particularly outside established democracies, no longer revolve around those topics in the first place. Especially in many divided societies, any reference to race, religion, or ethnicity in party platforms is grounds for banning parties, regardless of their democratic or anti-democratic tendencies.[7] Such anti-particularistic bans aiming at political aggregation have been widely adopted in sub-Saharan Africa.[8] But South Africa seems to be an exception, in that the discourse on political rights and liberties, as well as the debate about organizational features of political competition, such as party regulation, largely follows the lines of 'conventional' political reasoning. Party bans, for example, regardless of whether they are anti-extremist or anti-particularistic, have to be discussed in the broader context of the limitation of political rights. Thus, in this particular case it seems appropriate not to confine the analysis exclusively to anti-particularistic party bans, but rather to employ the more generic term 'party ban'.

In comparison to the more abstract anti-extremist conception, the 'negative-republican' understanding of party bans always refers to country-specific historical conditions and experiences.[9] From this point of view, party bans serve as a backward barrier against the regression to previous non-democratic practices, as well as a symbolic delimitation of an unjust past. Negative republicanism extracts its justification from a concrete negation of a historical regime. In the South African case apartheid rule might have served as such an unjust historical regime.

Possible justifications for party bans in post-apartheid South Africa

The South African constitutions of 1994 and 1997 contain no party ban provision, despite several threats to democratic government which arose during the transition period. In this section I shall discuss some of the reasons for both types of party bans. I shall start with some possible justifications for a negative-republican party ban.

Negative-republican party bans have to be understood first as a kind of politics of history or politics of memory, which demarcate both symbolically and factually the former unjust regime from the new democratic order. Ruti Teitel for example points to the party bans in the early Federal Republic of Germany in a broader context of 'transitional justice',[10] and the Italian constitution of 1948 provides an explicit demarcation from the predecessor regime. Likewise, the Portuguese constitution outlaws fascist organizations with the claim that the Republic was established by overthrowing the fascist regime. In the case of South Africa, this approach would have suggested an explicit ban on pro-apartheid organizations and maybe on other parties which referred to specific ethnic identities. Indeed, the 'constitutional guidelines' of the African National Congress (ANC) from 1988 proposed a regulation of political competition, which subordinated party politics to the overriding aim of fighting racial discrimination.[11] The guidelines emphasized the possibility of outlawing 'the advocacy and practice of racism, fascism, nazism or tribalism, or the incitement of ethnic or regional exclusiveness or hatred' (guideline k) explicitly. Furthermore, they stressed the constitutional duty of the state 'to eradicate racial discrimination' (guideline i). In addition to that, an 'intolerant' conception of democracy with a strong anti-particularistic bent was proposed.[12]

Party bans exhibit, secondly, the potential of ensuring freedom in societies that are undergoing a political transition. In this regard we have to consider the concept of 'liberatory intolerance' as a political guideline for a new South Africa. The later cabinet member Pallo Jordan proposed it towards the end of apartheid, claiming that 'liberatory intolerance' was an answer to a 'radically evil enemy', namely apartheid rule.[13] In his theory, Jordan rejected the liberal notion of tolerance since in his view apartheid could not be seen as another competitor in the market-place of ideas. The ANC guidelines discussed above, which may account for the exclusion of ethnic or racially based parties, drew on this line of reasoning.

A third strand of argument bridges the gap to the anti-extremist conception. The unstable conditions during the political liberalization period (1990–1994) posed serious threats to the success of democratic transition. Indeed, some observers speak of a 'low-intensity civil war' which was threatening the prospects of trans-formation.[14] Giovanni Sartori, for example, highlights the stabilizing impact of party bans in nascent democracies with regard to the Federal Republic of Germany. He argues that it was not only the 'five-percent clause' that brought about concentration and de-polarization of the party system but also the party bans imposed by the constitutional court on the neo-Nazi Sozialistische Reichspar-tei and the German Communist Party.[15] In this regard it might have been quite comprehensible if the newly adopted constitutional order had contemplated the possibility of party bans.

With respect to the South African case we have to consider, first, the COSAG parties (Concerned South African Group), a heterogeneous alliance of political actors[16] representing to some extent the division of South African society along ethnic and cultural affiliation. They ceased participation in the Multi Party Nego-tiation Process (MPNP) in June 1993. These parties intended neither to accept an interim constitution, nor to participate in the first free elections in 1994.[17] Basically the alliance had been kept together by what the parties involved regarded as a risk of marginalization, as a result of the close cooperation between the government and the ANC. This fear was based, for example, on the Record of Understanding, in which the National Party-led government and the ANC agreed to cooperate in the constitutional process and fixed some substantive provisions.[18] Thus, the COSAG parties which strengthened their internal organization in October 1993 as Freedom Alliance (FA) disagreed with the broad direction of the negotiation talks. In particular, the COSAG parties put forward three lines of criticism:

(1) They accentuated their opposition to the unitary state and invoked an explicit constitutional commitment to 'regionalism'.

(2) They argued for the devolution of central government powers to regional and 'traditional' entities.

(3) Finally, and most importantly, they refused to accept the outcome of the negotiations and peace process conducted by the South African government and the ANC.[19]

Each party in the alliance, however, pursued its own interests. The status of KwaZulu Natal (a sensitive issue for the traditionalistic and ethnic Inkatha Freedom Party), an Afrikaner 'volkstaat' (a sensitive issue for the white right-wing forces), and the opposition of the Bophuthatswana and Ciskei homeland administrations in the new dispensation mattered at most to two COSAG parties at a given time. But substantive differences were counterbalanced by a 'common hatred of ANC-government bilateralism, as epitomised by sufficient consensus in decision-making', and by the hope that a 'united front of malcontents would compel the ANC and the government to reconsider the way forward'.[20]

While the COSAG parties (i.e. Freedom Alliance) were officially committed to peaceful conduct, some of its members effectively followed a double-edged strategy, in that they threatened resistance if their proposals were not accepted. Two events showed that resistance and/or violence were not just empty threats. To begin with, quarrels between Inkatha and ANC adherents between 1990 and 1994 resulted in a civil war-like situation which caused approximately 15,000 casualties [21] White right-wing-extremists attempted to block the regime transition or at least to set up an independent 'volkstaat' based on apartheid rule. The most upsetting events were the attack by supporters of the Afrikaner Weerstandsbeweging (AWB) against the negotiation council in Kempton Park and the failed coup in the homeland of Bophuthatswana conducted by some AWB men. The AWB, a militant right-wing organization, had close ideological, personal, and even organizational connections to the right-wing Afrikaner parties Conservative Party (CP) and Afrikaner Volksunie (AVF) as well as to the umbrella organization Afrikaner Volksfront (AVF).[22] Ironically, the failed coup removed serious obstacles from the path to the first democratic election, because the white right-wing set up a new legalistic party, the Freedom Front, from which the rigid militants seceded. Until then, surprising electoral performances by the Conservative Party in by-elections threatened the dominant position of the National Party (NP) in the 'whites only' parliament. Furthermore the AWB's action embarrassed the black leaders in the Freedom Alliance. Spitz and Chaskalson state: 'No self-respecting black leader could live happily in an alliance with the AWB'.[23]

In addition to this, Inkatha's demand for a special position for KwaZulu Natal might have been interpreted as a challenge to the territorial integrity of the state. Its appeal to the importance of the 'traditional law' threatened further the ideal of an unconditionally valid rule of law.

Another party, the left-wing Pan Africanist Congress (PAC),[24] also played an important role within this scenario. This party opposed both the prospect of reform of the political system and the consensual orientation of the ANC. Hassen Ebrahim notes: 'According to the PAC, 'slaves have nothing to gain from negotiating with their masters ... We do not need reform. We need a complete overhaul of the entire economic and political system'.[25] Heribert Adam depicts the creed of extremist and particularistic actors of both sides: 'There were great doubts on the extreme (white) right as well on the extreme (black) left whether to join the political process at all and give up romanticized armed struggle. The racist AWB and their allies espoused the slogan *bullets instead of ballots*. On the other side, many in the SACP [South African Communist Party] and MK [the military wing of the ANC] argued that you cannot win at the negotiating table what you have not won at the battlefield'.[26]

Against this background, three arguments in favour of the adoption of party bans in post-apartheid South Africa can be summarized: (1) an explicit demarcation from the predecessor regime might have suggested a ban on pro-apartheid organizations; (2) the deep division of society along racial and ethnic lines might have justified the prohibition of particularistic racial and ethnic organizations; (3) unstable conditions, including massive violence during the transitional process, might have given rise to a curtailing of extremist and particularistic forces.

The applicable constitutional law[27]

In the following section I shall examine the applicable constitutional law and its dominant interpretation, especially with regard to the limitation of political rights and associational freedom. The South African Constitution hinges upon two underlying principles. The first principle is that of constitutional supremacy, which is embodied in irreversible fundamental rights (Bill of Rights). Thus, the South African democracy is an example of substantive democracy, as introduced above. The supremacy of the constitution and the rule of law are ensured by an independent constitutional court which fills a pivotal position in the South African political system. The second principle rests on a tolerant or accentuated liberal conception of these rights, establishing an unrestricted right to political association. Section 18 of the Final Constitution (FC), for instance, states simply that 'Everyone has the right to freedom of association'.

Section 19 FC (political rights) guarantees several political rights, namely:

(1) to form a political party;
(2) to participate in the activities of, or recruit members for, a political party;
(3) to conduct a campaign for a political party or cause.

In addition to this, section 19 FC guarantees free and fair elections, the right to vote and to apply for public office. According to section 36 FC the limitation of rights is bound to tight criteria. Nevertheless, the limitation clause provides possible arguments for placing restrictions on associational freedom. The limitation clause takes up some formulations of the International Covenant on Civil and Political Rights. Article 22 of the Covenant, which protects the freedom of association, admits restrictions when these are 'necessary in a democratic society'. Article 25 guarantees political rights 'without unreasonable restrictions'. Restrictions on these rights (e.g. refusal to register parties at the elections) are subject to less demanding criteria than restrictions on civil rights (e.g. banning and dissolving associations).[28]

Section 33(1) of the Interim Constitution (IC) allowed for restrictions on rights if it is 'reasonable and justifiable in an open and democratic society'. The limitation of several rights, e.g. freedom of association and political rights had to satisfy the higher standard of necessity: 'Rights which receive 'reasonable and necessary' protection should receive the greatest judicial solicitude'.[29]

The limitation clause of the Final Constitution rejected the standard of necessity in favour of a de-hierarchization of rights. Section 36(1) FC only states that limitation of rights should be 'reasonable and justifiable'. The tendency of the Interim Constitution to privilege liberal and procedural rights over more egalitarian guarantees has been adjusted. But this revision should not be misinterpreted as an attempt to weaken the requirements that limitations have to meet. Rather, according to Woolman, the revisions only aim at a 'non-preferential treatment of all rights under the limitation clause'.[30]

Let us now consider whether constitutional law allows for the *possibility* of banning parties under the provisions of section 18 FC. The concept of freedom of association has been developed in dissociation from apartheid rule which severely infringed upon everyone's general freedom to associate. Given this history of repression, 'great caution should be exercised before resort is had to the banning of any political entity'.[31] Legitimate bans on several kinds of associations require that there be concrete actions aiming at overthrowing the democratic government, and not simply ideological anti-democratic statements. It is not the ideological *militancy* of an association that can justify a ban on it, but rather its explicit intent to actually subvert the democratic order: 'This rule draws a distinction between associations which merely advocate the government's overthrow – which deserve at least prima facie protection – and associations which demonstrate through military preparation and action that they are bent on non-peaceable governmental change'.[32] To sum up, a ban on association is only legitimate if an organization resorts to massive violence, whereas an ordinary militant attitude is not a sufficient warrant. Thus, parties cannot be subjected to associational bans, provided they do not act as paramilitary organizations.[33]

The next question of interest points to the relationship between associational freedom and freedom of expression. According to section 16 (2) FC, freedom of expression might be restricted under three circumstances:

(1) Propaganda for war
(2) Incitement of imminent violence
(3) Advocacy of hatred that is based on race, ethnicity, gender or religion, and that constitutes incitement to cause harm.

For our purposes the question must be raised as to what extent the limitations of the freedom of expression has an impact on the freedom of association. But since section 18 FC, unlike section 16 FC, does not comprise limitation clauses, there is reason to believe that the limitation clause concerning freedom of expression should not be extended to freedom of association. However, it is controversial whether parties can held responsible for statements and actions of their members. The dominant view among South African constitutional lawyers emphasizes an individualistic interpretation of fundamental rights and rejects the notion of 'vicarious liability', according to which political parties can be held responsible for acts committed by their members.[34]

Both political rights and associational rights should be interpreted against the background of the previous apartheid system. According to de Waal, South Africa's history of denial of political rights provides the context within which section 19 FC must be read.[35] Yet in de Waal's analysis the illiberal past serves as justification for the tolerant conception of the constitution. Section 19 FC refers explicitly to the entitlement to form political parties, to participate in their activities, and to campaign for them. With regard to the right to set up a party and to participate there are no limitations emerging from a contextual interpretation of section 19 FC. But the interpretation of the right to campaign in the light of section 9 (equality) as well as section 16 (freedom of expression) upholds particular regularities controlling for the access to elections and public party financing (section 52 FC).

The Electoral Act and the Electoral Commission Act, as a specific body of law, enable courts to restrict the 'right to campaign'. The freedom of expression of political parties during campaigning is limited by section 9 (1) of the Electoral Code (schedule 2 of the Electoral Act). This code prohibits false or defamatory remarks, as well as the use of language which may lead to violence and intimidation. According to section 99 EA, every party and every candidate are required to subscribe the code of conduct. If parties or candidates fail to comply with the requirements of the code, section 96 EA provides for penalties ranging from fines to the cancellation of a party's registration.[36] Up to June 2008, the Independent Electoral Commission approved 12 instances of denied registration, concerning both national and provincial elections.[37] But none of those registrations had been denied because of defamation or intimidation during campaigns. Rather, they were due to the parties' failure either to fulfil the technical requirements expressed in section 15 ECA or to meet the rather procedural clause of section 16 (1a, i) ECA. To be sure, according to Section 16 (1a, ii), the Chief Electoral Officer is entitled to deny registration if a party name, distinguishing mark or symbol can be in some way linked to the propaganda or incitement of violence or hatred on the grounds of racial, cultural or ethnical affiliation. However, this clause, formulated along the lines of section 16 FC, has not been applied so far.

In order to draw a preliminary conclusion from this brief overview, it has to be stressed that the South African Constitution does not allow for the imposition of party bans, neither by invoking a traditional democracy protection nor by appealing to an anti-particularistic understanding about politics. Therefore, neither the government nor courts have legal means to dissolve parties. However, section 19 (1) FC and several clauses of the electoral law allow the denial of registration to parties in elections if they violate a fundamental code of conduct. This should not be misinterpreted as an implicit party ban provision, but denied registration may have serious consequences, for example, the cancellation of state funding.[38] Thus, suspension of parties can be considered as an utmost sanction.

Why there is no party ban provision in the South African Constitution

Despite several reasons to justify a party ban provision, the South African constitution adopts a liberal and tolerant conception of democracy. Drawing on the theoretical literature and using data from an expert survey conducted in 2007 I developed three hypotheses which may explain the absence of a party ban provision in the South African constitution. Thirty-two experts on South Africa's transition to democracy were selected to answer to an open questionnaire, which was distributed via e-mail. We had a return of nine questionnaires. In the first question the respondents were asked if they knew (1) of any discussions in any phase of the democratic transition about the introduction of a ban on political parties into the constitution, (2) who proposed the possibility of banning parties, (3) which types of parties were considered, and (4) which reasons were put forward in favour of a ban on certain political parties. If the respondents were not aware of any such discussion, they were asked, secondly, to specify the reasons for the absence of such debate. The third question pointed to discussions on the topic of party bans since the adoption of the Interim Constitution in 1994.

The empirical analysis of the following hypotheses essentially relies on additional in-depth expert interviews, which were conducted during a field research in South Africa in 2008. Where appropriate I shall directly quote from these interviews.[39]

Hypotheses

Despite obvious obstacles, the transition to democracy in South Africa followed a generally consensual and co-ordinated path, which included a variety of heterogeneous actors. Several studies on the topic emphasize the importance of actor beliefs,[40] rational conduct of the actors,[41] and specific mechanisms of the transformation process. Fundamental theoretical and empirical alternatives to the coordination model, which are common in other African countries, are managed transitions from above, externally induced reforms, and regime breakdowns, forced from below (revolution) or by external intervention.[42] But South African circumstances, as discussed below, allowed for a co-ordinated transition to democracy which diminished the reasonableness of party ban provisions.

On the basis of a review of the literature and the response to the survey (see above) three hypotheses can be developed. These hypotheses are not mutually exclusive in a strict analytically sense and operate rather in a heuristic manner:

(1) Actors' beliefs: in the context of the politics of memory, party bans were rejected due to the significance of bans on parties and other political organizations under apartheid rule. Unrestricted participation of political parties was upheld and political parties were warmly welcomed as institutions of an open democratic process.

(2) Nature of transition: South Africa followed the model of a co-ordinated transition. Inclusiveness and a broad consensus among the different participants played a pivotal role within this model. A party ban provision would have been a piecemeal element.

(3) Threats: political extremism and particularism were not considered as serious threats to the emerging democratic polity, notwithstanding the presence of the respective political actors. When these threats were compared to the costs of undermining the liberal ethos of the constitution, strong restrictions upon the freedom of association seemed disproportionate.

Analysis

The first aim of my analysis is to understand why party bans were not considered a proper instrument of a politics of memory. In this context, actors' beliefs play a central role. Secondly, it is necessary to analyse the basic structure of the transition process, thereby emphasising the specific features of the co-ordinated transition. Finally, I shall address the question of why the option of banning parties has not been adopted in the face of serious threats to the emerging democratic order. In particular, I shall argue that hypothesis 3 must be modified, especially in the light of the specific period under investigation and with regard to concrete actors' interests.

Politics of memory and actors beliefs

In the context of historical memory, one may justify the rejection of bans on association in the constitution as a deliberate dissociation from the past regime. Robert Mattes assesses the concept of 'liberatory intolerance': 'This idea never got very far at all, mostly because it smacked too much of what had gone on before'.[43] As a negotiated transition became the likely mode of democratization, the necessary prerequisites for both 'liberatory intolerance' and the constitutional guidelines of the ANC from 1988 vanished, since it could make sense only in the case of a regime breakdown foisted from above. But in the course of the transition process the party of the old regime, the National Party, tried to gain credibility by participating in the creation of the new political order. Intolerance was entirely reinterpreted[44] as an evil to do away with, for it posed a serious threat to a successful democratization. Gibson concludes with regard to 'liberatory intolerance' that theories of this kind divided supporters of apartheid and those struggling against it into 'categories of enemies and friends, evil and good' and lent a certain justification to intolerance in general.[45]

Many interviewees mention the negative experience with party bans as the most important reason for rejecting a party ban provision. Heribert Adam, for example, considers that 'inclusion of all political actors became the overriding goal of constitution making' because apartheid was a strongly 'exclusionary system'.[46] The majority of the anti-apartheid opposition had always campaigned for a culture of inclusion, even of its enemies. Therefore, a policy of prohibition would have been seen as a threat to the credibility of the main actors in the negotiation process.

In fact, the apartheid regime made extensive use of bans on organizations. In 1950, the SACP was the first party to be banned under the Suppression of Communism Act after the Afrikaner nationalists took over government.[47] In 1960 the ANC and the PAC were banned, followed by the Black Consciousness Movement (BCM) in 1977 and by the United Democratic Front (UDF) in 1988. The bans on anti-apartheid organizations have a great symbolic importance in South African collective memory. This is why restrictions on associational freedom always tend to be linked directly to the old regime. Even Nelson Mandela, in his autobiography, [48] qualifies the Suppression of Communism Act as one of the three pillars of apartheid, together with the Population and Registration Act and the Group Areas Act.[49] It is obvious that the adoption of association bans in the new constitution would have been seen as the repetition of the old regime mistakes, which would have damaged reputation and legitimacy of the main political actors.

The National Party government suspended the remaining bans on the ANC, PAC and SACP in 1990. A revitalization of bans on political enemies, albeit aimed at completely different groups, would have been nearly impossible to justify and might have triggered further conflicts. Indeed, both the white right-wing as well as the black opposition (the ethnically conservative and the left-wing pan-Africanist camp) would have been even more committed to violence and secession.

One interviewee highlighted the importance of the British constitutional tradition in South African political thought, in particular the legitimacy of a 'political party model of democracy' and the normative ideal of 'limited government under the rule of law'.[50] This observation can be strengthened by insights into the proceedings of the influential Technical Committees in the multiparty negotiation process. According to one member of the Technical Committee on the Bill of Rights, party bans had never been the object of debate.[51] These positions are echoed by a unique tradition of party politics, at least in the African context. The first South African parties were founded around 1900 and the first elections were held in 1910. This tradition may also account for the liberal mode of party regulation in functionalist terms.[52] Maybe we can extend this argument to the presence of formal democratic institutions under apartheid rule, which allows for the classification of South Africa as an 'exclusive democracy', a particular type of 'defective democracy'.[53] Even if large segments of the population were excluded from the civil right of universal suffrage and political competition was restricted to approximately the 25% of the population, South Africa exhibits nevertheless huge familiarity with democratic politics.

Although different conceptions of democracy have been advocated in the debate about the democratic prospects of South Africa,[54] the discussion has not focused primarily on the system of parliamentary democracy but rather on the exclusion of significant groups from its institutions. The legitimacy of the political party model was never thrown into question before and during the transition process. Eventually, then, the question arises to what extent functional equivalents of party bans have been applied. Ruti Teitel distinguishes several types of 'transitional justice' with 'militant democracy' as an attempt to catch up with 'administrative justice' On the other hand one could find several measures to bring about 'historical justice', among them truth commissions like the South African Truth and Reconciliation Commission (TRC).[55] Although the purpose of this article is not to reconstruct the debate about the TRC, it seems nonetheless suggestive to open up the question whether truth commissions represent an instance of transitional management which forecloses robust and repressive policies such as party bans. Hugh Corder distinguishes between repressive measures such as bans on association and 'lustration',[56] on the one hand and, on the other hand, truth and reconciliation commissions as distinct routes towards transitional justice. In the South African debate these were perceived as alternative models, and the commission model was eventually established.[57]

Nature of democratic transition

According to the literature on transformation towards democracy the South African case fits within the co-ordination model, which involves political elites reaching an agreement or a 'negotiated pact'.[58] The basic cause of change was the domestic crisis of the apartheid regime, which increasingly began to lose its credibility even among its alleged beneficiaries. In addition to this, the end of the Cold War and sanctions against South Africa could be interpreted as a loss of an external system of support.[59]

The attitudes of the old, 'outgoing' elite were a crucial element of the internal context of the transformation process. According to Jorge Heine these attitudes were rather in favour of democracy, or at least, not incompatible with a fundamental acceptance of democratic rule. Another important factor was the existence of a legitimate negotiation partner 'on the other side', namely the ANC and its allies.[60] The negotiation partners had started their talks long before the transformation process took place.[61] When the official negotiations began, four years of informal negotiation had provided a substantive shared basis for further agreement.[62] Meanwhile, the Afrikaner establishment and the ANC leadership developed mutual trust, which enabled the actors to cope with particularly critical situations.[63] Those fundamental agreements resulted in documents such as the Groote Schuur

Minute (4 May 1990), the Declaration of Intent of the First Convention for a Democratic South Africa (CODESA I) (21 December 1991) and the Agreement to Resume Bilateral Negotiations (25 November 1992) between the government and the ANC.[64] The capstone of this consensus-based process was the appointment of the Government of National Unity, in which each party that obtained more than the 5% of the votes was entitled to participate.[65]

Arato suggests seeing the 'co-ordinated transition' as the 'superior path to democracy'.[66] A coordinated transition is traversed by an internal tension between continuity with the legal tradition and critical rejection of it. Legality was maintained through a referendum in March 1992, in which only the white population was entitled to participate, as required by the old South African legal system. This referendum authorized the government to negotiate with formally non-constitutional partners, aiming at a new democratic constitution. The interim constitution, which served to a large extent as a definite blueprint for the final constitution, was adopted by the majority of the whites-only parliament in 1993. The constitutional assembly which eventually adopted the final constitution was then elected in accordance with the procedures required by this interim constitution.

It should be noted that a co-ordinated transition depends on comparatively sophisticated prerequisites, especially the existence of social forces capable of negotiation. In the South African case the two oldest African parties took part in the negotiations.[67] Therefore Jorge Heine concludes: 'South Africa would potentially be in the best position to consolidate its democratic institutions as its transition was very much a negotiated one (in which the rules of the previous regime were not broken) and the attitude of the outgoing elite was in favour of democracy'.[68] So the new government has been able to rely on an effective and loyal bureaucracy. Lustration was seldom enforced, and even the judiciary largely remained in charge. Despite some cases of forced retirements or 'golden handshaking' in the senior civil service ranks,[69] there was no systematic and coerced replacement of elites.[70]

The inclusive nature of the negotiations depended on the consensus of all parties involved, including the COSAG parties, which withdrew their participation from time to time.[71] This inclusive and open approach was part of the Declaration of Intent in the run-up to CODESA I: 'We agree that the present *and* future participants shall be entitled to put forward freely to the Convention any proposal consistent with democracy'.[72] In this regard we may also consider the intention of the constitution makers to ensure the future openness of the political process. Particularly in the light of a fragile and fragmented political scenario, the abandonment of party ban provisions can be seen as a credible confirmation to maintain democratic government in the future.

Closely bound to the second hypothesis is the role of constitutional review, which, however, became important later, namely in the period of democratic consolidation. The negotiated interim constitution of 1994 assigned vast competencies to the Constitutional Court in order to review the final constitution-making.[73]

The powerful role of the court was guaranteed by the 34 non-amendable constitutional principles of the interim constitution. Since the Constitutional Assembly
fell to some extent under control of the Constitutional Court, it could not deviate
significantly from the principles of the interim constitution.

Threats to the nascent democratic polity

With regard to a possible anti-extremist party ban, the argument of an extant objective threat during the period of liberalization and the early period of democratization has been already discussed. Only an objective threat or a clear and present
danger is recognized as an acceptable ground for banning parties.

One interviewee describes the starting point of the transition as 'a stalemate
where neither side could defeat the other'.[74] Therefore, neither side could
impose on the other any provision aimed at excluding certain parties from the political arena. Faced with threats from both sides of the political spectrum, the main
actors favoured inclusion over repression, since a militant demarcation within the
respective camps would have provoked a strengthening of antagonistic policies
supported by the opponents of a peaceful process, which exhibited at least
notable spoiling potential.[75] Thus, the legitimacy argument has to be supplemented
with a utility argument. Firstly, bans on organizations would have not been beneficial in the first place, since they would have raised violence to a greater
extent. Secondly, party bans might have threatened the common goal of the
main actors, namely a peaceful abolition of the apartheid regime within the framework of the existing legal order.

Both sides used to some extent their own extremist groups (for the ANC, PAC
and AZAPO;[76] for the NP, the COSAG parties) as a tool to put the other side under
pressure during the negotiations.[77] The NP, for example, used the uncompromising
position of COSAG for strong federalism[78] as a means to pressure the more cen-
tralistic ANC to accept a federalist structure.

When the interim constitution came into effect enabling the first democratic
elections, the emergency potential decreased significantly.[79] The most important
wings of COSAG/FA decided to participate in the elections. On the white right-
wing, the Freedom Front emerged as a legalist party from the moderate faction
of the AVF. Even Inkatha accepted the results of the negotiations. With regard to
the successful first democratic elections, one can agree with Heinz Klug's claim
that the remaining extremist militants did not have the potential to threaten the
democratic polity.[80] First of all, the armed forces and the administration proved
to be loyal in moments of crisis, such as the failed Bophuthatswana coup. The
more extreme groups of all political persuasions were not considered a serious
political or security threat to the new state. When these minor threats were compared to the costs of undermining the broad rights-based stand of the new constitution, it would have been considered unduly costly to restrict political rights.

Also, the weak electoral performance of most of the sceptics of the new order
contributed to weaken their political power. The Freedom Front in the role of the

legalist branch of the Afrikaner right-wing did not even manage to obtain 2% of the votes and failed to fulfil its own expectations. As a result, the Freedom Front had to postpone its volkstaat-plans for an Afrikaner homeland.[81]

While party bans were not useful for the NP government, the ANC-led Government of National Unity after 1994 and the ANC government after 1996 were 'simply not in any position to do this given the country's past and the experience of being banned itself'.[82] This reasoning might be supplemented by a tactical argument concerning the position of the ANC: 'Since the ANC command a huge majority anyway, it never felt threatened by smaller parties as potential targets of banning'.[83] Because the ANC enjoyed a dominant position in the party system and in the parliament since 1994, the ANC could be the only actor to impose a party ban. And although the absolute voter majority of the ANC would not have been at risk, at least in the intermediate term,[84] open repression against its weaker contenders would have strengthened the fear of dominant party rule.[85] A unilateral approval of democratic intolerance or militant democracy by the ANC would have immediately provoked the suspicion of a misuse of power.

With respect to actors' particular interests, the ANC as well as the National Party claimed to defend their reputation inside their respective camps. The ANC's 'broad church approach' aimed at the inclusion of several political groupings, with the expectation of obtaining an overwhelming majority in parliament.[86] The NP and its successor, the New National Party, adopted a similar, but eventually failed, strategy of remaining the main non-black party. Therefore, both parties tried to avoid being suspected of employing unpopular and illegitimate measures.

Conclusion

While there is substantial evidence to support hypotheses 1 and 2, hypothesis 3 stands in need of further clarification. Although the South African transition process was dominated by two actors (i.e. the government-led National Party and the ANC), those actors had been threatened by extremist forces before the adoption of the interim constitution. But those threats became much weaker after the election of the constituent assembly in 1994, in which all major groups finally participated. This, in turn, led to a marginalization of the remaining extremist forces.

Thus there are two main arguments that can explain the absence of party ban provisions. The first argument refers to actors' beliefs, which are strongly related to historical experience. The particular historical experience with bans during apartheid holds great symbolic importance in the South African collective memory. Hence, restrictions on associational freedom tend to be seen as an undesired legacy of the old, unjust regime. With regard to the condemnation of bans as a means of repression, the dominant view in South African constitutional law explicitly distinguishes the 'integration model' of the South African constitution from the model of 'militant democracy'.[87]

A second argument refers to specific structural characteristics of the South African democratic transition. A successful co-ordinated transition depends on four main features which were present in the South African case: inclusiveness of the transition process, willingness of the old elites to take part in the process, orientation of the prospective new elites toward consensus, and continuity of the legal order.

The dominance of two actors in the transition process did not undermine inclusiveness as one of its central pillars. Even the enemies of transition, respectively the course transition took, has been encouraged to participate in the process. The criterion, which required the old elites to play an active role, was satisfied as well. In fact, the pivotal force of the old regime – the National Party – was represented at the negotiation table. Therefore, demarcation from the apartheid regime had to be expressed in general terms, avoiding reference to particular associations or parties. It is obvious that even the prospect of debating about the adoption of a party ban provision in post-apartheid law would have been seen as a risk of falling back into the old mistakes, which, incidentally, would have damaged the reputation and legitimacy of the main political actors. The ANC, as the prospective dominant party, tried to avoid reinforcing conflicts about the emerging polity. By contrast, the ANC was keen to integrate as many interests and groups as possible while strengthening its broad church approach.

Even though it is impossible to provide a full analysis of the effects of the absence of party bans, I would like to add two more considerations on this point. First, the emergence of a dominant party, deeply rooted in civil society, which nevertheless adheres to the constitutional principles of pluralism and the rule of law, had a stabilizing impact in the short term. This provisional effect, however, might cease in the long run, since the effective restraint of political competition and alternatives breeds civic disappointment and alienation.[88] Corrections to those developments could be subject to institutional reforms, e.g. of the electoral system or party financing regulations. Still, political reforms should not resort to restrictive measures such as party bans. Secondly, political extremism and radical particularism are largely marginalized in the official political scene. So far, incidents of hate speech (sometimes from within the ANC[89]) have been successfully dealt with both by informal institutions and the courts.

The continuity of the legal order has been kept intact, because the transition occurred under existing rules. This distinguishes South Africa from cases of regime breakdowns, caused either by internal or external forces – a scenario that would have made the adoption of party bans more likely. And in contrast to managed transitions, the old legal order provided the basis both for the emergence of a new legitimacy and for its own abolition. While in managed transitions the old incumbents can be prone to resort to party bans as an instrument of political control, co-ordinated transitions are more likely to bring about open and liberal institutions. This is of particular interest from a comparative perspective. The structure of the South African transition seems unique in the African context, because South Africa is the only African country that has experienced a co-ordinated transition to democracy in a strict sense. This might help explain why the South African constitution differs significantly from other African constitutions. However, although we can certainly learn much from the South African case, we should resist the temptation of drawing general conclusions for political regulation in other deeply divided societies. The decision not to ban particularistic or extremist parties was successful because of the main transition actors' capacity to integrate spoilers. Furthermore, the state apparatus, which was necessary to cope with the challenges of transformation, remained largely intact and efficient. All these might be crucial elements[90] for successful transitions of divided societies, but are unfortunately not available in many instances.

Acknowledgements

The author would like to thank Martina Neunecker and Peter Niesen for helpful comments on an earlier version of this text as well as the two reviewers. I am particularly indebted to Enrico Zoffoli for his support of language editing.

Notes

1. But see Hartmann and Kemmerzell, 'Understanding Variations', on the difference between party ban *provisions* and the *implementation* of party bans.
2. For a more extensive account, see Bogaards, Basedau, and Hartmann, 'Ethnic Party Bans'.
3. Fox and Nolte, 'Intolerant Democracies'.
4. Loewenstein, 'Militant Democracy and Fundamental Rights'.
5. Fox and Nolte, 'Intolerant Democracies', 60.
6. Niesen, 'Zwischen Pfadabhängigkeit und Kommensuration: Verbote politischer Parteien in Europa'.
7. Rosenblum, 'Banning Parties'.
8. Cf. Moroff, 'Party Bans in Africa'.
9. Niesen, 'Zwischen Pfadabhängigkeit und Kommensuration: Verbote politischer Parteien in Europa'.
10. Teitel, *Transitional Justice*.
11. African National Congress (ANC), 'Constitutional Guidelines for a Democratic South Africa'.
12. I am thankful to Heinz Klug who directed me to this document.
13. Gibson, 'Does Truth Led to Reconciliation?'.
14. Kotzé and du Toit, 'Historical Contexts'.
15. Sartori, *Comparative Constitutional Engineering*, 19.
16. Members of COSAG were: Inkatha Freedom Party (IFP), Conservative Party (CP), Afrikaner Volksunie (AVU), KwaZulu Government, Homeland Governments of Bophutswana and Ciskei.
17. Spitz and Chaskalson, *The Politics of Transition*.
18. Ebrahim, *The Soul of a Nation*, 588–94.
19. Spitz and Chaskalson, *The Politics of Transition*, 213.
20. Ibid.
21. Indeed it would be historically misleading to assign responsibility for those events only to one faction. Violence has been conducted by Inkatha as well as ANC supporters. In addition to that the former secret service took part in the events as a 'third force', as the former President de Klerk had to admit later. Cf. Wilson, 'Justice and Legitimacy in the South African Transition', 194.

22. These organizations explicitly opposed the abandonment of apartheid rule by the National Party and became the agents of the old regime during the early 1990s.
23. Spitz and Chaskalson, *The Politics of Transition*, 245.
24. The Pan Africanist Congress (PAC) was founded in 1959, when several members broke away from the ANC because of its 'reformist' and inter-racial agenda, adopted in the Freedom Charter of 1955. After the tightening of apartheid rule and the significant leftwards trend of the ANC since the 1960s, both organizations converged, but PAC has remained an independent movement.
25. Ebrahim, *The Soul of a Nation*, 43.
26. Questionnaire Heribert Adam, cf. p. 695 for details of the questionnaire.
27. According to nomenclature of this chapter: Interim Constitution is abbreviated IC, Final Constitution is abbreviated FC, Electoral Act: EA, and Electoral Commission Act: ECA. The Interim Constitution came into effect by adoption of the 'whites only' parliament in 1993. The election of the Constitutional Assembly in 1994 based upon this constitution. Eventually, the Final Constitution was adopted by the Constitutional Assembly in 1996.
28. Fox and Nolte, 'Intolerant Democracies', 49.
29. Woolman, 'Section 12: Limitation', 37.
30. Ibid., 14.
31. Woolman, 'Section 22: Freedom of Association', 3.
32. Ibid., 7.
33. Currie and de Waal, *The Bill of Rights Handbook*, 427.
34. De Waal, 'Section 23: Political Rights', 6.
35. Ibid., 2.
36. In addition to that, public party funding is bound to mandates in assemblies. If a party is not registered than it does not qualify for any state funding.
37. Independent Electoral Commission, http://www.elections.org.za/Registered_Parties/Selection_Party.asp.
38. De Waal, 'Section 23: Political Rights', 7.
39. Interviews with the following experts were conducted by the author: Werner Böhler (Konrad Adenauer Foundation, Johannesburg, 28 May 2008), Hendrik Bussiek (journalist and consultant, Cape Town, 5 June 2008), Hugh Corder (Faculty of Law, University of Cape Town, 4 June 2008), Richard Calland (Faculty of Law, University of Cape Town, 4 June 2008), Robert Mattes (Department of Political Studies, University of Cape Town, 3 June 2008), Ursula Scheidegger (Department of Political Studies, University of the Witwatersrand, Johannesburg/EISA, Johannesburg, 26 May 2008). Additional interviews with Heribert Adam and Kogila Adam-Moodley were conducted in Darmstadt on 26 April 2007.
40. Sparks, *Tomorrow is Another Country.*
41. Sisk, *Democratization in South Africa.*
42. For a comprehensive elaboration on transition modes see Kis, 'Between Reform and Revolution' and Arato, 'The Occupation of Iraq and the Difficult Transition from Dictatorship'. For externally induced incomplete transitions to multiparty politics in sub-Saharan Africa see Kirschke, 'Informal Repression, Zero-Sum Politics and Late Third Wave Transitions'.
43. Interview with Robert Mattes, Cape Town, 3 June 2008.
44. IDASA, *Preparing for Democracy.*
45. Gibson, 'Does Truth Led to Reconciliation?'.
46. Interview with Heribert Adam, Darmstadt, 26 April 2007.
47. Ebrahim, *The Soul of a Nation*, 13–14.
48. Mandela, *Long Walk to Freedom.*

49. The Population Registration Act required that each South African inhabitant be classi-fied and registered in accordance with their racial characteristics. The 'Group Areas Act' assigned racial groups established by the 'Population Registration Act' to differ-ent residential areas. As an effect racial segregation was tightened.
50. Interview with Hugh Corder, Cape Town, 4 June 2008.
51. Ibid.
52. However, constitution-making in the 1990s referred not in the first instance to the British model, but, with regard to fundamental non-derogable rights, the separation of powers, and the importance of the constitutional court, to the German Grundgesetz or to the Canadian Constitution.
53. Merkel, 'Embedded and Defective Democracies', 49.
54. Horowitz, *A Democratic South Africa*.
55. Slye, 'Amnesty, Truth, and Reconciliation'; Villa-Vicencio and Verwoerd, *Looking Back, Reaching Forward*.
56. On lustration cf. Capoccia, *Defending Democracy*, 51–2, and Teitel, *Transitional Justice*, 149–91.
57. Interview with Hugh Corder, Cape Town, 3 June 2008.
58. O'Donnell and Schmitter, *Transitions from Authoritarian Rule*, 37.
59. Hoffmann, 'Legitimate Intervention and Illegitimate States'.
60. Heine, 'Institutional Engineering in New Democracies', 71.
61. Lawrence, 'Introduction: From Soweto to Codesa'.
62. Ebrahim, *The Soul of a Nation*, 19–27.
63. Atkinson, 'Brokering a Miracle?'
64. See for the most important documents Ebrahim, *The Soul of a Nation*, 363–655.
65. For a concise account of the key elements of the negotiated transition see Sisk and Stefes, 'Power Sharing as an Interim Step in Peace Building', 302f.
66. Arato, 'The Occupation of Iraq and the Difficult Transition from Dictatorship'.
67. On the genealogy of the NP cf. Kotzè, 'A Consummation Devoutly to be Wished?'; on the ANC cf. Lodge, 'The ANC and the Development of Party Politics in Modern South Africa'.
68. Heine, 'Institutional Engineering in New Democracies', 71–2.
69. Interview with Hugh Corder, Cape Town, 4 June 2008.
70. This should not be confused with longer term policies of 'racial redress' which aims at a transformation of the public sector; see Ndletyana, 'Affirmative Action and the Public Sector'.
71. Spitz and Chaskalson, *The Politics of Transition*, 228–31.
72. Ebrahim, *The Soul of a Nation*, 530.
73. Arato, 'Post-Sovereign Constitution Making and Democratic Legitimacy', 99.
74. Interview with Heribert Adam, Darmstadt, 26 April 2007.
75. On the concept of 'spoiler' see Stedman, 'Spoiler Problems in Peace Processes'.
76. The Azanian People Organization (AZAPO) was founded in 1978 and draws its ideas from socialism and the Black Consciousness Movement. Similar to the PAC, it stands to the left of the ANC.
77. Spitz and Chaskalson, *The Politics of Transition*, 212–50.
78. On the significance of federalism see Egan and Taylor, 'South Africa'.
79. Du Toit, *South Africa's Brittle Peace*.
80. Questionnaire, Heinz Klug.
81. Succeeding President Nelson Mandela promised that there would be negotiations about the 'volkstaat' if the election result suggested this; interview with Hendrik Bussiek, Cape Town, 5 June 2008.
82. Interview with Robert Mattes, Cape Town, 3 June 2008.
83. Interview with Heribert Adam, Darmstadt, 26 April 2007.

84. Lodge, 'The Future of South Africa's Party System', 164.
85. Giliomee et al., 'Dominant Party Rule, Opposition Parties and Minorities in South Africa'.
86. Interview with Hendrik Bussiek, Cape Town, 5 June 2008.
87. Woolman, 'Section 22: Freedom of Association', 3.
88. Mattes, 'South Africa: Democracy Without the People?'
89. Vena, 'Is This What All Those Men and Women Died For?'
90. Lemarchand, 'Managing Transition Anarchies'.

Notes on the contributor

Jörg Kemmerzell is Lecturer and Research Associate at the Department of Political Science, Technical University Darmstadt (Germany). His research focuses on comparative politics, particularly political parties and change and stability of political regimes.

Bibliography

African National Congress (ANC). 'Constitutional Guidelines for a Democratic South Africa, 1988'. Digital Innovation South Africa. http://www.disa.ukzn.ac.za/index. php?option=com_displaydc&recordID=pam19890000.026.021.000.

Arato, Andrew. 'The Occupation of Iraq and the Difficult Transition from Dictatorship'. *Constellations* 10 (2003): 408–24.

Arato, Andrew. 'Post-Sovereign Constitution Making and Democratic Legitimacy'. In *Souveränität, Recht. Moral. Die Grundlagen politischer Gemeinschaften*, ed. Tine Stein, Hubertus Buchstein and Claus Offe, 92–105. Frankfurt and New York: Campus, 2008.

Atkinson, Doreen. 'Brokering a Miracle? The Multiparty Negotiation Forum'. In *The Small Miracle. South Africa's Negotiated Settlement*, ed. Steven Friedman and Doreen Atkinson, 13–43. Johannesburg: Ravan Press, 1994.

Bogaards, Matthijs, Matthias Basedau, and Christof Hartmann, 'Ethnic Party Bans in Africa. An Introduction'. *Democratization* 17, no. 4 (2010): 599–617.

Capoccia, Giovanni. *Defending Democracy: Reactions to Extremism in Interwar Europe*. Baltimore and London: The Johns Hopkins University Press, 2005.

Currie, Iain and Johan de Waal. *The Bill of Rights Handbook*, 5th ed. Cape Town: Juta, 2006.

De Waal, Johan. 'Section 23: Political Rights'. In *Constitutional Law of South Africa*, ed. Matthew Chaskalson et al. Cape Town: Juta, 1999.

Du Toit, Pierre. *South Africa's Brittle Peace. The Problem of Post-Settlement Violence*. Houndmills: Palgrave, 2001.

Ebrahim, Hassen. *The Soul of a Nation. Constitution-making in South Africa*. Cape Town: Oxford University Press, 1998.

Egan, Anthony, and Rupert Taylor. 'South Africa. The Failure of Ethnoterritorial Politics'. In *The Territorial Management of Ethnic Conflict*, ed. John Coakley, 99–117. London and Portland: Frank Cass, 2003.

Fox, Gregory H., and Georg Nolte. 'Intolerant Democracies'. *Harvard International Law Journal* 36 (1995): 1–70.

Gibson, James L. 'Does Truth Lead to Reconciliation? Testing the Causal Assumptions of the South African Truth and Reconciliation Process'. University of Texas at Austin. http://www.utexas.edu/law/news/colloquium/papers/UTVersio.pdf.

Giliomee, Hermann, James Myburg, and Lawrence Schlemmer. 'Dominant Party Rule, Opposition Parties and Minorities in South Africa'. In *Opposition and Democracy in*

South Africa, ed. Roger Southall, Roger, 161–82. London and Portland: Frank Cass, 2001.

Hartmann, Christof, and Jörg Kemmerzell. 'Understanding Variations in Party Bans in Africa'. *Democratization* 17 (2010): 642–65.

Heine, Jorge. 'Institutional Engineering in New Democracies'. In *Democracy Under Construction: Patterns from Four Continents*, ed. Ursula J. van Beek, 65–94 Bloomfield Hills and Opladen: Barbara Budrich, 2005.

Hoffman, John. 'Legitimate Intervention and Illegitimate States. Sanctions against South Africa'. In *Political Theory, International Relations, and the Ethics of Intervention*, ed. Ian Forbes and Mark Hoffman, 157–66. London: Macmillan, 1993.

Horowitz, Donald. *A Democratic South Africa? Constitutional Engineering in a Divided Society.* Berkeley: University of California Press, 1991.

IDASA. 'Preparing for Democracy'. *Die Suid-Afrikaan* No. 43 (1993).

Independent Electoral Commission, http://www.elections.org.za/Registered_Parties/Selection_Party.asp.

Kirschke, Linda. 'Informal Repression, Zero-Sum Politics and Late Third Wave Transitions'. *The Journal of Modern African Studies* 38 (2000): 383–405.

Kis, János. 'Between Reform and Revolution'. *Eastern European Politics and Societies* 12 (1998): 300–83.

Kotzé, Hennie. 'A Consummation Devoutly to be Wished? The Democratic Alliance and Its Potential Constituencies'. In *Opposition and Democracy in South Africa*, ed. Roger Southall, 117–34. London and Portland: Frank Cass, 2001.

Kotzé, Hennie, and Pierre du Toit. 'Historical contexts'. In *Democracy Under Construction: Patterns from Four Continents*, ed. Ursula J. van Beek, 259–304. Bloomfield Hills and Opladen: Barbara Budrich, 2005.

Lawrence, Ralph. 'Introduction: From Soweto to Codesa'. In *The Small Miracle. South Africa's Negotiated Settlement*, ed. Steven Friedman and Doreen Atkinson, 1–12. Johannesburg: Ravan Press, 1994.

Lemarchand, René. 'Managing Transition Anarchies: Rwanda, Burundi, and South Africa in Comparative Perspective'. *The Journal of Modern African Studies* 32 (1994): 581–604.

Lodge, Tom. 'The ANC and the Development of Party Politics in Modern South Africa'. *The Journal of Modern African Studies* 42 (2004): 189–219.

Lodge, Tom. 'The Future of South Africa's Party System'. *Journal of Democracy* 17 (2006): 152–166.

Loewenstein, Karl. 'Militant Democracy and Fundamental Rights'. *American Political Science Review* 31 (1937): 417–32.

Mandela, Nelson. *Long Walk to Freedom.* Boston: Little, Brown and Company, 1994.

Mattes, Robert. 'South Africa: Democracy Without the People?' *Journal of Democracy* 13 (2002): 22–36.

Merkel, Wolfgang. 'Embedded and Defective Democracies'. *Democratization* 11 (2004): 33–58.

Moroff, Anika. 'Party Bans in Africa – An Empirical Overview', *Democratization* 17, no. 4 (2010): 618–41.

Ndletyana, Mcebisi 2008: 'Affirmative Action and the Public Service'. In *Racial Redress and Citizenship in South Africa*, ed. Adam Habib and Kristina Bentley, 77–98. Cape Town: HSRC Press, 2008.

Niesen, Peter. 'Zwischen Pfadabhängigkeit und Kommensuration: Verbote politischer Parteien in Europa'. In *'Schmerzliche Erfahrungen' der Vergangenheit und der Prozess der Konstitutionalisierung Europas*, ed. Christian Joerges, Matthias Mahlmann, and Ulrich K. Preuß, 258–73. Wiesbaden: VS-Verlag, 2008.

O'Donnell, Guillermo, and Philippe Schmitter. *Transitions from Authoritarian Rule. Tentative Conclusions about Uncertain Democracies*. Baltimore and London: The Johns Hopkins University Press 1986.

Rosenblum, Nancy L. 'Banning Parties: Religious and Ethnic Partisanship in Multicultural Democracies'. *Journal of Law and Ethics of Human Rights* 1 (2007): 17–75.

Sartori, Giovanni. *Comparative Constitutional Engineering*. London: Macmillan, 1994.

Sisk, Timothy D. *Democratization in South Africa. The Elusive Social Contract*, Princeton: Princeton University Press, 1995.

Sisk, Timothy D., and Christoph H. Stefes. 'Power Sharing as an Interim Step in Peace Building: Lessons from South Africa'. In *Sustainable Peace. Power and Democracy after Civil Wars*, ed. Philip G. Roeder and Donald Rothchild, 293–319. Ithaca and London: Cornell University Press, 2005.

Slye, Ronald C. 'Amnesty, Truth, and Reconciliation. Reflections on the South African Amnesty Process'. In: *Truth vs. Justice. The Morality of Truth Commissions*, ed. Robert I. Rotberg and Dennis Thompson, 170–88. Princeton: Princeton University Press, 2000.

Sparks, Allister. *Tomorrow is Another Country. The Inside Story of South Africa's Road to Change*. Chicago: University of Chicago Press, 1996.

Spitz, Richard and Matthew Chaskalson. *The Politics of Transition. A Hidden History of South Africa's Negotiated Settlement*. Oxford: Hart Publishers, 2000.

Stedman, Stephen John. 'Spoiler Problems in Peace Processes'. *International Security* 22 (1997): 5–53.

Teitel, Ruti. *Transitional Justice*. Oxford and New York: Oxford University Press, 2000

Vena, Vuvu. 'Is This What All those Men and Women Died For?' *Mail & Guardian Online*. http://www.mg.co.za/article/2010-03-19-is-this-what-all-those-men-and-women-died-for.

Villa-Vicencio, Charles, and Wilhelm Verwoerd. *Looking Back, Reaching Forward. Reflections on the Truth and Reconciliation Commission in South Africa*. Cape Town & London: Cape Town University Press, 2000.

Wilson, Richard A. 'Justice and Legitimacy in the South African Transition'. In *The Politics of Memory. Transitional Justice in Democratizing Societies*, ed. Alexandra Barahona de Brito, Carmen Gonzales-Enriquez, and Paloma Aguilar, 190–217. Oxford and New York: Oxford University Press, 2001.

Woolman, Stuart. 'Section 12: Limitation'. In *Constitutional Law of South Africa*, ed. Matthew Chaskalson et al. Cape Town: Juta, 1999.

Woolman, Stuart. 'Section 22: Freedom of Association'. In *Constitutional Law of South Africa*, ed. Matthew Chaskalson et al. Cape Town: Juta, 1999.

Political party bans in Rwanda 1994–2003: three narratives of justification

Peter Niesen

Institute of Political Science, Technical University of Darmstadt, Darmstadt, Germany

This article discusses the public justifications brought forward for three waves of bans on political parties in Rwanda after the regime change of 1994. While the standard narrative of protecting democracy from its enemies ('militant democracy') was not invoked, two alternative narratives carried the burden of justification. The first is that of banning strongly particularistic parties, i.e. parties that discriminate or incite hatred and violence along ethnic or similar lines. The second is that of banning the former ruling party, responsible for mass atrocities, and its successor organizations. While both justification narratives have strong initial plausibility against Rwanda's history of ethnic conflict and genocide, and mirror analogous justifications for banning parties elsewhere, a detailed discussion of the evidence suggests that Rwanda's bans mainly served the purpose of repressing political opposition. The justifications brought forward in the later waves of bans remain unconvincing and cannot claim political legitimacy.

Among the most prominent cases of political party bans in sub-Saharan Africa in recent decades are the bans on Hutu parties that took place in Rwanda between 1994 and 2003. The Rwandan bans occurred in three waves. The first wave comprises the immediate post-genocidal bans on the former state party Mouvement Révolutionaire Nationale pour le Developpement (MRND) and the radical Hutu party Coalition pour la Défense de la République (CDR) in 1994. The second wave consists of a single case, the outlawing of the formation of a new party, Party for Democracy and Regeneration (PDR) 'Ubuyanja', in 2001. In a third wave, the largest opposition party, Mouvement Démocratique Républicain (MDR), was banned in 2003 and a successor organization barred from registering in the upcoming elections.

One striking feature of the various bans on parties in post-genocide Rwanda is that they cannot easily be integrated into the standard framework in which party bans have been understood in the past: militant democracy. Since the mid-twentieth century, governments have justified bans on parties as ways of 'defending democracy', and constitutional lawyers and democratic theorists have tended to approve of such bans if and only if parties could be shown to have the aim of destroying democratic institutions.[1] In the Rwandan cases, this understanding was irrelevant. In fact, the Rwandan authorities invoked two different justification narratives for banning Hutu parties.[2] First, they have justified them as restrictions on particularistic political parties. Particularistic parties are composed of, seek the support of, and act on behalf of the interests of a particular identity group.[3] Agreements before and after regime change in Rwanda emphasized a broad anti-particularistic approach, ruling out political organizations operating on the basis of ethnic, linguistic, regional or religious division. The public justifications of Rwanda's party bans have more specifically stressed parties' alleged 'strong particularism', i.e. their display of aggression or incitement of hatred, discrimination and violence on a particularistic basis. Second, the government has drawn on arguments from Rwanda's immediate history of violence, and presented bans on parties as means of averting a relapse into past atrocities. The first and third wave of bans were framed as disbanding the former ruling parties and their successor organizations. In this, they resemble party bans in a number of post-conflict states around the world that have occurred since the mid-twentieth century, as outlined below.

This study concentrates on the bans' defences 'on the ground', guided by the idea that only arguments actually put forward in favour of a policy can contribute to its political legitimacy.[4] It attempts to take seriously the claims of the bans' proponents without thereby endorsing them, and to trace, understand, and delimit the potential of the justifications advanced. While militant democracy has been explored in both comparativist and normative terms,[5] the two alternative narratives have not yet been broadly debated or evaluated in the literature. Political theory has only tentatively started discussing anti-particularistic bans or bans on former ruling parties.[6] Especially where bans are criticized, as in this article, it is important to see in how far their justifications hold up in general, or in analogous cases. This study comes to a negative result as to the legitimacy of the second and third waves of bans discussed, and questions aspects of the first. It concludes that Rwanda's repression of political parties after regime change is a showcase of how the implementation of party bans, though based on impressive arguments, can contribute to the failure of a process of democratization.

Three waves of party bans in Rwanda

Background: one party rule and attempted reform

Before presenting the party bans between 1994 and 2003, some brief historical background to the Hutu-Tutsi conflict needs to be given.[7] Under German and then Belgian rule from 1916, the economic and political upper class in Rwanda was recruited exclusively from the Tutsi population. The Belgian colonial regime sealed the ethnic identities of Rwandans in 1933 by incorporating ethnic affiliation (Hutu, Tutsi, and Twa) into identity cards. Widespread Hutu resistance, often referred to as Hutu 'revolution', started in 1959 and marked the end of both the colonial period and Tutsi dominance. The Belgians shifted their loyalty to the Hutu, who described themselves as the indigenous population and the Tutsi as immigrants.[8] After Rwandan independence on 1 July 1962, many Tutsi were forcibly expatriated to Uganda. The most important political force in the Hutu Revolution was MDR-Parmehutu (Mouvement Démocratique Républicain-Parmehutu), an emphatically majoritarian movement with Hutu-supremacist ideology.

In 1973, the Hutu general Juvénal Habyarimana took power.[9] He officially declared Rwanda a one party state two years later and abolished MDR-Parmehutu, which had been suspended before. The MRND became the state party, led by Habyarimana both as party chairman and Rwandan president. Under the auspices of a changed geopolitical climate toward the end of the 1980s, his regime came under significant internal and external pressure. In 1990, a national commission was founded to install processes of democratization. It was designed to secure the political survival of Habyarimana through a reform process toward power sharing, but the situation was already one of escalating civil war. The Rwanda Patriotic Army (RPA), representing the interests of half a million exiled Rwandan Tutsi, mounted an attack from Uganda. Under pressure from the RPA, the Hutu opposition, human rights groups, and donor nations, Habyarimana was forced to accept a constitutional settlement that introduced a multiparty system in June 1991. By April 1992 the coalition government under Habyarimana included most of the newly founded parties, including the re-formed MDR, which shed its suffix '-Parmehutu'. At the same time, the MRND started building a militant youth organization, the notorious Interahamwe, which was to become a key actor in the genocide of April 1994. From its foundation, the renewed MDR fought the MRND over representing the Hutu population, while their respective youth organizations, Inkuba and Interahamwe, clashed violently. Both parties were characterized by bitter infighting of rivalling factions.

Ceasefire talks with the Rwanda Patriotic Front (RPF, the political arm of the Tutsi army RPA) were started only under the new multiparty government in 1992. The Arusha agreements of August 1993 envisaged splitting governmental powers three ways: between Habyarimana's MRND and its allies; the exiled RPF; and the emerging 'new democratic forces' of the newly founded parties surrounding the MDR. The rapid escalation of armed conflict prevented the agreements from being implemented. In neighbouring Burundi, presidential elections had taken place in June 1993. Against the expectations of the governing, Tutsi-dominated party, the Hutu Melchior Ndadaye defeated the incumbent Pierre Buyoya. When a Tutsi faction of the Burundian army murdered Ndadaye on 21 October 1993, radical Hutu in Rwanda, led by extremists in the army and the former state party, formed the party-transcending Hutu-Power (or -PAWA) movement that united activists from MRND with an MDR faction opposed to the Arusha agreements. Ethnic conflict escalated to genocide when President Habyarimana was shot down in his plane on 6 April 1994. In the ensuing massacres, between 500,000 and 800,000 men, women and children were killed within 12 weeks. Seventy-five percent of the Tutsi population within Rwanda were murdered, as were many moderate Hutu, among them Prime Minister Agathe Uwilingiyimana, a former member of the MDR. The genocide only ended with the successful military advance of the RPA from Uganda, taking Kigali on 4 July 1994.

Banning MRND and CDR

When the RPF, speaking for the victorious army, declared the formation of a transitional government on 17 July 1994, it invoked the ideals of democracy, pluralism, and the rule of law and signalled a qualified commitment to the power-sharing logic of the Arusha accords. In the same breath, it declared the state party MRND and the small Hutu party Coalition pour la Défense de la République (CDR) to be immediately excluded 'from all participation in the institutions'.[10] In May 1995, this ban was ratified by the MDR and the other 'new democratic forces' when the transitional national assembly agreed to make the RPF 'Déclaration' the cornerstone of a transitional 'Fundamental Law'.[11] The reason for the ban given in the Déclaration was that the political and military apparatus of Habyarimana's 'régime de feu' (government of fire)[12] and its CDR associates in the interim government prepared and executed the genocide. Unlike the MRND, which was to take up a third of government posts, the CDR had not been considered for participation in the transitional government, as it was the only significant political party to have persistently campaigned against the Arusha agreements.[13] Besides banning MRND and CDR, which left the RPF to claim additional ministerial portfolios, the Déclaration modified the constitutional balance toward a presidential system and pencilled in a vice-presidential office, to be claimed by the leader of the RPF, Paul Kagame. The new president was Pasteur Bizimungu, RPF, a Hutu and former government official under Habyarimana. The prime minister was Faustin Twagiramungu of the MDR, as envisaged before the genocide. Fourteen of the 20 new government ministers were Hutu. The RPF ostensibly took on a role as one force among several in a power-sharing government, but had in fact already changed the terms of cooperation.[14] It is also worth mentioning that the RPF, asserting itself as the dominant force in post-genocide politics, did not initially follow an overall strategy of lustration, but was more interested in incorporating former opponents. It invited defection from enemy militias and made offers to members of the radical Interahamwe militia and the MDR.[15]

Outlawing PDR 'Ubuyanja' (Party for Democracy and Regeneration)

The next case of outlawing a political party in Rwanda occurred with the thwarted formation of the PDR 'Ubuyanja' in 2001. Pasteur Bizimungu had stepped down from the presidency under pressure in early 2000 and was replaced by Paul Kagame. Kagame had effectively been controlling the government, 'a Hutu super-structure behind which he exercised final authority',[16] as vice-president since 1994. In May 2001, one year after his resignation, Bizimungu prepared the founding assembly of a new party, the PDR, but was arrested and imprisoned with several of his allies. Kagame's cabinet charged him with offending against Rwandan party law in founding the PDR.[17] It was argued that the law disallowed the founding of new parties during the transitional period, and that Bizimungu's activities were a threat to public safety. Cabinet ministers accused the PDR founders of stirring up ethnic 'divisionism'. A number of supporters were arrested and charged with 'endangering national security' and inciting ethnic hatred. Leading activists were imprisoned, detained or attacked.[18]

Dissolving MDR

In the run-up to the 2003 parliamentary and presidential elections, on 30 December 2002, the Rwandan transitional parliament commissioned seven parliamentarians with investigating what it called 'the problems of the MDR'.[19] In the ensuing weeks, the Parliamentary Commission collected several hundred pages of material from a variety of sources, most of which remains unpublished.[20] A 35-page report by the commission, delivered to parliament on 17 March 2003, accuses the MDR of a comprehensive twofold 'divisionist' strategy: first, in the sense of provoking internal party divisions, and second, of fostering the resilient ethnic division of the population. On 14 April 2003, the Transitional National Assembly adopted the report's recommendation to dissolve Rwanda's second largest party. No further formal act of dissolution occurred; observers therefore advisedly speak of a 'de facto dissolution'.[21] Formally, the MDR ceased to exist when it did not apply for renewed registration after a new law was passed, requiring all existing parties to re-register before the presidential and parliamentary elections.[22] Only one successor organization, the Party for Peace and Concord (PPC), was admitted to the parliamentary elections, but failed to reach the required threshold of 5% of the vote.[23] The registration of another successor party, Alliance pour la démocratie, l'équité et le progress (ADEP-Mizero), led by a former cabinet minister of MDR, was rejected because its statutes allegedly did not comply with the law on political parties. The party was not allowed to change its statutes.[24] Not only were both parties, MDR and ADEP-Mizero, barred from campaigning on their own behalf in the parliamentary elections, they were also kept from participating in the presidential campaign, where the former MDR prime minister Faustin Twagiramungu challenged the incumbent, Paul Kagame. Deprived of mass party support, and under harassment from the government, Twagiramungu's campaign faltered. In the immediate aftermath of the proceedings against MDR, a number of former ministerial members of the party and other high-ranking politicians named in the parliamentary report disappeared, others were held or arrested.

Justifying party bans in Rwanda: three narratives

Militant democracy

Legal and democratic theory have in recent decades largely focused on one justification for bans on parties, namely their danger to democratic government. This is the original understanding of militant democracy as introduced by Karl Loewenstein and adopted *inter alia* in the post-World War II constitution of the Federal Republic of Germany.[25] According to this understanding, party bans are preemptive instruments used against forces that seek to abolish democratic rule, especially if they operate within the law and ostensibly respect the democratic process. The organizations targeted by such provisions attempt to take over political power in a legalist strategy involving elections. Once they have taken over, they show their true colours and abolish elections, eliminating the danger of being voted out by 'locking the door' they used to gain entry.[26] Parties that do not respect their competitors' equal chances of winning political power can thus be excluded from political competition. Militant democracy has in recent years been reformulated within the categories of international law and accordingly globalized,[27] relying on the support for political liberties in the International Covenant on Civil and Political Rights, and on the emergence of democracy-protecting activities within the UN Security Council.[28] If states commit to securing democratic rights, the argument goes, they should be permitted to use legal restrictions against parties or movements that would do away with those democratic rights once in power.[29]

The Rwandan bans only superficially connect with this abstract and general justification narrative,[30] and the proponents of bans on Hutu parties did not enter into an argument of defending democracy against its enemies. True, ethnic Hutu parties have broad appeal and may indeed have been successful in their attempts at mass mobilization. But it would have been implausible to accuse the Hutu parties of planning to do away with elections after getting into power. From the Hutu parties' point of view, abolishing democratic structures would have been irrational, as they had little to fear from subsequent elections for demographic reasons. To put the contrast bluntly, it would not be amiss to ascribe a more radical commitment to electoral democracy to the incriminated Hutu parties than to their opponents in government. In the semantic minefield that is Rwandan public discourse, opponents and defenders of the bans on Hutu parties divide along a simple line: their opponents invoke the value of 'democracy', while their defenders point to '(national) unity'. Invoking 'democracy' expresses the hope that an electoral polarization of ethnic plurality will determine access to power, while a recourse to 'unity' or a shared national identity entails the repressive depoliticization of ethnic plurality.[31] The argument that Hutu parties, once voted into power, will 'lock the door' behind them and abolish elections, in order not to be voted out again, has not been publicly made.[32] The Rwandan constellation thus exemplifies Nancy Rosenblum's recent complaint that 'the justifications for banning parties with overtly antidemocratic political ideologies, fascism or communism, cannot be neatly applied to ... parties defending or attacking benefits to ethnic groups'.[33] Although many '[p]arties based on religion, ethnicity, and cultural community are as ardent and potentially uncompromising as parties avowing radical, antidemocratic political ideologies', they need not be anti-democratic.[34] Because it has not been argued, let alone proved, that the Hutu parties were anti-democratic, an argument from militant democracy cannot shed any political legitimacy on the Rwandan party bans.

Anti-particularism

A second, as yet underdeveloped approach to the justification of party bans focuses on parties' particularistic nature. Like the militant democracy paradigm, this narrative can point to overt formulations in state constitutions.[35] After 1990, many African states introduced bans on particularistic parties of varying description into their constitutions and legal codes. One straightforward example comes from the Algerian constitution, which states that 'political parties cannot be founded on a religious, linguistic, racial, sexual, corporatist or regional basis' (Art. 42). Under this provision, what might be termed 'weak particularism' is a sufficient reason for a party ban. Parties are 'weakly particularistic' if their set-up (name, membership, leadership, etc.) exclusively reflects an identity group, and 'strongly particularistic' if they additionally pursue particularistic interests by attacking, discriminating against or suppressing other identity groups. This definition makes clear that 'mere' discrimination or incitement, unconnected to a particularistic party basis, will not suffice to make a party 'strongly particularistic'.[36] Still, where such behaviour is incriminated in a particularistic party, the connection to the party's set-up should not be obscured.

One characteristic feature of the Rwandan cases is the authorities' blurring of lines between weak and strong particularism. A statute against ethnic parties was first introduced in 1991. It reads: 'Parties are not to institute discrimination based on ethnic, regional, professional or other allegiances into their principles, programs and behaviour.'[37] The Arusha agreements, with their quasi-constitutional status during the transitional period, contain a similar provision. Parties must abstain from discrimination based on 'ethnic, regional, sexual or religious difference' (Art. 80). Art. 54 of the new Rwandan constitution of 2003, ratified after the bans discussed here took place, states that 'political organizations are prohibited from basing themselves on race, ethnic group, tribe, clan, region, sex, religion or any other division which may give rise to discrimination'.[38] It seems safe to say that the earlier formulations of the party law and Arusha accords and their later constitutional variant express the same concern: All draw a connection between ethnic affiliation and discrimination. All are clear anti-particularistic provisions, but they all remain ambiguous between a strong and a weak understanding of their anti-particularistic intents. It seems analytically conceivable that weakly particularistic parties do not fall victim to the provisions if their particularistic set-up does not 'institute' or 'give rise to' discrimination. However, it cannot be ruled out that the very formation along ethnic lines is itself considered to constitute discrimination. It is further unclear whether discrimination must be intended or even caused by the parties in order to invite prosecution. In their vagueness, the Rwandan statutes assimilate the categories of weak and strong particularism, and thus set the stage for prosecuting all ethnic parties under a pretence of clamping down on strong particularism.

Discriminatory appeals to ethnicity are captured in Rwandan public discourse under a narrative of 'divisionism', which has further served to blur the lines between strong and weak particularism. On one understanding, 'divisionism' is a criminal offence. Law 47/2001, published only after the prosecution of PDR 'Ubuyanja', punishes 'divisionism', i.e. 'the crime of discrimination and of division', understood as 'speech, written statement or action that causes conflict ... that may degenerate into strife among people'.[39] Parties offending against Law 47/2001 can be suspended or banned. Although the provision is, again, not very clear, it seems reasonable to read it as criminalizing incitement. Inciting violent conflict, if provoked on the basis of particularistic cleavages, qualifies as strong particularism. On the other hand, 'divisionism' has been invoked in a very broad and unspecific sense, both in public debate and in criminal prosecution. The RPF has based electoral campaigns and programmes of re-education on the notion of fighting divisionism and protecting national unity.[40] The government has prosecuted as 'divisionist' public support for opposition candidates, advocacy on behalf of ethnic groups (*inter alia* for the minority Twa population), and media reports critical of the government.[41] The charge of 'divisionism' has been used to discourage any reference to an ethnically divided citizenry.[42] Even staunch defenders of the RPF regime agree that mere references to the ethnic identities of Hutu, Tutsi, and Twa have served as the basis for accusations of divisionism.[43] If to refer to divisions is to propagate divisions, then all ethnic particularism is strong particularism.

Both PDR 'Ubuyanja' and MDR were charged with divisionism. In the parliamentary report against the MDR, the party is said to practice 'ethnic discrimination and regional favouritism'.[44] The main references to 'divisions' in the report, however, concern intra-party splits, and it is true that divisions within the party have in the past preceded the radicalization of its wings. The report is less specific on 'divisionism' between the ethnic groups of Hutu and Tutsi allegedly propagated by the party. Apart from references to reviving Parmehutu ideology, to be treated below, the main objection is to the parties' framing of political interests in ethnic terms. In the case against PDR 'Ubuyanja', Bizimungu was charged with propagating 'divisionist' ideology in an interview to *Jeune Afrique* magazine. He was quoted as follows:

> We are persuaded that if things continue, the Hutus will prepare for war and in 15 or 20 years, they will have driven out the Tutsis, with the conceivable consequences that would entail. Mechanisms need to be set up so that each community can truly have a hand in the government, until we have forged a national identity that transcends Hutu/Tutsi divisions.[45]

In the absence of a power-sharing arrangement between ethnic groups, Bizimungu predicts that the Hutus will revolt and 'drive out' the Tutsis. Commentators disagree about whether this is a warning or a threat,[46] yet the statement admits of an interpretation as prognosis, not incitement. What is uncontroversial is that Bizimungu's statement evokes Rwanda's experiences of escalating conflict, expulsion and murder, and that he formulates grievances and articulates cleavages along ethnic lines.[47]

Sanctioning parties for inciting violent conflict or racial hatred is a powerful and widely recognized justification narrative,[48] and the Rwandan government has insisted on this core argument when pressed.[49] We must therefore ask whether anti-particularism, in its variant of fighting incitement, can substitute for the militant democracy narrative in the Rwandan bans. Such a narrative need not commit to repressing weakly particularistic parties, but can remain neutral on that question.[50] What it rejects, after all, is not identity groups pursuing the interest of their members, but putting in jeopardy the rights and well-being of non-members. However, the Rwandan government's strategy of staking their public justification of the bans on PDR and MDR on an opposition to incitement appears deeply flawed. Three considerations seem especially relevant. The first is the lack of detail provided in the incitement charges. In both the PDR and MDR cases, the party's initiators or leading members were blamed for the incitement of ethnic hatred and the propagation of violent conflict along ethnic lines. As a legal category, incitement relates to situations of clear and present danger and involves the advocacy of illegal acts.[51] The government in no way attempted to show the danger to be immediate, or the likelihood of 'strife among people' to be imminent. The lack of open advocacy of illegal acts was explained by the use of coded language.[52] Nor has the government made the case that the parties' ethnic references amounted to incitement to racial hatred. The quote given from Bizimungu above illustrates that ethnic mobilization concerns the distribution of political power, not racial stratification. Neither of the banned parties had revived the racist propaganda that lead up to the genocide in 1994. The second consideration concerns the inflationary use of 'divisionism' as an all-purpose weapon, which detracts from the specificity and credibility of the charges against both parties. Party bans were embedded in a variety of official and unofficial strategies of repression, and the government has not been able to rebut the charge that it 'interprets divisionism to mean any form of opposition to its policies'.[53] Under an overbroad construal of 'divisionist' activity, the prosecution of allegedly divisionist parties must be regarded as arbitrary. The third consideration relates to the government's attempt to isolate itself from critique through administering anti-particularistic bans. By criminalizing political associations' ethnicity-based appeals, it has ruled out challenges of ethnic favouritism against its own composition and policies. It has thereby sought to silence any organized articulation of the main oppositional grievance. A central element of ethnicity-based campaigning by PDR and MDR was the protest against what was perceived as 'reverse' ethnic discrimination under a Tutsi supremacy replicating the colonial social stratification of the country.[54] The prosecution of 'divisionism' cannot escape the charge that it makes a renewed Tutsi predominance unassailable. Taken together, these considerations strongly suggest that the anti-particularist justification narrative cannot establish political legitimacy for the party bans discussed.

Banning the former ruling party

While anti-particularistic arguments are phrased in general, viewpoint-neutral terms, it is obvious that a more concrete historical frame for party bans is available in the Rwandan experience of genocide in 1994. The memory of ethnic persecution and of genocide does not point toward abstract dangers to democracy, as under the militant democracy narrative, nor does it envisage one particularistic discriminatory threat among many possible others. Rather, it could serve as a freestanding justification for introducing, in Ulrich Preuß' phrase, a 'backward barrier'.[55] Such 'backward barriers' are not in principle incompatible with transitions to democracy. By outlawing a historically dominant party, Ruti Teitel has argued, new regimes can refer to a 'distinctive former tyranny, while at the same time and through this reaction redefin[ing] democracy'.[56] Banning former ruling parties in or after political rupture, and the subsequent inclusion of such bans into post-conflict constitutions, are common practices during regime change. Parallel cases can be found in post-World War II Italy, where the 1947 constitution rules out the reorganization of the Partito Nazionale Fascista (PNF),[57] but also in the occupation of Iraq, where the first Coalition Provisional Order banned the Ba'ath Party.[58] Other examples display more clearly the ambivalence of bans on former ruling parties, as when democratic predecessor parties are outlawed in authoritarian takeovers.[59] Though they may play important functional roles in the politics of transition, we cannot simply assume that all bans on former ruling parties are legitimate.

The Rwandan authorities have defended bans against Hutu parties as strikes against the perpetrators of grave injustice and against the danger of relapse into the former condition of violence and tyranny. Both the immediate post-genocide ban on MRND and CDR in 1994 and the later ban on MDR in 2003 were justified as bans on (a revival of) the former ruling party. The time elapsed suggests that they represent two variants of such bans: the outlawing of ruling parties during regime change, and the banning of a presumptive successor party well into the process of regime consolidation. While the first variant can build on recent evidence of crimes and injustice, a ban of the second kind is more difficult to justify and depends on the relevant identity of the predecessor and successor organizations.

The immediate post-genocide ban on MRND and CDR

Both the former state party MRND and the CDR, partners in the *genocidaire* government, were banned as former ruling parties in the first public declaration of the victorious RPF.[60] The rejection of Hutu-supremacist ideology and the organizations that embodied it were central to the new regime's endeavours to build a new political identity on the ruins of its predecessor. Accordingly, the bans of the first wave have strong claims to legitimacy. First, outlawing the parties followed upon crimes and injustices on a massive scale. In cases where a new regime is founded after massive state crimes and grave human rights violations, banning a former ruling party responsible for the moral catastrophe assumes a special moral urgency. There is nothing frivolous in permanently disbanding an organization that has advocated, abetted or perpetrated genocide. Second, responsibilities have been clearly established in the Rwandan case. While scholars still debate how far the genocide was a state-driven project and how far the dynamic of hostility 'spontaneously' escalated into mass murder, ascribing responsibility to the MRND and CDR is not controversial. The parties put the administrative and military resources of the Rwandan state into the service of the killers.[61]

There is, however, a serious concern to be addressed. The permanent disbanding of a former ruling party, like any ban, has to be seen in the context of other measures introduced in the politics of transition to a new regime. On the one hand, the concrete identification of the organization(s) to be outlawed (by proper names 'MRND' and 'CDR' in the RPF Déclaration) appears to rule out possible abuses. It gives the repressive measures an exceptional status, with very limited apparent general applicability. Compare the case of Italy, where the constitutional provision against re-forming the formerly ruling PNF has not led to a repressive or overly restrictive practice, not least because the sheer individuality of the party identified has all but ruled out its invocation against other parties.[62] Granting a historically motivated, narrowly circumscribed exception to associative liberty can turn out to be less damaging to overall political freedom than operating under a general conception of militant democracy.[63] On the other hand, there exist cases where banning the former ruling party out of a sense of moral urgency has facilitated the overall repression of political pluralism. In the occupied territories that became the German Democratic Republic (GDR) after World War II, the Soviet Military Administration of Germany explicitly admitted only anti-fascist parties, combining a ban on the former ruling Nationalsozialistische Deutsche Arbeiterpartei (NSDAP) with a repressive registration system for all other parties, only to develop into a de-facto one party regime.[64] In Rwanda, likewise, the immediate post-genocide bans on MRND and CDR did not lead to a narrow or exceptional understanding of justified repression. Prosecution of parties and individuals continued, and parties' independence was compromised when they were coerced into an ostensibly consensual, but RPF-dominated 'Forum for Political Parties'.[65] The later Rwandan party system, based on excluding the parties responsible for national catastrophe, and with only notional independence of existing parties alongside the RPF, is thus reminiscent of single party states of the socialist era.[66]

The ban on the MRND, far from being an exceptional limit to free political association, established a pattern of behaviour on the part of the new ruling party. The RPF Déclaration dissolving the former state party went on to state that the government posts originally reserved for the MRND were to go to the RPF, thereby awarding it a blocking minority within the transitional government.

Together with other unilateral modifications, outlawing the former state party in the declaration allowed the RPF 'to exercise a political monopoly' that doomed attempts at introducing a viable democratic system.[67] Although a broad consensus of reformist forces supported the public de-legitimization of the genocidal forces, the redistribution of their powers unilaterally rewarded the dominant party, and irreversibly skewed the ensuing political process.

The proceedings against the MDR

In itself, the repression of a former ruling party in the immediate aftermath of a murderous regime need not compromise a new regime. Still, it cannot be taken for granted that similar policies can be applicable in later periods of consolidation. Though later procedures directed against former ruling parties and their successors can often rely on more complex legal and constitutional institutions, and thereby improve on spontaneous decisions taken under conditions of political rupture, the immediate evidence, urgency, and moral pressure of massive crimes may not be present at a later stage. The crucial question is how it can be shown that a targeted party is indeed continuous with the past regime. The Parliamentary Commission investigating the MDR, nine years into the transitional process, attempted to establish such a narrative. The Commission traced elements of a Hutu-supremacist ideology to origins in MDR-Parmehutu, and drew a link between disagreements arising within the party and the emergence of radicalized discriminatory agendas against the Tutsi population.[68] During the reign of the state party, the Parmehutu ideology was allegedly kept alive by the MRND, only to be taken over unmodified by the re-founded MDR, the party, according to its own statutes, of the 'peuple majoritaire'. The report concedes that in 1994 the MDR participated in the transitional multiparty government as it 'had not been tainted by genocide',[69] and that it changed its flag and symbol in 1999 to distance itself from past wrongdoings. However, in the immediate aftermath of its 1999 reform, the party allegedly split into two factions again and displayed symptoms of its 'chronic disease'. It campaigned against government programmes, national unity, and reconciliation.[70] The report charges the MDR with 'minimizing' the genocide: 'If they do not altogether deny that it took place, they argue that there was a double genocide (Hutu and Tutsi) and that the Hutu were the only ones to have been imprisoned.'[71] The MDR is argued to defend a culture of impunity for the perpetrators of genocide and to induce collective intoxication in the population, thus bringing about a situation 'like before the election of Ndadaye in Burundi in 1993'.[72] The report claims that MDR ideology is continuous with both MDR-Parmehutu and MRND, as well as its earlier radical Hutu-Power wing.[73] It concludes with an old Rwandan saying, that in the case of the MDR 'the disease that killed your cow has not yet left the cadaver'.[74]

The German Federal Constitutional Court had faced a similar constellation when the government applied to have the neo-Nazi Sozialistische Reichspartei (SRP) banned in 1952. The Court built the case against the SRP on the party's 'essential affinity' with the NSDAP. An 'essentially affine' organization is an unmistakeable successor party, sharing the personnel, programme, worldview and overall style of an historical role model.[75] The Court noted that the SRP communicated by 'camouflaged and encrypted statements', unobjectionable on the surface, but meaning different things to the uninitiated and the initiated. It stressed the continued use of symbols and signals, flags and uniforms. The successor organization revealed itself through 'the apology of NS crimes, the decoration of its representatives ... and the cultivation of National Socialist tradition'.[76] An essential affinity with National Socialism was also displayed in the 'belittlement and apology of its crimes' for example, in relativizing the genocide of the European Jews.[77] The German Court concludes that 'a party which has an essential affinity with a clearly anti-constitutional political movement of the past in its worldview and all essential forms of articulation, will seek to realize the same – or at least kindred – goals if it is left to continue in operation'.[78]

Mutatis mutandis, 'essential affinity' is what the Rwandan Parliamentary Commission attempted to establish in the MDR case. Its historical pedigree and contemporary physiognomy were to prove its commitment to the pursuit of Hutu-supremacist policies along the lines of MDR-Parmehutu and MRND. It is important to note that, independently of the merits of the case, the historical analogy does not presuppose any ideological similarities between National Socialism and Hutu supremacism. While the MDR has been likened to the NSDAP in political debate,[79] such sweeping indictments have no basis. Establishing 'essential affinity' with a former ruling party does not turn on a specific ideology.

The justification narrative employed by the Rwandan parliamentary commission appears internally coherent. If banning MRND was legitimate, how could outlawing an essentially identical party be objectionable? From a more comprehensive perspective, objections prevail. These objections turn on contradictions in the parliamentary report and on factual questions. How could the MDR have been considered a bona fide coalition partner in the transitional government, if its affinity to the *genocidaires* had been so obvious? Why is the fact that current personnel were 'untainted by the genocide' not taken into consideration? It is also unconvincing to claim that the MDR is both a successor organization of MDR-Parmehutu and MRND, as both movements were mutually exclusive. Finally, even support for Parmehutu-type ideals cannot be taken to entail either genocide revisionism or an intended or imminent relapse into genocidal persecution. In sum, the report did not successfully establish 'essential affinity' with the alleged predecessor party. Human rights organizations have univocally criticized the identification of MRD with the genocidal movements, concluding that 'the government is far from having convincing proof of these broad and extremely serious charges'.[80] Some political commentators have weighed in to support the RPF's strategy against the MDR,[81] and the ban only briefly irritated the donor community.[82] Yet it has found no defenders in the scholarly literature. Some authors have toned down their criticism in view of the considerable moral pressure of the past catastrophe, and of what they see as a persistent 'danger of conflagration';[83]

others have castigated the regime's abuse of its 'genocide credit'.[84] Even authors sympathetic to the RPF regime have based their greater indulgence on the stability and economic promise of an authoritarian order, and not on claims to political legitimacy.[85] What hopes remained for the country's transition to democracy evaporated when, with the MDR, the only remaining opposition party was banned. In the absence of organized support for opposition candidates, the reported vote of 95% in the ensuing elections for the incumbent president Paul Kagame, even if resting on a turnout of 96%, has been rendered meaningless from a democratic point of view.[86] Rwanda has effectively been a one-party state since 2003.

Conclusion

Before briefly reviewing again the argument, two additional remarks seem apt, since they apply to all three justification narratives. The first concerns the legal and political context in which party bans take place. It seems that the justificatory burden incurred in repressing freedom of association can only be discharged by demonstrating the policies' narrowly targeted, exceptional character. The Rwandan bans, in contrast, occurred in a comprehensive context of persecution, both official and unofficial. The official context was characterized by severe restrictions on freedom of expression and assembly, by administrative and police harassment of parties, candidates and party members, and by a lack of independent judicial control of security services, police, and government executive. Human rights organizations have added that the bans took place in an environment of systematic intimidation, disappearances and killings.[87] Both official and unofficial contexts strongly indicate the use of party bans as a regular means of managing political opposition, despite their enormous cost for the credibility of an ostensibly pluralist system. A second remark concerns the bans' procedural credentials. Of course, the prosecution of PDR 'Ubuyanja' and the outlawing of MDR do not reflect the more sophisticated party ban proceedings that were only implemented in the 2003 constitution,[88] as they occurred before the constitutional referendum took place. But earlier law had already installed procedural safeguards. The existing party law during the MDR case constrained the interior minister to apply at a tribunal of the first instance for the dissolution of a party.[89] In the Arusha agreements, the contracting parties empowered the Supreme Court to exclude parties from participating in public office (Art. 80). Law 47/2001, which was mentioned in the MDR ban application, does not envisage suspending or dissolving parties by parliamentary resolution, but by decision of a tribunal of the first instance.[90] Thus, although Rwandan law has consistently delegated the authority to dissolve parties to courts, no evidence was found of the judiciary participating in any of the three waves of party bans. Courts did play an active role in the criminal prosecution of opposition figures for 'divisionism', but the outlawing of MRND and CDR, as well as the pre-emptive ban on the formation of PDR 'Ubuyanja', were executive-driven, while the MDR was de facto disbanded by its competitors in parliament. Rwandan president Paul Kagame is quoted as saying that 'courts have banned some opposition parties . . . only because they stirred up group hatred, not because they posed a political threat',[91] but courts did not have an independent say in the dissolutions. For party bans to be legitimate, it seems necessary that governments can fail in their attempts to bring them about.

This study has discussed three waves of party bans in Rwanda and the justifications offered for them. In the absence of a manifest link to militant democracy, two justification narratives have been examined: banning strongly particularistic parties and banning the former ruling party, responsible for grave human rights violations, and its successor organizations. While the exclusion of two former government parties compromised by genocide, MRND and CDR, still appears unobjectionable, the unilateral mode of their disbandment helped establish a continuous pattern of political repression. Later charges of inciting ethnic discrimination and reconstituting a discredited former ruling party remained unconvincing both procedurally and substantively. The charges brought forward against PDR and MDR for inciting ethnic hatred and violence suffered not only from a lack of specificity and a lack of evidence, but also from their role in protecting the regime against challenges of ethnic privilege. In disbanding the MDR, the prior ban on MRND lent initial plausibility to banning any 'essentially affine' party, but the Parliamentary Commission fell short of identifying the MDR with the genocidal former ruling party. Seen together, the three successive waves of bans indicate the new ruling party 'learned' from experience and gradually took to managing political opposition through the routine application of political party bans. In the sequence of the waves, the regime divested itself of its challengers and competitors, one by one, until no effective competition was left. The final dissolution of the MDR, the one remaining major opposition party, did not put up a 'backward barrier', but put a lasting obstacle into the path of post-conflict transition.

Acknowledgements

The drafting of this study has profited from criticism by Anika Moroff, Giovanni Capoccia, Giovanni Carbone, Oda van Cranenburgh, Philip Dann, Günter Frankenberg, Matthias Goldmann, Jörg Kemmerzell, and two reviewers for this journal.

Notes

1. For the historical roots of the doctrine in interwar Europe, see Capoccia, *Defending Democracy*.
2. Justification narratives are comprehensive public attempts to found or secure the legitimacy of orders or decisions, containing both narrative and argumentative elements. For an exposition of the notion, see Forst, 'Der Grund der Kritik', 150–64.
3. Cf. Basedau et al., 'Ethnic Party Bans in Africa'.
4. In understanding political legitimacy as Janus-faced (combining actual justification and justifiability beyond the immediate context), my approach follows Habermas, *Legitimation Crisis*, 102.
5. Thiel, *'Militant Democracy' Principle*, esp. 379–424; Leggewie & Meier, *Republikschutz*.

6. Rosenblum, 'Banning Parties'; Niesen, 'Anti-Extremism'.
7. This article is not intended to contribute to the extended debate on how 'substantialist' or 'constructivist' ethnic allegiances in Rwanda might be understood. Some critical observers have argued against applying the categories of ethnic difference to the Hutu-Tutsi opposition at all and have instead spoken of caste-like differences (Hankel, 'Wir möchten, dass ihr uns verzeiht', 141). However, the question of the exact nature of the Hutu-Tutsi cleavage is caught up in the political controversy that is at issue here. While the ruling Tutsi-dominated Rwanda Patriotic Front (RPF) party propagates the constructivist view of ethnic difference (Buckley-Zistel, 'Dividing and Uniting', 108), oppositional Hutu groups propagate a substantialist understanding (see fn. 8). A commitment to either of these views is beyond the aims of this article.
8. This was the position advanced in the Manifeste des Bahutu, 'Note sur l'aspect sociale racial indigène au Rwanda', drafted under the auspices of the leading Hutu party MDR-Parmehutu. For the later relevance of the manifesto to the ban on the MDR, see Commission Parlementaire, *Rapport*, 5.
9. This and the next paragraph rely on DesForges, *Leave None to Tell the Story*, 31–141.
10. Déclaration du Front patriotique rwandais, 2. All translations by PN.
11. Loi fondamentale du 26 mai 1995, Art. 1.
12. Déclaration du Front patriotique rwandais, 2.
13. DesForges, *Leave None to Tell the Story*, 124–6.
14. Reyntjens, 'Constitution-Making in Situations of Extreme Crisis', 237.
15. DesForges, *Leave None to Tell the Story*, 694–7.
16. Kinzer, *A Thousand Hills*, 221.
17. For details, from the point of view of the prosecuted individuals, see Bizimungu, Letter to the President of the Republic, 5 June 2001. No corroboration of the claim of illegality has been found in the Arusha accords or Rwandan party law.
18. International Crisis Group, 'End of Transition in Rwanda', 31; Human Rights Watch, *Preparing for Elections*, 13.
19. Commission Parlementaire, *Rapport*, 1.
20. Human Rights Watch, *Preparing for Elections*, 5.
21. Kimonyo et al., 'Supporting the Post-Genocide Transition in Rwanda', 25.
22. US Department of State, *Country Reports* (2003).
23. Meierhenrich, 'Presidential and Parliamentary Elections in Rwanda', 631.
24. US Department of State, *Country Reports* (2003).
25. Loewenstein, 'Militant Democracy and Fundamental Rights'; cp. the Basic Law of the Federal Republic of Germany, Art. 21, 2.
26. Schmitt, *Legalität und Legitimität*, 33, 37–8.
27. For the international law perspective, see Fox & Nolte, 'Intolerant Democracies'.
28. Rwanda had acceded to the Covenant on 16 April 1975. For democracy-protecting intervention, see Fox & Roth, *Democratic Governance and International Law*.
29. Fox & Nolte, 'Intolerant Democracies', 64–5.
30. It could be argued that the militant democracy justification for party bans is not applicable to the Rwandan bans because Rwanda was not a democracy during the period investigated (July 1994–May 2003; the Transitional Government and Parliament were scheduled for mid-2003). While the premise is true, the conclusion does not hold. The militant democracy justification of party bans is a forward-looking one: it would justify banning presumed anti-democratic actors even under a dictatorship preparing elections. An example of this is Algeria, where a regime of questionable democratic standards banned the presumptively anti-democratic Front Islamique du Salut (FIS). Fox & Nolte, 'Intolerant Democracies', 55, 65.
31. Buckley-Zistel, 'Dividing and Uniting'; see also Kimonyo et al., 'Supporting the Post-Genocide Transition in Rwanda'.

32. It might be claimed that a more substantive concept of militant democracy contains a defence of minority claims, as in its German version, which protects not just free elections, but a 'free democratic basic order'. The narrower concept delineated here concurs with Fox & Nolte, 'Intolerant Democracies', 6, who identify democracies by the recurrence of free elections.
33. Rosenblum, 'Banning Parties', 23.
34. Ibid.
35. See Basedau et al., 'Ethnic Party Bans in Africa'; Janda, *Political Parties and Democracy in Theoretical and Practical Perspectives*; Moroff, 'Party Bans in Africa – An Empirical Overview'.
36. Moroff, 'An Empirical Overview'.
37. Law 28/91 of 18 June 1991.
38. Art. 54 goes on to require parties to 'constantly reflect the unity of the people of Rwanda ... whether in the recruitment of members, putting in place organs of leadership and in their operations and activities'.
39. Human Rights Watch, *Preparing for Elections*, 12; cf. Commission Parlementaire, *Rapport*, 2.
40. Human Rights Watch, *Preparing for Elections*, 2–4.
41. See the evidence collected in Immigration and Refugee Board of Canada, *Rwanda: Legislation Governing Divisionism*.
42. Buckley-Zistel, 'Dividing and Uniting', 110.
43. This is the position of Kinzer, *A Thousand Hills*, a book written in broad solidarity with Paul Kagame's politics.
44. Commission Parlementaire, *Rapport*, 18.
45. International Crisis Group, 'End of Transition in Rwanda', 30, quoting *Jeune Afrique*, 3–9 July 2001.
46. International Crisis Group, 'End of Transition in Rwanda', reads it as a warning. Kimonyo et al., 'Supporting the Post-Genocide Transition in Rwanda', read it as a threat. Kinzer, *A Thousand Hills*, 225, allows both readings.
47. Bizimungu was later convicted and imprisoned under the broad understanding of 'divisionism'; he was pardoned after serving five years of his 15-year sentence in 2007.
48. The leading cases come from Israel and Belgium. See Navot, 'Fighting Terrorism in the Political Arena', 749, and Brems, 'Belgium', 706. Within Africa, one other example is the banning of the Union des Forces Dèmocratiques (UFD-A) in Mauritania in November 2000 for inciting racism and violence; see US State Department, *Country Reports* (2001). Not all of these cases concern incitement by particularistic parties. See also the International Covenant on Civil and Political Rights, which recognizes that 'advocacy of national, racial or religious hatred that constitutes incitement to discrimination, hostility or violence shall be prohibited by law' (Art. 20 (2)).
49. Kinzer, 'Big Gamble in Rwanda'.
50. A possible exception is the non-registration of ADEP-Mizero, which is unfortunately not well documented.
51. Rosenblum characterizes incitement as 'intent to instigate violence', with 'a close connection between speech and action. Incitement is express provocation to a violent or criminal act, *now.*' Rosenblum, 'Banning Parties', 50.
52. Commission Parlementaire, *Rapport*, 18.
53. Immigration and Refugee Board of Canada, *Rwanda: Legislation Governing Divisionism*; quoting an unnamed senior HRW adviser.
54. Reyntjens, 'Rwanda, Ten Years On', 188.
55. Preuß, *Legalität und Pluralismus*, 163–4.
56. Teitel, *Transitional Justice*, 177.

57. See Art. XII of the Transitory and Final Dispositions, and Niesen, 'Anti-Extremism'.
58. Coalition Provisional Order No. 1, De-Ba'athification of Iraqi Society. The ban has since been included into the Iraqi constitution of 2005, Art. 7.
59. In Gambia, the Armed Forces Provisional Ruling Council banned the formerly ruling People's Progressive Party after a *coup d'état* in 1994.
60. Déclaration du Front patriotique rwandais, No. 3.
61. On premeditation and spontaneity, see Mann, *The Dark Side of Democracy*, 472. On the role of the Rwandan state institutions in the perpetration of genocide in general, see Mann, *The Dark Side of Democracy*, 449; Strauss, *The Order of Genocide;* and DesForges, *Leave None to Tell the Story.*
62. See Leggewie & Meier, *Republikschutz*, 308.
63. Niesen, 'Anti-Extremism', Pt. C.
64. Weber, *Die DDR*, 6–7.
65. Through the Forum, 'the RPF ... controls all political life, sanctioning any politician who challenges the government's line or calls for a new, credible alternative'. International Crisis Group, 'End of Transition in Rwanda', 8.
66. The militant democracy focus of most research has obscured this obvious starting point for further comparative work on party bans.
67. Reyntjens, 'Constitution-making in Situations of Extreme Crisis', 238.
68. Commission Parlementaire, *Rapport*, 7.
69. Ibid., 10.
70. Ibid., 16, 15.
71. Ibid., 19.
72. Ibid.
73. Ibid., 15.
74. Ibid., 16.
75. BVerfG 2.1., 70. The argument from 'essential affinity' with the NSDAP was taken up and developed in a later party ban motion of the German parliament, the (unsuccessful) attempt to have the neo-Nazi party Nationaldemokratische Partei Deutschlands (NPD) outlawed in 2001. See the motion drafted by constitutional lawyers Frankenberg & Löwer, *Verbotsantrag*, and the academic and political discussion in Leggewie & Meier, *NPD-Verbot.*
76. Frankenberg & Löwer, *Verbotsantrag.*
77. Ibid.
78. BVerfG 2.1., 68.
79. The allegations were made by the president of the Rwandan constitutional commission, Tito Rutaremara, a politician close to the RPF, in a BBC debate with MDR presidential candidate Faustin Twagiramungu. Human Rights Watch, *Preparing for Elections*, 14.
80. Human Rights Watch, *Preparing for Elections*, 12. See also the references in Immigration and Refugee Board of Canada, *Rwanda.*
81. The former British secretary for international development, Clare Short, made it clear that she supported the ban. Short, 'Webchat'. See also Kimonyo et al., 'Post-Genocide Transition in Rwanda', 18 fn. 25. The author Dr Kimonyo had already participated in the report of the Parliamentary Commission as an expert witness, recommending the dissolution of the MDR (Commission Parlementaire, *Rapport*, 30).
82. See the EU Rapport Final.
83. Kinzer, *A Thousand Hills*, 330. Cp. also Paul, 'Schuld, Strafe und Moral in Ruanda', 59.
84. Reyntjens, 'Rwanda Ten Years On', 199.
85. Again, see Kinzer, *A Thousand Hills.*

86. Meierhenrich, 'Presidential and Parliamentary Elections in Rwanda', 630, 633; Reyntjens, 'Rwanda, Ten Years On', 186.
87. Human Rights Watch, *Preparing for Elections*, 8–9.
88. The application to have a party outlawed now needs to be made by the Senate and adjudicated by the High Court of the Republic, with a possible appeal to the Supreme Court (Art. 54).
89. Party Law 28/91.
90. Commission Parlementaire, *Rapport*, 2; Human Rights Watch, *Preparing for Elections*, 12.
91. Kinzer, 'Big Gamble in Rwanda'.

Notes on contributor

Peter Niesen is Professor of Political Theory and History of Ideas at Technische Universität Darmstadt and a member of the research cluster EXC 243, 'Formation of Normative Orders', at Goethe Universität, Frankfurt. He has worked on limits to political liberty in the political philosophy of the enlightenment (Kant, Bentham) and in twentieth century political thought. He is currently studying bans on former ruling parties in the politics of transition.

Bibliography

Basedau, Matthias, Matthijs Bogaards, Christof Hartmann, and Peter Niesen. 'Ethnic Party Bans In Africa: A Research Agenda'. *German Law Journal* 8, no. 6 (2007): 617–34.
Bizimungu, Pasteur. Letter to the President of the Republic, 5 June 2001. http://grandlacs. net/doc/2037.pdf (accessed 6 July 2008).
Brems, Eva. 'Belgium: The Vlaams Blok Political Party Convicted Indirectly of Racism'. *International Journal of Constitutional Law* 4, no. 4 (2006): 702–11.
Buckley-Zistel, Susanne. 'Dividing and Uniting: The Use of Citizenship Discourses in Conflict and Reconciliation in Rwanda'. *Global Society* 20, no. 1 (2006): 101–13.
BVerfGE (*Entscheidungen des Bundesverfassungsgerichts*). No. 2, Tübingen: Mohr Siebeck, 1952.
Capoccia, Giovanni: *Defending Democracy. Reactions to Extremism in Interwar Europe*, Baltimore: Johns Hopkins UP, 2005.
Coalition Provisional Order No. 1, De-Ba'athification of Iraqi Society. http://www. iraqcoalition.org/regulations/20030516_CPAORD_1_De-Ba_athification_of_Iraqi_ Society_.pdf (accessed 3 February 2010).
Commission Parlementaire. *Rapport de la commission parlementaire sur les problemes du MDR*. MS, Kigali, 17 March 2003. http://www.grandslacs.net/doc/2856.pdf (accessed 6 July 2008).
Déclaration du Front patriotique rwandais relative à la mise en place des institutions du 17 juillet 1994. http://mjp.univ-perp.fr/constit/rw1994.htm (accessed 8 January 2010).
DesForges, Alison. *Leave None to Tell the Story. Genocide in Rwanda*. New York: Human Rights Watch, 1999.
EU Rapport Final: Rwanda Election Presidentiélle 25 Aout 2003/Elections législatives 29 et 30 Septembre. 2 October 2003.
Forst, Rainer, 'Der Grund der Kritik. Zum Begriff der Menschenwürde in sozialen Rechtfertigungsordnungen'. In *Was ist Kritik?* ed. Rahel Jaeggi and Tilo Wesche, 150–64. Frankfurt: Suhrkamp, 2009.
Fox, Gregory H., and Brad R. Roth, eds. *Democratic Governance and International Law*. Cambridge: Cambridge UP, 2001.

Fox, Gregory H., and Georg Nolte. 'Intolerant Democracies'. *Harvard International Law Journal* 36, no. 1 (1995): 1–70.

Frankenberg, Günter, and Wolfgang Löwer, *NPD-Verbotsantrag des Deutschen Bundestages*. MS 2001 (shortened version at http://www.extremismus.com/dox/antrag-bt.htm, accessed 1 February 2008).

Habermas, Jürgen. *Legitimation Crisis*. Cambridge: Polity, 1988 [1973].

Hankel, Gerd. 'Wir möchten, dass ihr uns verzeiht'. In *Nach Kriegen und Diktaturen*, ed. Alfons Kenkmann and Hasko Zimmer, 141–52. Essen: Klartext, 2005.

Human Rights Watch. *Preparing for Elections: Tightening Control in the Name of Unity*. MS 2003. http://hrw.org/backgrounder/africa/rwanda0503bck.pdf (accessed 2 February 2009).

Immigration and Refugee Board of Canada. *Rwanda: Legislation Governing Divisionism and its Impact on Political Parties, the Media, Civil Society and Individuals*. 3 August 2007. http://www.unhcr.org/refworld/docid/474e895a1e.html (accessed 4 February 2010).

International Crisis Group. 'End of Transition in Rwanda: A Necessary Political Liberalisation'. *ICG Africa Report* 53, 13 November 2002. http://www.crisisgroup. org/library/documents/report_archive/A400817_13112002.pdf (accessed 2 February 2009).

Janda, Kenneth. *Political Parties and Democracy in Theoretical and Practical Perspectives. Adopting Party Law*. New York: NDI, 2005.

Kimonyo, Jean-Paul, Noel Twagiramungu, and Christopher Kayumba. 'Supporting the Post-Genocide Transition in Rwanda. The Role of the International Community'. *Clingendael Center Working Paper* 32, December 2004. www.clingendael.nl/ publications/2004/20041200_cru_working_paper_32.pdf (accessed 2 February 2009).

Kinzer, Stephen. 'Big Gamble in Rwanda'. *New York Review of Books* 54, no. 5, 29 March 2007. http://www.nybooks.com/articles/article-preview?article_id=19996 (accessed 2 May 2007).

Kinzer, Stephen. *A Thousand Hills. Rwanda's Rebirth and the Man Who Dreamed It*. Hoboken, NJ: Wiley, 2008.

Leggewie, Claus, and Horst Meier. *Republikschutz. Maßstäbe für die Verteidigung der Demokratie*. Reinbek: Rowohlt, 1995.

Leggewie, Claus, and Horst Meier. *Verbot der NPD oder: mit Rechtsradikalen leben?* Frankfurt: Suhrkamp, 2002.

Loewenstein, Karl. 'Militant Democracy and Fundamental Rights'. *American Political Science Review* 31, no. 2 & 3 (1937), 417–32, 638–58.

Loi fondamentale du 26 mai 1995. http://mjp.univ-perp.fr/constit/rw1995.htm (accessed 8 January 2010).

Manifeste des Bahutu. 'Note sur l'aspect sociale racial indigène au Rwanda'. www. grandlacs.net/doc/0982.pdf (accessed 2 February 2009).

Mann, Michael. *The Dark Side of Democracy. Explaining Ethnic Cleansing*. Cambridge: Cambridge UP, 2005.

Meierhenrich, Jens. 'Presidential and Parliamentary Elections in Rwanda, 2003'. *Electoral Studies* 25, no. 3 (2006) 627–34.

Moroff, Anika. 'Party Bans in Africa – An Empirical Overview'. *Democratization* 17, no. 4 (2010): 618–41.

Navot, Suzie. 'Fighting Terrorism in the Political Arena: The Banning of Political Parties'. *Party Politics* 14, no. 6 (2008): 745–63.

Niesen, Peter. 'Anti-Extremism, Negative Republicanism, Civic Society: Three Paradigms for Banning Political Parties'. *German Law Journal* 3, no. 7 (2002).

Paul, Axel T. 'Schuld, Strafe und Moral in Ruanda'. *Leviathan* 34, no. 1 (2006): 30–60.

Preuß, Ulrich K. *Legalität und Pluralismus*. Frankfurt: Fischer, 1973.

Reyntjens, Filip. 'Constitution-Making in Situations of Extreme Crisis: The Case of Rwanda and Burundi'. *Journal of African Law* 40, No. 2 (1996): 234–42.

Reyntjens, Filip. 'Rwanda, Ten Years on: From Genocide to Dictatorship'. *African Affairs* 103, no. 411 (2004): 177–210.

Rosenblum, Nancy L. 'Banning Parties: Religious and Ethnic Partisanship in Multicultural Democracies'. *Journal of Law & Ethics of Human Rights* 1, no. 1 (2007): 17–75.

Schmitt, Carl. *Legalität und Legitimität*. Berlin: Duncker & Humblot, 1993 [1932].

Short, Clare. 'Webchat'. *BBC 4 Today Programme International Report*, 3 July 2003. http://www.bbc.co.uk/radio4/today/reports/international/rwandawebchat_20030703.shtml (accessed 2 February, 2009).

Strauss, Scott. *The Order of Genocide. Race, Power, and War in Rwanda*. Syracuse: Cornell UP, 2006.

Teitel, Ruti. *Transitional Justice*. Oxford & New York: OUP, 2000.

Thiel, Markus, ed. *The 'Militant Democracy' Principle in Modern Democracies*. Farnham, Surrey: Ashgate, 2009.

US Department of State. *Country Reports on Human Rights Practices*, 2001–2003. Released by the Bureau of Democracy, Human Rights, and Labor, 2002–2004.

Weber, Hermann. *Die DDR 1945–1990*. München: Oldenbourg, 2006.

Ethnic party bans and institutional engineering in Nigeria

Matthijs Bogaards

School of Humanities and Social Sciences, Jacobs University Bremen, Bremen, Germany

Nigeria is the African country that implemented ethnic party bans most systematically. At different points in time, a total of at least 64 parties has been denied registration for failing to demonstrate 'national presence'. Nigeria is also the African country with the longest record in institutional engineering. Ethnic party bans are one instrument in a broader repertoire of incentives for the creation of national parties that transcend the manifold socio-cultural differences. This article provides an overview of the often highly innovative ways in which successive Nigerian leaders, especially military, have sought to control the political organization of ethnicity in the process of democratization.

Introduction

While most African constitutions contain a ban on ethnic parties, only a minority have implemented these bans.[1] Nigeria is the country in sub-Saharan Africa that enforced its ethnic party ban most rigorously. Between 1989 and 2002, electoral commissions denied registration to no less than 64 parties for failing to establish a national presence. This record makes Nigeria a particularly interesting case to analyse in this special issue on ethnic party bans in Africa. A second reason why Nigeria merits closer attention is that ethnic party bans in Africa's most populous country have been part of a broader menu of institutional innovation, thereby constituting a veritable laboratory for the analysis of political engineering for ethnic conflict management. Several of these institutional innovations have since been adopted elsewhere, such as spatial distribution requirements for presidential elections and party organizations.[2] This article embeds the analysis of ethnic party bans in a comprehensive overview of the ways in which a succession of Nigerian leaders, both military and civilian, have sought to create a national party system that would transcend regional, religious, linguistic, and ethnic differences.

The starting point is the conceptualization of parties and the party system as an intermediary between society and politics. In a heterogeneous society, in which people differ from each other in language, religion, colour of skin, or other socio-cultural attributes, parties can perform three functions. Parties can articulate or *translate* socio-cultural divisions by organizing as, for example, ethnic, religious, or regional parties. Parties can *aggregate* differences that exist in society by organizing as multi-ethnic or cross-regional parties that bridge at least some divisions. Finally, parties can organize on another basis, such as ideology and thereby *block* the political organization of socio-cultural issues. In designing the electoral system and regulating political parties, policy makers should be clear about the desired role of political parties and the function of the party system. The choice is between interventions that promote the functions of articulation, aggregation, or blocking.[3]

At one time or another, Nigeria has tried all three of the main approaches. Moreover, it has done so through intriguing combinations. The main instrument for blocking has been the ethnic party ban introduced in the 1979 constitution, 'characterized by a vigorous determination to curb and control the potential of ethnicity as a force of national disintegration'.[4] The first parties were only denied registration in the 1980s, after the electoral commission started to implement strict requirements for 'national presence'. Because these criteria constituted a set of incentives for building national parties, not simply a prohibition of ethnic parties, they are best viewed as a 'positive' ethnic ban aimed at aggregation rather than blocking.[5] Other arrangements to promote aggregation were the distribution requirements for presidential elections and local elections. Since 1979, the successful contestant of presidential elections in Nigeria has to win not just an overall majority, but also a minimum percentage of the vote in a minimum number of states to ensure the winning candidate has national support. In 1998, distribution requirements for local elections were used to decide which parties would win permanent registration. It is more difficult to detect traces of translation in Nigeria. Translation is associated with consociational democracy, a type of democracy that secures political stability and social harmony in divided societies through elite collaboration in the government, autonomy for the constituent groups, a mutual veto to protect vital interests, and a proportional division of spoils and offices.[6] The key to consociational interpretations is the so-called 'federal character' principle that was included in the 1979 constitution. According to the federal character principle, government and administration at all levels should reflect the composition of the nation. However, whether this requirement was meant to promote translation or rather aggregation is controversial. The only clear evidence of translation comes in the form of a rotation of the highest offices among the main regions, especially the Muslim north and the mostly Christian south. Rotation has been an informal practice since the 1970s, but an attempt to write it into the constitution in the mid-1990s failed.

All this makes Nigeria a fascinating case of institutional engineering, which allows us to understand ethnic party bans in the context of the broader menu of institutional design. The sections below examine the Nigerian experience with the main party system functions of blocking, aggregation, and translation, respectively. Each section is organized in a rough chronological order. The conclusion summarizes the experience with the various institutions that have been introduced by successive regimes and rulers to deal with Nigeria's diversity, highlighting the synergies and contradictions, and offering a tentative evaluation of their effectiveness.

Blocking in Nigeria: ethnic party bans

After the breakdown of Nigeria's First Republic in 1966, the internecine power struggle between a small number of powerful federal units and their political parties, was identified as the main problem and the 1979 Constitution of the Second Republic sought to provide a remedy. The three, later four, regions that made up Nigeria during the First Republic were broken up into 12, then 19 states. The three main national groups – Yoruba in the Southwest, Igbo in the southeast, and the Hausa-Fulani in the north – were thus dispersed over various states. In addition, several minority groups obtained their 'own' state.[7] The number of states has continued to rise and now stands at 36. At the same time, the powers of the states have declined, reaching their lowest level during periods of military rule (1967–1978; 1984–1998).[8]

The then head of state, General Murtula Muhammed, instructed the Constitution Drafting Committee in 1975 to seek ways to build 'genuine and truly national parties'.[9] In the section entitled 'Fundamental Objectives and Directive Principles of State Polity' of the 1979 Constitution, one reads it is 'the duty of the State to... promote or encourage the formation of associations that cut across ethnic, linguistic, religious, or other sectional barriers'. The Constitution contained four clauses that aim to create national parties. Article 202(b) stipulated that for an association to function as a party, 'the membership of the association is open to every citizen of Nigeria irrespective of his place of origin, circumstance of birth, sex, religion or ethnic grouping'. Article 202(e) required that 'the name of the association, its symbol or logo does not contain any ethnic or religious connotation or give the appearance that the activities of the association are confined to a part only of the geographical area of Nigeria'. Article 203/1(b) demanded that the constitution and rules of the party 'ensure that the members of the executive committee or other governing body of the political party reflect the federal character of Nigeria'. Article 203/2(b), finally, specified that the executive committee or other governing body can be said to reflect the federal character 'only if the members thereof belong to different States not being less in number than two-thirds of all the States comprising the Federation'.

Already prior to the adoption of the new constitution, the Federal Military Government issued Electoral (Amendment) Degree No. 32 of 1978 requiring a party to demonstrate 'that it had established branch offices where officers had been elected or appointed to handle its affairs in at least two-thirds of the states' and that 'it could there present a political platform effectively in the local-government areas'.[10] It was up to the Federal Electoral Commission to verify whether these requirements had been met by the 19 associations that sought to register as parties in the run-up to the 1979 elections. The deadline for applications was 18 December 1978. Four days later, the electoral commission announced that only five had been successful. Clearly, there had been no time for the electoral commission to visit local government areas to check whether parties had indeed established local party organizations that were, moreover, able to 'effectively present' their platforms.[11] Quite likely, 'at the time of registration of parties none of the political associations could be said to have met the requirements of registration'.[12] The five parties that won registration were all headed by 'communal champions' linked to the politics of the First Republic.[13] There is thus no evidence that the requirement of national presence played a decisive role in the decision to register or not register a party.

The Second Republic was terminated in 1983 by a military coup. The next round of party registrations took place in 1989, when the ban on parties was lifted by head of state General Babangida as part of a democratization process for the Third Republic. The National Electoral Commission produced a 96-page report detailing its criteria for registration and providing scores for the 13 parties seeking registration.[14] Scores were added up according to a weighting formula: number (25%) and geographical spread (25%) of party membership; number (15%) and geographical spread (15%) of the party's administrative organization; and articulation of the issues in the party manifesto (20%). The criteria pertaining to party membership and organization are said to be 'objective in the sense that claims made by each political association in respect of the conditions and requirements in question can be empirically verified and quantified'.[15] The report then explains in great detail how scores were calculated for each of the parties for each of the five items. It claims that '3,000 researchers were involved nationwide in the verification exercise'.[16] The outcome is a ranking in which the first-ranked party, the Peoples' Solidarity Party, scored 43.90 out of 100. Parties evidenced most difficulties in demonstrating national membership. The National Electoral Commission recommended granting the first six parties registration, even though the sixth party only scored 17.70 out of 100. The military regime rejected all for failing to pass the mark of 50% and then created two new parties, the National Republican Convention and the Social Democratic Party, by itself. This decision might have been facilitated by the very critical conclusions in the report about the state of the parties, noting that 'all of the associations performed poorly. They made exaggerated claims about their membership size and organizational strength ... Most associations are poorly organized at all levels of government in spite of the obvious evidence of window dressing. ... Virtually all the associations derive their roots from the politics of the First and Second Republics, in varying degrees'.[17] The registration process of 1989 and the 'scientific survey' carried out by the National Electoral Commission to verify parties' claims is surely the most thorough attempt at enforcing the criteria for national parties competing on national issues in Nigeria and quite possibly in Africa.[18] Whether seven or 13 parties were denied registration for failing to demonstrate national presence depends on whether one looks at the recommendation of the National Electoral Commission or the final verdict of the head of government, General Babangida.

The next attempt at multiparty politics came in 1996. As part of the timetable for a return to democracy under General Sani Abacha, parties were invited to register after the 'no-party' local elections in March. They had to face stringent requirements. They were to have at least 40,000 members in all 31 states and no less than 14,000 in the capital territory of Abuja. In addition, parties had to establish offices in all states plus the capital down to the 690 local government councils and most of the country's 7,000 electoral wards.[19] Apparently, the National Electoral Commission (NECON) 'specified even the type of furniture and number of employees in each party office'.[20] Eighteen parties tried to register and all but five failed to satisfy the requirements. How those five managed to, among other things, recruit more than a million card-carrying members in a couple of months is not clear. The government produced a score card recording the extent to which parties fulfilled the requirements. According to the chairman of the National Electoral Commission, 'not less than 50% of the conditions is regarded as the basic qualification for registration'.[21] This narrowly excluded three parties that each achieved between 48.65% and 49.28%.[22] How these scores were calculated is not clear. In the end it appears preference was given to parties favourable to the military dictatorship, fuelling suspicion about the commitment of Abacha to democracy. The five parties legalized in 1996 were dissolved in 1998 under General Abdusalam Abubakar, who headed the transitional government after the sudden death of Abacha.[23]

Abubakar embarked upon a new democratization process. Parties could register in preparation for the 1998 local elections. Twenty-six parties applied and nine were successful.[24] It appears that the 17 parties which failed to obtain registration by the Independent National Electoral Commission stumbled over a requirement to demonstrate national presence.[25] The 1998 guidelines, as those of 1978, required parties to have 'functional branches' in at least 24 out of the 36 states.[26] As explained below, the nine parties registered in 1998 only earned the right to compete in local elections.[27] Depending on their performance in these elections, they could acquire permanent registration.[28] In the end, only three succeeded. These were the parties that contested the presidential and parliamentary elections of 1999 which marked the return to democracy. The 1999 constitution currently in force is closely modelled on the 1979 constitution and contains the exact same clauses on parties.[29]

In the run up to the 2003 parliamentary and presidential elections, many new parties sought registration. At one point, it seemed that no new parties were allowed to register under the new electoral law, but this clause was removed.[30] The Independent Electoral Commission (INEC), as in 1998, demanded the establishment of offices in at least 24 states of the federation and evidence of occupation of office accommodations in 24 states of the federation and a national headquarter in Abuja.[31] Under these rules, only three new parties were registered. Twenty-one parties were denied registration for failing to demonstrate national presence.[32] However, these guidelines, which cannot be found in the constitution but were adopted by successive electoral commissions, were criticized as 'draconian' and an infringement on the right of freedom of association.[33] In November 2002, the Supreme Court invalidated these additional requirements upon the appeal of five parties that had been denied registration on the grounds of insufficient national organizational presence (SC.228/2002).[34] As Obeagu notes, 'INEC has no power to make stringent guidelines, outside the Constitution, that will shut the door on associations seeking to be registered as political parties'.[35] This conclusion was corroborated in January 2003 when the Supreme Court made public the reasons behind its ruling. Since then, no party has been denied registration for failing to demonstrate national presence.

In the light of the experience of party registration under Generals Babangida and Abacha, it is no wonder that the whole notion of party registration became highly controversial. Agbese complains that the military, by imposing impossible conditions encouraged corruption and fraudulent practices, subverted democracy, weakened parties, and delegitimized them in the eyes of the voters, sustaining 'the myth that the military is a corrective institution determined to lay down rigid conditions for the establishment of a viable democracy'.[36] The Nigerian experience confirms the relationship between authoritarian regimes and the implementation of ethnic party bans also observed in other contributions to this special issue. At four points in time the electoral commission enforced the requirement for national parties first introduced in the 1979 constitution: in 1989 under General Babangida, in 1996 under General Abacha, in 1998 under General Abubakar, and in 2002 under President Obasanjo. Tellingly, the last attempt failed as the decision of the electoral commission was overturned by the Supreme Court. For the country's highest judicial body to exhibit such an independent stance would have been unthinkable under the previous military dictatorships.

Aggregation in Nigeria: distribution requirements

Since the Second Republic, the promotion of crosscutting cleavages has been most pronounced in the new rules for the election of the national president. In order to win, a presidential candidate not only has to win a majority of the vote nationally, but also a quarter of the vote in at least two-thirds of the states. Horowitz presents this as an example of successful 'vote pooling' whereby candidates are encouraged to reach out beyond their own community to attract votes.[37] Distribution requirements have the disadvantage of potential indecisiveness, when no candidate fulfils the requirements. This happened in 1979 and a constitutional crisis was only narrowly avoided through an imaginative interpretation of the rules by the electoral commission, upheld by the Supreme Court.[38] This incident highlights the need for 'a reliable back-up formula'.[39] If no candidate musters the required geographical spread of the vote, an electoral college composed of all federal and state legislators chooses the president.

The most radical case of party system design is undoubtedly Nigeria's abortive Third Republic. In 1987 the military regime embarked upon a five-year plan for a return to democracy. A two-party system was written into the Constitution and parties were invited to register, following strict guidelines. As we saw, none qualified and the military government decided to create two parties: the Social Democratic Party (SDP) and the National Republican Convention (NRC). The party programmes and statutes were drafted by the government. The SDP was designed to be a 'little bit to the left' and the NRC 'a little bit to the right'.[40] The two-party system was thought to offer the best chances for democratic legitimacy, political stability, and effective government.

The 1989 Constitution retained distribution requirements for the presidential elections. Chief Abiola of the SDP won the 1993 presidential elections with an estimated 58.4% of the vote. Chief Abiola's support dropped below one-third in only two of the then 30 states. His opponent, Alhaji Bashir Othman, also satisfied the requirements of geographical spread. In the view of a commentator, 'though the North-South regional divide did not totally disappear, the two-party system weakened the tie between ethnic/regional affiliation and political parties. For the first time, Nigerians had no options but to vote in significant numbers for candidates and parties that were not strongly affiliated with their ethnic groups'.[41] Unwilling to surrender power, the military dictatorship annulled the outcome of the elections, breaking off the transition to democracy.

In the subsequent round of constitutional innovation, the military government under General Abubakar decided that parties must gain a least 10% of the vote in 24 of 36 states in order to qualify for permanent registration after the December 1998 local government elections. Many politicians from the parties that had registered after the liberalization of 1998 criticized this rule and the Independent National Electoral Commission (INEC) later relaxed the threshold to 5%. Only three parties received permanent registration: the People's Democratic Party (PDP), the All People's Party (APP) – currently known as All Nigeria People's Party (ANPP) – and the Alliance for Democracy (AD).[42] The AD, whose support is restricted to the Yoruba South West, won more than 5% of the vote in only 13 of the 36 states in the local government elections of 1998, but was still allowed to participate in subsequent elections.[43] General Obasanjo, running for the PDP won the 1999 presidential elections, acquiring more than a quarter of the vote in no less than 32 of the 36 states.[44]

The extension of distribution requirements to local elections is innovative, but problematic. It seems contradictory to have parties prove their national character in local government elections. More importantly, after parties have obtained permanent registration there is no further incentive for moderation and cross-ethnic appeal. Making continued party registration dependent on future election results is not an attractive alternative, as this may lead to major disruptions of the party system when existing parties slip under the threshold and have to disband.[45]

Before the 2002 Supreme Court decision at least, the distribution requirement for party registration corresponded with distribution requirements in presidential elections, a good example of what Reynolds calls 'institutional alignment' or institutions that work in concert.[46] Still, Diamond suggests 'there is room for further innovation – for example, to find means of electing the National Assembly (perhaps especially the Senate) that generate the kind of transethnic political appeals and constituencies that are fashioned in presidential elections'.[47] One suggestion is to elect deputies in the House of Representatives through constituency pooling.[48] For that purpose, the country could be divided into a moderate number of regions or zones. The idea of 'zones' is not new and has been part of reform debates in Nigeria for a long time.[49] Following the draft 1995 constitution, the country could be divided into six zones. Each zone would be further divided into electoral districts. Candidates would have to run simultaneously in six districts: one from each zone. To decide the winner, the votes from all six zones would be added, making sure that the winning candidate had support from all over the country. How precisely constituencies are pooled is not decisive, as long as they are of roughly equal size, with a fair mix of urban and rural localities.[50] Constituency pooling for parliamentary elections in Nigeria would be the logical next step in the country's attempt to create parties that transcend ethnic, religious, and regional cleavages. Constituency pooling fits with the strong tradition of constituency representation in Africa and can be used with the electoral system of first-past-the-post, which 'is deeply embedded in the Nigerian political culture'.[51] It is said that distribution requirements require a relatively high level of party institutionalization.[52] This is even more true for constituency pooling, as only well-organized parties would be able to coordinate the cross-country election campaigns of its candidates.

Translation in Nigeria: the federal character principle and rotation

Translation or the political articulation of socio-cultural differences can be achieved through a variety of mechanisms, most prominently the electoral system of proportional representation.[53] Translation is often combined with consociationalism, a particular package of formal or informal rules for power sharing. These are a grand coalition of segmental leaders in the executive, proportional representation and allocation of resources and offices, segmental autonomy, and a mutual veto.[54] Advocacy for proportional representation in Nigeria is rare,[55] but there is a surprisingly large literature on consociationalism in Nigeria. Lijphart himself reviews the experience of the Nigerian First Republic (1960–1966) in light of first Apter's conception of consociationalism and then his own.[56] He notes how the grand coalition with parties representing all three regions that prepared the way for independence in 1960 was never repeated; how the delaying powers of the Senate, composed of an equal number of representatives of the three regions, did not amount to a proper veto power and how federalism was lopsided, thereby aggravating political tensions.[57] His cautious conclusion is that 'the chances for the survival of democracy in Nigeria might have been better if a consociational pattern had been adopted'.[58]

For Lijphart, the strongest claim to consociational status of Nigeria was its federal system, which initially left much power to the states.[59] However, it failed to provide for segmental autonomy because the original three states did not correspond to ethnic boundaries and smaller groups did not get their own states. While the number of states has since increased, the powers of the states have declined and there is still an imperfect correspondence between ethnic boundaries and state boundaries, with the implication that any allocation based on the states would be imperfectly proportional from an ethnic point of view.[60] Moreover, the current system discriminates against internal migrants and has failed to break through the domination of majority group elites.[61]

Williams identifies several consociational features in the Second Republic (1979–1983). In his view, the requirement in the 1979 Constitution (section 135(3)) that the president in choosing a cabinet 'appoint at least one minister from each State, who shall be an indigene of such a State' led to an 'ethnic grand coalition'.[62] However, in terms of parties, this was still a coalition of the North and the East with the main party of the West, the United Party of Nigeria (UPN), excluded. The ever increasing size of cabinets in Nigeria has made it easier to accommodate diversity, a longstanding concern.[63] Proportionality in resource allocation and representation was at least partially satisfied by the federal character principle. Proportionality is also visible in the application of the federal character principle to political parties and appointments.[64] Segmental autonomy, despite 'impressive guarantees' in the constitution for state power, was weak in practice due to financial constraints, with 90% of the state budget coming from the federal government.[65] A mutual veto was absent, although Jinadu interprets the double plurality requirement in presidential elections as a 'mild form of the mutual veto'.[66] Views on the Second Republic differ. For some, 'the Second Republic was pronouncedly consociational',[67] while for others it 'never embodied more than superficial elements of consociationalism'.[68]

Agreement exists that the key consociational element in Nigerian politics has been the federal character.[69] Article 14(3) of the 1979 Constitution stipulated that 'the composition of the government of the federation or any of its agencies and the conduct of its affairs shall be carried out in such manner as to reflect the Federal Character of Nigeria and the need to promote national unity, and also to command national loyalty thereby ensuring that there shall be no predominance of persons from a few states or a few ethnic or other sectional groups in the government or any of its agencies'. Is the federal character principle, described as 'the soul of the 1979 Nigerian constitution', a consociational principle, promoting translation, or an aggregative measure, promoting integration?[70] The background, nature, and impact of the federal character principle are contested.[71] This goes back to the contradictions inherent in the principle itself which have been exposed in commentary and the problem that in spite of 'extensive regulations and provisions, the federal character principle has remained a profoundly nebulous and contentious concept'.[72] Ayoade views the adoption of the federal character principle by the Constitution Drafting Committee in 1979 as another victory for the North, allowing it to further strengthen its presence in government and bureaucracy, after having gained the political upper hand through the steady increase of its share of the states in the federation.[73] Concerns have been voiced that 'although the federal character principle was intended to promote national integration, its politics have proved to be extremely divisive in regional, ethnic, and religious terms',[74] that it revolves around the distribution rather than the generation of wealth, and that it undermines standards and professionalism.[75]

Although designed to ensure a proportional representation of ethnic groups within parties and the federal government through the proxy of states, there are reasons to doubt that these aims were achieved and that the result amounted to the consociational principles of proportionality and a grand coalition of segmental leaders. First, states cannot be equated with the socio-political entities that make up Nigerian society, thereby providing an inadequate mode of representation.[76] At the same time, the shift of loyalties from ethnic groups or regions towards the states counts as aggregation.[77] In classic consociationalism, socio-cultural diversity is translated through political parties. But since the electoral law provides incentives for national parties and the constitution bans ethnic parties, Nigeria's diversity is channelled politically through the federal system. This is bound to be incomplete and to a certain extent arbitrary, no matter how many states are recognized. Second, the federal character does not specify how 'representatives' are selected. This problem already plagued cabinet formation in the First Republic, when 'it was the Head of the Federal Government who solely exercised the right of who to include in his cabinet from each of the parties'.[78] The paradox is thus that while the federal character principle 'makes for weak national leadership, since leaders are seen first as ethnic and regional elites' it also fails to ensure the election of the segmental leaders stipulated by consociational theory.[79]

The 1995 draft constitution was said to have an 'underlying consociational logic' because of the principle of rotation and the idea of proportional representation of parties in the cabinet.[80] Already in the Second Republic, the top positions within the main parties at both the federal and the state level were divided among recognized groups according to an allocation formula.[81] In the build up to the abortive Third Republic and again during the Constitutional Conference of 1994–1995, more extensive use of the principle of rotation was discussed.[82] The recommendation of the Constitutional Conference to have the presidency rotate between the North and South was modified by the Abacha government to a proposal whereby the offices of the president, vice-president, prime minister, vice-prime minister, president of the Senate, and speaker of the House of Representatives would rotate among six newly created geographical zones.[83] These are the Northwest, Northeast, Middle Belt, Southeast, South-South, and Southwest.[84] In the end, the 1995 draft constitution provided for rotation of offices at all levels of government, from the president to the governor and even the chairman of the Local Government Councils. In addition, article 229(5) required political parties to reflect the principle of rotation in their constitution. In 1998, the guidelines of the Independent National Electoral Commission in article 6(a) required of a party 'evidence of its resolution to confirm with the principle of Power Sharing and Rotation of Key Political Offices'.[85] None of these innovations made it into the 1999 Constitution, which merely repeated the requirement that each state be represented with at least one indigene in the cabinet.[86]

Several scholars have claimed consociational democracy as indispensable for a democratic and peaceful future of Nigeria.[87] Joseph, after a critical review of the consociational literature, nonetheless admits that for Nigeria 'it has been apparent that some combination of consociational devices will have to be introduced if the country is ever to develop a recognizably democratic system of government and politics'.[88] Adekanye concurs, but adds that power-sharing is bound to be different and more difficult in conditions of poverty and inequality and after violent conflict has occurred.[89] Consociationalism is often criticized for treating the symptoms rather than the root causes, using ethnic groups as building blocks rather than breaking down existing barriers. For Nigeria and African states at large, Williams turns this into an advantage, arguing that an approach which does not necessitate changes in the existing fabric of society and which does not rely on integration, is more feasible.[90] The desirability of consociationalism, however, says nothing about the chances of its adoption. The favourable factors for consociational democracy are largely absent in Nigeria: Nigeria has a large population and its many ethnic groups are unequal in size and economic resources; there is no external threat than can induce national solidarity and the presence of an overarching loyalty to the Nigerian nation is doubtful; ethnic groups are not completely geographically concentrated; and a history of compromise and accommodation is sorely lacking.[91] An unfavourable context for consociationalism is not an insurmountable obstacle, as everything ultimately depends on the political will of the elites, but precisely this political will has been found wanting.[92] As Onyeoziri notes, there is little point in identifying formal elements of consociationalism when elite behaviour is adversarial, uncompromising, impatient, and follows a winner-take-all strategy, thereby negating both the spirit and practice of accommodation.[93]

Conclusion

Institutional design in Nigeria has been a process of trial and error, but 'after decades of political experimentation, the country has established norms that include competitive federalism, ethnic rotation, and power sharing', observe Joseph and Kew.[94] In the process, a variety of approaches have been experimented with. Situating Nigerian constitutional engineering in-between the 'integrationist' prescriptions of scholars such as Horowitz and Reilly and the 'accommodationist' recommendations of Lijphart, Ejobowah classifies the 1979 constitution as mainly integrationist in contrast to the more accommodationist 1995 draft constitution.[95] However, the main lesson from Nigeria's recent political history is that 'these strategies are not mutually exclusive'.[96]

In our terminology, political engineering in Nigeria has combined blocking, aggregation, and translation. Blocking occurred in the form of a ban on ethnic parties first included in the 1979 constitution. Aggregation occurred in the form of distribution requirements for presidential elections, local elections, and party organizations. Translation occurred in the form of the constitutional requirement that each state is represented with one minister in the federal cabinet. To complicate matters even further, the 'federal character' principle combines elements of aggregation (the requirement of national parties) with that of translation (proportional allocation of offices and resources), and even blocking (because it rules out mono-ethnic parties). This has led many scholars to detect elements of consociationalism in Nigeria, especially since the Second Republic. However, as Table 1 shows, most efforts have focused on aggregation.

The Nigerian case has helped to demonstrate the importance of a conceptual distinction between what for lack of a better term can be called 'negative' versus 'positive' ethnic party bans. Negative party bans simply aim to remove ethnicity from politics. Positive party bans provide incentives for parties to organize across communal boundaries. In Horowitz's framework, negative ethnic party bans correspond to the illusion of a 'non-ethnic' society, whereas positive ethnic party bans provide stimuli similar to vote pooling.[97] Nigeria has had both types of ethnic party bans. Since 1979, the constitution has contained a mainly negative party ban, with the application of the federal character principle to the composition of party leadership as a positive element. More important was the requirement of national presence in terms of offices and officers imposed by the military government even prior to the adoption of the 1979 Constitution. All 64 denials of registration between 1989 and 2002 were based on the guidelines of the respective electoral commissions, guidelines that went much further than the constitution demanded. These distribution requirements for party organization constitute an example of what we call a positive ethnic party ban. Still, only military rulers in the end had the power to enforce these guidelines. Perhaps distribution requirements would be less controversial if instead of following the command and

Table 1. Institutional engineering of the party system in Nigeria.

Measure	Blocking	Aggregation	Translation	Period
Ethnic party ban	X	–	–	Since 1979
Distribution requirement for presidential elections	–	X	–	Since 1979
Distribution requirement for local elections	–	X	–	1998
Distribution requirement for party organizations	–	X	–	1978–2002
Mandatory two-party system	–	X	–	1987–1993
Federal character	–	X	–	Since 1979
Rotation	–	–	X	1995–1998

Source: Own compilation.

control style typical for party regulation, parties would receive benefits in case they satisfied the regulations, for example in the form of state subsidies.[98]

Successive military leaders have invested much time, effort, and ingenuity in creating national parties. This is probably the best evidence that political parties do matter in Nigeria. Nigeria's current party system has been shaped decisively by the institutional engineering of previous regimes, especially military. Party regulation in Nigeria has contributed to a concentration of the party system and has reinforced the tendency towards national parties emanating from the constitution and the electoral law. The three parties that contested the transition elections of 1999 were the same three parties that managed to register in 1998 and subsequently demonstrated their national electoral support in the local elections. In this way, Abubakar's legacy can still be detected.

After the Supreme Court in 2002 invalidated the organizational distribution requirement adopted by the electoral commission, no parties have been denied registration for failing to demonstrate national presence. The result is a record number of registered parties, 59 at the last count.[99] It is testimony to the progress made since the Second Republic that the recent discussion about party (de-)registration concerns the number of parties, not their ethnic character or national presence.

Since 1999, the People's Democratic Party (PDP) has been in power at the national level. Its presidential candidates have convincingly demonstrated national appeal. The three consecutive victories make it a dominant party according to Sartori's definition.[100] Sadly, this dominance has been established and deepened through increasingly dubious means. While the outcomes of the 2003 elections could still be qualified as 'hardly credible, but acceptable',[101] the 2007 elections 'were marred by extraordinary displays of rigging and the intimidation of voters in many areas'.[102] On the positive side, Suberu notes the 2007 elections were 'happily well-insulated from Nigeria's combustible internal divisions'.[103] The informal rotation among the leading presidential candidates, this time coming from the North instead of the South, helped to prevent the politicization of this divide in the 2007 elections. The PDP is 'impressively multiregional' at the national level but at the same time 'remains a fractious and ideologically inarticulate congeries of politicians whose great common enterprise is the doling out of patronage along ethnographical lines'.[104] With regular intervals violent clashes between Muslims and Christians make the headlines as does the ongoing controversy about the adoption of the Sharia by 12 northern, predominantly Muslim, states and the armed rebellion in the oil-producing Niger delta.[105] While institutional engineering has thus contributed to a national party system, it has not eradicated ethnic violence or transformed the underlying dynamics of patronage politics.[106]

Acknowledgements

A previous version of this paper was presented at the workshop on Democratization and Ethnic Communities: Conflict, Protection, and Accomodation at the Munk Centre for

International Studies, University of Toronto, April 2009. The author wishes to thank the participants for their helpful comments!

Notes

1. Moroff, 'Party Bans in Africa', this issue. Consistent with other contributions to this special issue, the term 'ethnic' is used in the broad sense to refer to any socio-cultural difference.
2. Bogaards, 'Comparative Strategies'.
3. Bogaards, 'Electoral Systems and the Management of Ethnic Conflict in the Balkans'; Bogaards, 'Electoral Systems, Party Systems and Ethnic Conflict Management in Africa'; Bogaards, 'Comparative Strategies'. These functions resemble the three models of coping with ethnicity in conflicts identified by Azarya: avoidance, acceptance, and prevention. He uses Nigeria as an example of prevention. Azarya, 'Ethnicity and Conflict Management'.
4. Kirk-Greene, 'Ethnic Engineering', 461.
5. See Moroff, 'Party Bans in Africa', and Moroff and Basedau, 'An Effective Measure of Institutional Engineering?', both this issue.
6. Lijphart, *Democracy in Plural Societies*.
7. These include the Middle Belt, Ilorin-Kabba, Kanuri, Ibibio-Annang, Efik, and Ijaw minorities. See Suberu, *Federalism and Ethnic Conflict*, 82–94.
8. Paden, 'Unity with Diversity'.
9. Omoruyi, 'Federal Character', 190.
10. Koehn, 'Competitive Transition', 412.
11. Omoruyi, 'Federal Character', 197.
12. Ibid., 198.
13. Ibid., 197.
14. National Electoral Commission, 'Report and Recommendations'.
15. Ibid., 5.
16. Ibid.
17. Ibid., 15.
18. Aina, 'Party and Electoral Politics', 89.
19. Economist Intelligence Unit, *Country Report Nigeria, 3rd Quarter 1996*.
20. Agbese, 'Party Registration', 64.
21. Economist Intelligence Unit, *Country Report Nigeria, 4th Quarter 1996*, 11.
22. Aina, 'Party and Electoral Politics', 90.
23. Economist Intelligence Unit, *Country Report Nigeria, 4th Quarter 1998*.
24. Ibid.
25. Bergstresser, 'Nigeria', 140.
26. Obiyan, 'Political Parties', 42.
27. The second change is an additional requirement for 'rotation of offices' within the party and is discussed below in the section on translation.
28. This is described in more detail below in the section on aggregation
29. Ejobowah, 'Constitutional Design'; Bah, *Breakdown and Reconstitution*. The respective clauses in the 1999 constitution can be found in articles 222(b) and (e), 223/1(b), and 223/2(b).
30. Economist Intelligence Unit, *Nigeria at a Glance*.
31. Article 3(e) of the INEC Guidelines for the Registration of Political Parties requires parties to submit 'a register showing the names, residential addresses of persons in at least 24 states of the federation and FCT who are members of the association. Article 3(h) demands 'the address of its headquarters office at Abuja and the addresses of its

offices, list of its staff, list of its operational equipment and furniture [sic] in at least 24 states of the federation'.

32. See the US Department of State country report on Nigeria for 2002 at: http://www. state.gov/g/drl/rls/hrrpt/2002/18220.htm.

33. Oluyerni-Kusa, 'Electoral Reform'; Citizens' Forum for Constitutional Reform, *The Position of the Citizens' Forum*.

34. *Vanguard* (Lagos), 11 November 2002.

35. Obeagu, 'Supreme Court Verdict'.

36. Agbese, 'Party Registration', 65.

37. Horowitz, *Ethnic Groups in Conflict*, 635–38.

38. Dudley, *An Introduction to Nigerian Government*, 169–78.

39. Horowitz, *A Democratic South Africa?*, 184.

40. Akinola, 'Manufacturing the Two-Party System'.

41. Bah, *Breakdown and Reconstitution*, 122.

42. Nwosu, 'Nigerian Local Government Elections'.

43. Economist Intelligence Unit, *Country Report Nigeria, 1st Quarter 1999*.

44. The idea to make party registration dependent on electoral performance has resurfaced recently in discussions about the deregistration of 'under-performing' parties with less than 2.5% of the seats in the Nigerian parliament. The ostensible aim is to reduce fragmentation of the party landscape. The controversial proposal was made by a presidential committee composed of the four main parties. See Ohuegbe, 'Committee Recommends De-Registration'; Okoronkwo, 'Politicians' Huge Debate Over De-Registration'.

45. Bogaards, 'Electoral Systems, Party Systems, and Ethnic Conflict Management in Africa'.

46. Reynolds, 'Building Democracy After Conflict', 60.

47. Diamond, 'Nigeria: The Uncivic Society', 474.

48. Bogaards, 'Electoral Choices for Divided Societies'.

49. See below.

50. Bogaards, 'Electoral Choices for Divided Societies'.

51. Barkan, 'Elections in Agrarian Societies'; IDEA, *Democracy in Nigeria*, 225.

52. McMenamin, 'Party Regulation'. On the other hand, the requirement to demonstrate national presence and even more the need to run an expensive multitude of cross-country campaigns under constituency pooling increases the need for money and may lead to personalistic parties. See Randall, 'Party Regulation in Conflict-Prone Societies'.

53. Bogaards, 'Electoral Systems and the Management of Ethnic Conflict in the Balkans', 'Electoral Systems, Party Systems and Ethnic Conflict Management in Africa', 'Comparative Strategies'.

54. Lijphart, *Democracy in Plural Societies*.

55. For an exception, see Electoral Reform Network, *Proportional Representation*.

56. Lijphart, *Democracy in Plural Societies*, 161–64.

57. For a concurring view, see Jinadu, 'Federalism'.

58. Lijphart, *Democracy in Plural Societies*, 164.

59. Ibid., 163.

60. Nolte, 'Federalism and Communal Conflict'; Mustapha, 'Ethnicity and the Politics of Democratization'; Bah, *Breakdown and Reconstitution*.

61. Ejobowah, 'Integrationist and Accommodationist Measures', 246.

62. Williams, 'Accommodation in the Midst of Crisis?', 104; see also Jinadu, 'Federalism', 89.

63. Osaghae, 'The Federal Cabinet, 1951–1986'.

64. Williams, 'Accommodation in the Midst of Crisis?', 107; Jinandu, 'Federalism'.
65. Williams, 'Accommodation in the Midst of Crisis?', 110.
66. Jinandu, 'Federalism', 89.
67. Ibid.
68. Williams, 'Accommodation in the Midst of Crisis?', 113.
69. Kellas, *The Politics of Nationalism;* Beckett, 'Legitimizing Democracy'; Bah, *Breakdown and Reconstitution;* Ejobawah, 'Integrationist and Accommodationist Measures'.
70. Ekeh, 'The Structure and Meaning of Federal Character', 21.
71. See especially Kirk-Greene, 'Ethnic Engineering'.
72. Suberu, 'Nigeria's Muddled Elections', 115.
73. Ayaode, 'The Federal Character Principle'.
74. Suberu, 'Nigeria's Muddled Elections', 138.
75. Ekeh, 'The Structure and Meaning of Federal Character'.
76. Osaghae, 'The Complexity of Nigeria's Federal Character', 15.
77. Cf. Ekeh, 'The Structure and Meaning of Federal Character', 29.
78. Onyeoziry, 'Consociationalism', 426.
79. Ekeh, 'The Structure and Meaning of Federal Character', 29.
80. Uwazurike, 'Politics and the Search for Accommodation in Nigeria', 331; see also Agbaje, 'The Ideology of Power Sharing'.
81. Joseph, 'Political Parties and Ideology in Nigeria'.
82. Akinola, *Rotational Presidency.*
83. Olaitan, 'Rotational Presidency and State-Building in Nigeria', 143.
84. Paden, 'Unity with Diversity', 25–6.
85. As reprinted in the report of the Commonwealth Observer Group, *The Report of the Commonwealth Observer Group (1999).*
86. Ejobowah, 'Constitutional Design and Conflict Management in Nigeria', 151.
87. Abubakar, 'The Federal Character Principle'; Adebowale, 'The Bane of Consociational Politics'.
88. Joseph, *Democracy and Prebendal Politics*, 32.
89. Adekanye, 'Power-Sharing in Multi-Ethnic Political Systems'.
90. Williams, 'Accommodation in the Midst of Crisis?', 116.
91. Njoku, 'Consociationalism: Its Relevance for Nigeria'.
92. Bogaards, 'The Favorable Factors'.
93. Onyeoziry, 'Consociationalism'.
94. Joseph and Kew, 'Nigeria Confronts Obasanjo's Legacy', 169.
95. Ejobowah, 'Integrationist and Accommodationist Measures'; Horowitz, *Ethnic Groups in Conflict*; Lijphart, *Democracy in Plural Societies*; Reilly, *Democracy in Divided Societies.*
96. Ejobowah, 'Integrationist and Accommodationist Measures', 257.
97. Horowitz, *A Democratic South Africa?*
98. McMenamin, 'Party Regulation'.
99. See: http://www.inecnigeria.org/index.php?cateid=3&contid=93. This is the figure for April 2010.
100. Sartori, *Parties and Party Systems.*
101. Kew, 'The 2003 Elections'.
102. Rawlence and Albin-Lackey, 'Nigeria's 2007 General Elections', 497.
103. Suberu, 'Nigeria's Muddled Elections', 96.
104. Ibid., 101.
105. Mustapha, 'Ethnicity and the Politics of Democratization in Nigeria'.
106. See Reno, 'The Roots of Sectarian Violence'.

Notes on contributor

Matthijs Bogaards is Professor of Political Science in the School of Humanities and Social Sciences, Jacobs University Bremen

Bibliography

Abubakar, D. 'The Federal Character Principle, Consociationalism and Democratic Stability in Nigeria'. In *Federalism and Political Restructuring in Nigeria*, ed. A. Amuwo, Agjabe, R. Suberu, and G. Hérault, 164–76. Ibadan: Spectrum Books, 1998.

Adebowale, T. 'The Bane of Consociational Politics in Nigeria'. In *Political Democratisation and Economic De-regulation in Nigeria under the Abacha Administration 1993-1998*, ed. D. Kolawole and O. Mimiko, 147–57. Ado-Ekiti: Department of Political Science, Ondo State University, 1998.

Adekanye, J. 'Power-Sharing in Multi-Ethnic Political Systems'. *Security Dialogue* 29, no. 1 (1998): 25–36.

Agbaje, A. 'The Ideology of Power Sharing: An Analysis of Content, Context and Intent'. In *Federalism and Political Restructuring in Nigeria*, ed. A. Amuwo, A. Agjabe, R. Suberu, and G. Hérault, 121–35. Ibadan: Spectrum Books, 1998.

Agbese, P. 'Party Registration and the Subversion of Democracy in Nigeria'. *Issues* 27, no. 1 (1999): 63–7.

Aina, A. 'Party and Electoral Politics'. In *Nigeria's Struggle for Democracy and Good Governance: A Festschrift for Oyeleye Oyediran*, eds. A. Agbaje, L. Diamond, and E. Onwudiwe, 83–100. Ibadan: Ibadan University Press, 2004.

Akinola, A. 'Manufacturing the Two-Party System in Nigeria'. *Journal of Commonwealth & Comparative Politics* 28, no. 3 (1990): 309–27.

Akinola, A. *Rotational Presidency*. Ibadan: Spectrum Books, 1996.

Ayaode, J. 'The Federal Character Principle and the Search for National Integration'. In *Federalism and Political Restructuring in Nigeria*, ed. A. Amuwo, A. Agjabe, R. Suberu, and G. Hérault, 101–20. Ibadan: Spectrum Books, 1998.

Azarya, V. 'Ethnicity and Conflict Management in Post-Colonial Africa'. *Nationalism and Ethnic Politics* 9, no. 3 (2003): 1–24.

Bah, Abu Bakarr. *Breakdown and Reconstitution: Democracy, the Nation State, and Ethnicity in Nigeria*. Oxford: Lexington Books, 2005.

Barkan, J. 'Elections in Agrarian Societies'. *Journal of Democracy* 6, no. 4 (1995): 106–16.

Beckett, P. 'Legitimizing Democracy: The Role of the Highly Educated Elite'. In *Dilemmas of Democracy in Nigeria*, ed. P. Beckett and C. Young, 111–34. Rochester, NY: University of Rochester Press, 1997.

Bergstresser, Heinrich. 'Nigeria'. In *Afrika-Jahrbuch*, 135–51. Hamburg: Institut für Afrika-Studien, 1998.

Bogaards, M. 'The Favorable Factors for Consociational Democracy: A Review'. *European Journal of Political Research* 33, no. 4 (1998): 475–96.

Bogaards, M. 'Electoral Choices for Divided Societies: Multi-Ethnic Parties and Constituency Pooling in Africa'. *Commonwealth and Comparative Politics* 41, no. 3 (2003): 59–80.

Bogaards, M. 'Electoral Systems and the Management of Ethnic Conflict in the Balkans'. In *Nationalism after Communism: Lessons Learned*, ed. A. Mungiu-Pippidi and I. Krastev, 247–68. Budapest: CEU Press, 2004.

Bogaards, M. 'Electoral Systems, Party Systems, and Ethnic Conflict Management in Africa'. In *Votes, Money and Violence: Political Parties and Elections in Africa*, ed. M. Basedau, G. Erdmann, and A. Mehler, 168–93. Uppsala: Nordiska Afrikainstitutet, 2007.

Bogaards, M. 'Comparative Strategies of Political Party Regulation'. In *Political Party Regulation in Conflict-Prone Societies*, ed. B. Reilly and P. Nordlund, 48–66. Tokyo: United Nations University Press, 2008.

Citizens' Forum for Constitutional Reform. *The Position of the Citizens' Forum for Constitutional Reform (CFCR) on the Review of the 1999 Constitution of the Federal Republic of Nigeria*. Lagos: CFCR, 2001.

Commonwealth Observer Group. *The National Assembly and Presidential Elections In Nigeria, 20 and 27 February 1999: The Report of Commonwealth Observer Group (1999)*. London: Commonwealth Secretariat, 1999.

Diamond, L. 'Nigeria: The Uncivic Society and the Descent into Praetorianism'. In *Politics in Developing Countries: Comparing Experiences with Democracy* (2nd ed.), ed. L. Diamond, J. Linz, and S. Lipset, 417–91. Boulder, CO: Lynne Rienner, 1995.

Dudley, B. *An Introduction to Nigerian Government and Politics*. Bloomington: University of Indiana Press, 1982.

Economist Intelligence Unit. *Country Report Nigeria, 3rd Quarter 1996*. London: Economist Intelligence Unit, 1996.

Economist Intelligence Unit. *Country Report Nigeria, 4th Quarter 1996*. London: Economist Intelligence Unit, 1996.

Economist Intelligence Unit. *Country Report Nigeria, 4th Quarter 1998*. London: Economist Intelligence Unit, 1998.

Economist Intelligence Unit. *Country Report Nigeria, 1st Quarter 1999*. London: Economist Intelligence Unit, 1999.

Economist Intelligence Unit. *Nigeria at a Glance: 2002–03*. London: Economist Intelligence Unit, 2002.

Ejobowah, J. 'Constitutional Design and Conflict Management in Nigeria'. *Journal of Third World Studies* 18, no. 1 (2001): 143–60.

Ejobowah, J. 'Integrationist and Accommodationist Measures in Nigeria's Constitutional Engineering: Successes and Failures'. In *Constitutional Design for Divided Societies: Integration or Accommodation?*, ed. Sujit Choudhry, 233–57. Oxford: Oxford University Press, 2008.

Ekeh, P. 'The Structure and Meaning of Federal Character in the Nigerian Political System'. In *Federal Character and Federation in Nigeria*, ed. P. Ekeh and E. Osaghae, 19–44. Ibadan: Heinemann Educational Books, 1989.

Electoral Reform Network. *Proportional Representation: New Electoral System for Nigeria*. Abuja: Electoral Reform Network, 2005.

Horowitz, D. *Ethnic Groups in Conflict*. Berkeley: University of California Press, 1985.

Horowitz, D. *A Democratic South Africa? Constitutional Engineering in a Divided Society*. Berkeley: University of California Press, 1991.

IDEA: International Institute for Democracy and Electoral Assistance. *Democracy in Nigeria*, Capacity Building Series 10. Stockholm: International Institute for Democracy and Electoral Assistance, 2001.

Jinadu, L. 'Federalism, the Consociational State, and Ethnic Conflict in Nigeria'. *Publius* 15, no. 2 (1985): 71–100.

Joseph, R. 'Political Parties and Ideology in Nigeria'. *Review of African Political Economy* 13 (1978): 78–90.

Joseph, R. *Democracy and Prebendal Politics in Nigeria: The Rise and Fall of the Second Republic*. Cambridge: Cambridge University Press, 1987.

Joseph, R. and D. Kew. 'Nigeria Confronts Obasanjo's Legacy'. *Current History* 107, no. 708 (2008): 167–73.

Kellas, J. *The Politics of Nationalism and Ethnicity*. London: Macmillan, 1991.

Kew, D. 'The 2003 Elections: Hardly Credible, but Acceptable'. In *Crafting the New Nigeria: Confronting the Challenges*, ed. R. Rotberg, 139–73. Boulder, CO: Lynne Rienner, 2004.

Kirk-Greene, A.H.M. 'Ethnic Engineering and the "Federal Character" of Nigeria: Boon of Contentment or Bone of Contention?' *Ethnic and Racial Studies* 6, no. 4 (1983): 457–76.

Koehn, Peter. 'Competitive Transition to Civilian Rule: Nigeria's First and Second Experiments'. *The Journal of Modern African Studies* 27, no. 3 (1989): 401–30.

Lijphart, A. *Democracy in Plural Societies*. New Haven: Yale University Press, 1977.

McMenamin, I. 'Party Regulation and Democratization: Challenges for Further Research'. In *Political Parties in Conflict-Prone Societies: Regulation, Engineering and Democratic Development*, ed. B. Reilly and P. Nordlund, 223–41. Tokyo: United Nations University Press, 2008.

Moroff, A. 'Party Bans in Africa – An Empirical Overview'. *Democratization* 17, no. 4 (2010): 618–41

Moroff, Anika, and Matthias Basedau. 'An Effective Measure of Institutional Engineering? Ethnic Party Bans in Africa'. *Democratization* 17, no. 4 (2010): 666–86.

Mustapha, A.R. 'Ethnicity and the Politics of Democratization in Nigeria'. In *Ethnicity and Democracy in Africa*, ed. B. Berman, D. Eyoh, and W. Kymlicka, 257–75. Oxford: James Currey, 2004.

National Electoral Commission. 'Report and Recommendations on Party Registration'. *Lagos: A National Electoral Commission Publication*, no. 3 (September 1989).

Njoku, R. 'Consociationalism: Its Relevance for Nigeria'. *Nationalism & Ethnic Politics* 5, no. 2 (1999): 1–35.

Nolte, I. 'Federalism and Communal Conflict in Nigeria'. *Regional and Federal Studies* 12, no. 1 (2002): 171–92.

Nwosu, N. 'The Nigerian Local Government Elections of 1998'. *Commonwealth & Comparative Politics* 38, no. 1 (2000): 93–104.

Obeagu, O. 'Supreme Court Verdict on Inec: Hopes and Impediments'. *This Day Online* (19 November 2002).

Obiyan, A. 'Political Parties under the Abubakar Transition Program and Democratic Stability in Nigeria'. *Issues* 27, no. 1 (1999): 41–3.

Ohuegbe, C. 'Committee Recommends De-Registration of Parties'. *Leadership* (Abuja), 17 April 2008.

Okoronkwo, K. 'Politicians' Huge Debate Over De-Registration of Political Parties'. *Guardian* (Nigeria), 18 April 2008.

Olaitan, W. 'Rotational Presidency and State-Building in Nigeria'. In *Federalism and Political Restructuring in Nigeria*, ed. A. Amuwo, Agjabe, R. Suberu, and G. Hérault, 137–46. Ibadan: Spectrum Books, 1998.

Oluyemi-Kusa, D. 'Electoral Reform in Nigeria: A Critique'. In *Development Policy Management Network Bulletin* 13, no. 3 (2001): 27–9.

Omoruyi, O. 'Federal Character and the Party System in the Second Republic'. In *Federal Character and Federalism in Nigeria*, ed. P. Ekeh and E. Osaghae, 188–220. Ibadan: Heinemann, 1989.

Onyeoziri, F. 'Consociationalism and the Nigerian Political Practice'. In *Federal Character and Federalism in Nigeria*, ed. P. Ekeh and E. Osaghae, 411–38. Ibadan: Heinemann, 1989.

Osaghae, E. 'The Complexity of Nigeria's Federal Character and the Inadequacies of the Federal Character Principle'. *The Journal of Ethnic Studies* 16, no. 3 (1988): 1–25.

Osaghae, E. 'The Federal Cabinet, 1951–1984'. In *Federal Character and Federalism in Nigeria*, ed. P. Ekeh and E. Osaghae, 128–63. Ibadan: Heinemann, 1989.

Paden, J. 'Unity with Diversity: Toward Democratic Federalism'. In *Crafting the New Nigeria: Confronting the Challenges*, ed. R. Rotberg, 17–37. Boulder, CO: Lynne Rienner, 2004.

Randall, V. 'Party Regulation in Conflict-Prone Societies: More Dangers than Opportunities?' In *Political Party Regulation in Conflict-Prone Societies*, ed. B. Reilly and P. Nordlund, 242–60. Tokyo: United Nations University Press, 2008.

Rawlence, B., and Chris Albin-Lackey. 'Nigeria's 2007 General Elections: Democracy in Retreat'. *African Affairs* 106/424 (2007): 497–506.

Reilly, B. *Democracy in Divided Societies: Electoral Engineering for Conflict Management*. Cambridge: Cambridge University Press, 2001.

Reno, W. 'The Roots of Sectarian Violence, and Its Cure'. In *Crafting the New Nigeria: Confronting the Challenges*, ed. R. Rotberg, 219–38. Boulder, CO: Lynne Rienner, 2004.

Reynolds, A. 'Building Democracy After Conflict: Constitutional Medicine'. *Journal of Democracy* 16, no. 1 (2005): 54–8.

Sartori, G. *Parties and Party Systems: A Framework for Analysis*. Cambridge: Cambridge University Press, 1976.

Suberu, R. *Federalism and Ethnic Conflict in Nigeria*. Washington, DC: United States Institute of Peace Press, 2001.

Suberu, R. 'Nigeria's Muddled Elections'. *Journal of Democracy* 18, no. 4 (2007): 95–110.

Uwazurike, C. 'Politics and the Search for Accommodation in Nigeria: Will Rotational Consociationalism Suffice?'. In *Dilemmas of Democracy in Nigeria*, ed. P. Beckett and C. Young, 329–40. Rochester, NY: University of Rochester Press, 1997.

Williams, D. 'Accommodation in the Midst of Crisis? Assessing Governance in Nigeria'. In *Governance and Politics in Africa*, ed. G. Hyden and M. Bratton, 97–119. Boulder, CO: Lynne Rienner, 1992.

Comparing ethnic party regulation in East Africa

Anika Moroff

GIGA Institute of African Affairs, Hamburg, Germany

Since 1990 the banning of ethnic and other identity-based parties has become
the norm in sub-Saharan Africa. This article focuses on three East-African
countries – Kenya, Tanzania, and Uganda – which opted for different ways
of dealing with such parties. The analysis shows that the laws have actually
been enforced by the responsible regulatory institutions. However, they
have only marginally influenced the character of the political parties in the
three countries: a comparison of regional voting patterns suggests that bans
on particularistic parties have not ensured the emergence of aggregative
parties with a national following in Tanzania and Uganda. In Kenya on the
other hand, where such a ban has been absent until 2008, parties proved not
to be more regionally based. In all three countries governing parties were
clearly more nationalized than opposition parties, while the overall level of
party nationalization is lower than in other world regions.

Introduction

When reintroducing multiparty politics in the 1990s, most African countries
decided to regulate political parties. Forty out of 46 countries adopted specific
party laws or regulated parties in their electoral laws and/or their constitutions.[1]
A specific feature of such regulation in Africa has been the widespread distrust
of ethnic, religious or other identity-based parties. In order to avert the emergence
of such particularistic parties, which are feared to foster violent conflict, most
countries simply banned them.[2] Additionally, numerous countries have regulated
the organization and membership structure of parties through spatial distribution
requirements in order to promote aggregative parties with nationwide support.
Such broad-based national parties are thought to help stabilize a peaceful
democracy.[3]

   While party bans and spatial distribution requirements are very common and
seldom questioned, little is known about their enforcement and effectiveness in

preventing particularistic parties and violent conflict.[4] However, if the regulations are supposed to influence levels of conflict, they first have to be enforced and indeed influence the character and behaviour of political parties. Given the low regulatory capacity of many African institutions, the impact of informal practices and other factors influencing political parties, such as social cleavages and the electoral system, such an influence cannot be taken for granted.[5]

This article, therefore, takes a closer look at the impact of party regulations on political parties in East Africa. While party bans and spatial distribution requirements initially target the party programme, organization and membership structure, ultimately, if successful, they promote parties with a national electorate.[6] The analysis thus concentrates on the following question: Do such regulations foster aggregative parties with a national support base?

The article applies the concept of party nationalization, which allows for assessing the extent to which a party's support is equally distributed over the country or has regional strongholds. Such a focus on a party's electorate makes sense analytically for at least two reasons. On the one hand, other party characteristics seem less suited for our analysis: while data on party membership is notoriously difficult to obtain and often unreliable, party programmes of most African parties tend to be very vague and similar to each other. On the other hand, the electoral support of a party is not only more easily obtainable, it is also the most straightforward and most common indicator. If a country aims at the prevention of particularistic parties and manages to foster parties with a multi-ethnic membership and leadership structure but parties still receive voter support only in specific areas of the country, this might be considered a failure to prevent particularistic parties.

In order to answer the research question, this article adopts a regional approach and takes a closer look at three East African countries, namely Kenya, Tanzania, and Uganda. While they are geographically close and share a number of historical and structural similarities (such as ethnic heterogeneity, low income, partly free political regime, British colonial background), these countries opted for very different strategies to deal with particularistic parties in the 1990s. A careful comparison of the regulations' enforcement and the degree of party nationalization gives us first hints whether the different regulations actually led to different levels of nationalization of their political parties.

After a brief overview of the regulation on particularistic parties in the three countries, the article presents original findings on the enforcement of the regulations.[7] Finally, it assesses the impact of the regulations on the degree of party nationalization in the countries under investigation. The analysis shows that while the regulations have been enforced, particularly with regard to party registration, their impact on voter support of political parties has remained limited.

The regulation of particularistic parties in East Africa

During the 1990s Kenya, Tanzania, and Uganda opted for three different approaches to regulate particularistic parties. Kenya had no party law at all;

parties were regulated under the Societies Act of 1968. After several failed attempts to change this situation, a political party law was enacted in July 2008, including strict registration requirements and outlawing particularistic parties.[8]

Tanzania, in contrast, passed a party law in 1992, which banned particularistic parties and included spatial distribution requirements. The same provisions were included in the constitution. Finally, Uganda outlawed party activities under the so-called 'movement system' until 2005. The movement system was introduced in 1986 by President Museveni and the National Resistance Movement (NRM) and was initially thought to represent a transitional form of government. However, it was then introduced in the 1995 Constitution, which not only prohibited party activities as long as the movement system was in place, but also included regulations regarding particularistic parties. In 2002 a party law was enacted, but it was soon superseded by a new law in 2005. Table 1 provides a brief overview of previous and current regulations regarding particularistic parties in the three countries.

The enforcement of party regulation in East Africa

If party regulations are supposed to have an impact on political parties, they first have to be enforced by the responsible institutions. However, this enforcement cannot be taken as a given: many scholars of African politics have questioned the relevance of all types of formal institutions in sub-Saharan Africa.[9] Additionally, African institutions often lack funds which could also prevent an effective enforcement of the law.

The following section shows that the regulations have clearly been enforced in all three countries; however the enforcement focused mainly on party registration. Numerous parties failed to meet the registration requirements and were unable to prove their national character. In some cases, party registration was politically influenced by the government. The outlawing of existing parties was more seldom: only Tanzania de-registered existing parties, while in Kenya all parties that failed to fulfil the requirements of the new Political Parties Act of 2007 were de-registered. In all three countries, informal practices also played a role in dealing with particularistic parties.

Tanzania

Tanzania re-introduced multiparty politics in July 1992. The incumbent government aimed at a controlled liberalization of the political system and thus regulated parties extensively. Article 20 of the constitution as well as the Political Parties Act prohibit the registration of a party that aims at promoting only the interests of particular groups or advocates for the break-up of the Republic, whose membership is not open to all citizens or that intends to carry on its activities in only one part of the republic.[10] Groups that want to register as a political party have to apply for provisional registration first, and then for full registration within 180 days. In order to be fully registered, the party has to fulfil the spatial distribution requirements.[11]

Table 1. Party regulation in Kenya, Tanzania and Uganda since 1990.

	Legal source	Outlawed identity	Spatial distribution requirement	Responsible institution (registration)	Responsible institution (dissolution)
Kenya 1992	Societies Act	–	–	Registrar of societies	Registrar of societies
Kenya 2008	Political Parties Act	colour, ethnicity, faith, language, race, region, tribe	200 members from each province, one member from each province in the governing body, one founding member from each district; party branches in each district	Registrar of political parties	Registrar of political parties
Tanzania 1992	Constitution Political Parties Act	religion, place of origin, race, tribe	200 members each from 10 regions, including Pemba and Zanzibar; leadership from mainland and Zanzibar	Registrar of political parties	Registrar of political parties (agreed to by the responsible minister)
Uganda 1995	Constitution	ethnicity, faith or other sectarian division	'national character'		
Uganda 2002	The Political Parties and Organisations Act	colour, ethnicity, faith, race, region, tribe	50 members from each of at least half of all the districts*	Registrar general	Registrar general may apply to High Court
Uganda 2005	The Political Parties and Organisations Act	colour, ethnicity, faith, race, region, tribe	50 members from each of at least 2/3 of all the districts in each region	Electoral Commission	Electoral Commission may apply to High Court

Source: Author's compilation.
Notes: *In order to be registered, parties had to bring a list with the names and addresses of at least 50 members from only one-third of the districts.

The registrar of political parties registers parties and can – with the consent of the responsible minister – cancel the registration of a party that has violated any provision of the act or that otherwise ceases to qualify for registration under the act. Like the deputy registrar, he is nominated directly by the president, while several assistant registrars are nominated by 'the responsible minister', currently the prime minister.[12]

The registration process began in 1992 under the first registrar of political parties, George Liundi. The party law proved to be an effective tool for controlling the opening of the political system: 31 political parties received provisional registration in the first year, but only 12 were ultimately registered. According to official information, all of the others were unable to get the necessary 2000 member signatures. No party was registered between March 1994 and November 2001. Only when Liundi retired and John Tendwa was named registrar of political parties, in 2001, did new registrations take place. Between 1992 and 2005, a total of 71 parties received provisional registration and 20 were fully registered.[13] The existing parties fail to fulfil numerous requirements of the act, such as holding regular internal elections or reporting on their accounts.[14] Despite various threats by both registrars to deregister non-complying parties, however, only three parties were de-registered for not holding internal elections.[15]

While 51 parties failed to get the necessary signatures, no party was denied registration because of its religious, 'tribal' or racial character. However, this seems to be partly the result of a deliberate strategy of the registrar, who considered the signature requirements as less controversial than the other rules.[16] Therefore, Liundi denied registration to two parties on grounds of lacking signatures, while he could as well have relied on other criteria. One example is the Democratic Party (DP) of Reverend George Mtikila, who applied for registration in 1992. Mtikila was openly critical of the union of Tanzania mainland and Zanzibar and considered the latter not to be part of Tanzania. Additionally, at public rallies, he employed a xenophobic rhetoric against the Asian business community, accusing them of corruption and theft from the poor African majority. One of these speeches led to riots in Dar es Salaam in January 1992, with his supporters attacking vehicles and other properties belonging to Asian residents. At the same time, Muslims argued that if a party founded by a Christian reverend were registered, a Muslim party should likewise be allowed.[17] Finally, the DP was denied registration because Mtikila did not get the necessary signatures in Zanzibar.[18] When asked why he had not banned the DP on the basis of its religious or discriminatory policy, Liundi argued that this would have fuelled additional conflicts. On a later occasion he followed the rationale of his initial decision regarding the DP, denying registration to a Muslim party because of its inadequate membership.[19]

The registration process has never been without problems and critiques. Particularly in the first years, the Office of the Registrar encountered difficulties in trying to enforce the regulations: for example, it lacked the staff and resources to travel to ten regions to verify member signatures of all the parties that applied for full registration. It therefore only verified the party members in some regions during the first years.[20] While the Office of the Registrar justified this as a measure of support for the young parties,[21] some parties criticized the sporadic control and claimed that the registrar applied requirements and regulations in a discriminatory manner.[22]

It has sometimes been argued that the requirements were not effective because many of the signatures were 'bought' with food and tea or small gifts.[23] While it is difficult to test this claim, it is clear that not all parties were able to obtain the necessary signatures this way: 51 parties failed to meet the requirements. In at least one case, in 1992, two groups even merged to form a party, the Civic United Front (CUF), in order to have the required geographic presence in both Zanzibar and Tanzania mainland.[24] Opposition parties have continuously reported difficulties to comply with spatial distribution requirements and questioned their necessity.[25] They complained especially of harassment by the governing parties and civil service agents during public rallies as well as a lack of resources, which made it difficult to travel the country in order to mobilize potential members.[26] In their eyes, the restrictive party regulation has been an obstacle to further democratization in Tanzania.[27]

Kenya

Until 2008 the regulation of political parties in Kenya followed the Societies Act of 1952. It prohibited associations of which the registrar of societies had 'reasonable cause to believe that the society [had] among its objectives, or [was] likely to pursue or to be used for, any unlawful purpose or any purpose prejudicial to or incompatible with peace, welfare or good order in Kenya'.[28] The registrar of societies, who was nominated by the president, could also cancel a party's registration for the same reasons. The act left considerable discretionary power to the registrar of societies and did not specify any time limits for the registrar's decision.[29]

The registrar denied registration to various parties and functioned as a political instrument of the regime by registering government-friendly parties and various splinter groups, which had names and symbols similar to existing opposition parties, while delaying or even denying the registration of opposition parties considered politically threatening.[30] Between 1992 and 1996 alone the registrar denied registration to 23 parties. One of them, the Islamic Party of Kenya (IPK), was denied registration due to its presumed religious character in June 1992. The decision revealed the unclear legal situation: when the party complained about the refusal to the attorney general (AG), Amos Wako, he justified the decision on the grounds that the constitution outlaws religious parties. However, there is no such article in the constitution and the decision was harshly criticized by many opposition parties.[31] The IPK tried unsuccessfully to challenge the denial before the court and finally allied with FORD-Kenya for the 1992 elections. The conflict about its registration led to clashes in Mombasa between party supporters, security forces and – since mid-1993 – members of the government-sponsored organization United Muslims of Africa, which lasted over two years.[32]

In other cases, the registration was simply delayed over a very long time. Safina, an opposition party founded by reformist opposition politicians around Paul Muite and Richard Leakey, waited for its registration from June 1995 to November 1997. AG Wako even tried to introduce a political party law, which according to observers was directed primarily against Safina (meaning 'the ark' in Swahili). His bill, which was proposed three days after Safina had applied for registration, included a ban on ethnic and religious party names and proposed a registration process of at least seven months. Wako finally backed down on bringing the bill to parliament due to a wave of national and international criticism.[33]

Despite the restrictive registration practices of the registrar, the number of parties grew from 12 to 26 in 1997 and to 51 in 2002. Since 2007 the number of parties increased rapidly from 85 in February to 161 in December. However, most of these parties only existed on paper, and many were created in order to allow candidates who had not been nominated by their original party to stand in the 2007 elections.[34]

The Political Parties Act of 2008 transferred the responsibility for political parties to the registrar of political parties, located within the (now defunct) electoral commission. It rules that no party shall be registered that is founded on a particularistic basis, uses divisive slogans or symbols or carries on its activities in only part of Kenya.[35] As is the case in Tanzania, the registration process has two steps; in order to become fully registered, the party must fulfil the spatial distribution requirements. If a party breaches these regulations or has obtained its regulations in a fraudulent manner, the registrar of political parties shall warn the party and – if the party does not comply with the regulations – de-register it within 90 days.

In 2008 all parties had to apply for full registration before the end of the year. Only 47 parties managed to fulfil all the criteria, including getting the necessary members, opening party branches in every district and paying a registration fee of KSh 600,000 (US$7,770).[36] It is likely that this number will decrease even more over the years as the Political Parties Act provides for the cancellation of a party's registration that has failed to gain at least 5% of the national vote in two consequent elections.[37]

Uganda

When the NRM came to power in 1986 after a five-year civil war, its leadership abolished parts of the 1967 constitution in their Legal Notice 1 of 1986 and thereby banned political party activities.[38] The 1995 constitution continued this ban and regulated parties under the 'movement system' by Article 270. However, it also included an article that would regulate parties if a multiparty system were reintroduced, as occurred in 2005. This article requires parties to 'have a national character' and rules that 'membership of a political party shall not be based on sex, ethnicity, religion or other sectarian division'.[39]

Under the movement system, no new political party could register, while a political party law was not in place. Only in 2002, the Political Parties and

Organisation Act (PPOA) was adopted. The very restrictive act was immediately challenged before the courts by two opposition parties. In 2003, the Constitutional Court declared large sections of the act unconstitutional and annulled them, declaring that they would make Uganda into a de facto one-party-state.[40] A new and significantly altered PPOA was then passed in 2005 as part of the preparation for a new referendum on the re-introduction of multiparty politics in Uganda. Both laws ruled that no party should be registered whose membership was not open or which used divisive slogans or symbols. In order to be registered, a party had to prove its national character by fulfilling the spatial distribution requirements.[41] When the responsible institution – since 2005 the Electoral Commission (EC) – finds that a party does not comply with the act, it may require the party to take steps to do so and, in case of persistent non-compliance, may apply to the High Court for an order winding up the party.

The registration on parties only started after the passing of the PPOA in 2002. Nevertheless, in April 1993, a Muslim group around Idris Muwonge and the Tabliq Youth Movement announced the foundation of the Uganda Islamic Revolutionary Party (UIRP). The attempt was immediately condemned by Museveni, who argued that the NRM would 'not allow religion to be brought into politics'.[42] Muwonge declared that the UIRP would operate clandestinely but the group did not appear to enjoy strong support from the Muslim population and seems to have disappeared.[43]

The first group seeking to register as a political party, in June 2003, was the NRM itself. Initially rejected by the registrar general (RG) because of unconstitutional passages in the party statute, the National Resistance Movement-Organisation was registered in October 2003.[44] No other party registered in 2003 as most parties questioned the legitimacy of the act. Prior to the elections in 2006, 33 parties registered; today the number has increased to 36.[45] However, a number of opposition parties had difficulty registering. Some of the problems resulted from internal leadership wrangles, as in the case of the Democratic Party (DP), others apparently from the delaying strategies of the RG, as in the case of the Forum for Democratic Change (FDC), which represented a serious political challenge to the NRM.[46]

The RG's office argued that registration delays were due to a lack of funds: it complained about having insufficient resources to ensure that the extensive membership requirements were met.[47] While it is unclear if this was actually the case, the RG was certainly not in the best position to enforce the law as his office was based solely in Kampala. The PPOA 2005 therefore transferred the responsibility for political parties to the EC. In order to verify that a party complies with the law, the EC first checks the party constitution and then samples several districts per region as well as several villages per district, where member signatures are checked and the existence of the signing members is verified.[48] By 2008 the EC had discovered fake names on the membership lists of three parties.[49] Such an infringement does not automatically lead to the denial of registration: when the EC discovers non-compliance it indicates this to the party, which is permitted to rectify the situation. Nonetheless, apparently none of the three parties with faked names is still registered. Despite the fact that most parties do not comply with the requirement of an annual declaration of their assets, no party has been deregistered up to now.

Since the beginning of the registration process in 2003 only one party has effectively been denied registration, namely a group called 'Kabaka Yekka' (KY; which means 'king only' in Luganda). The original KY was founded in 1961 as the party of the Baganda and governed the country in a coalition with Obote's Uganda Peoples Congress (UPC) from 1962 to 1966. The new KY sought registration in 2004 but was advised by the RG to change its name. The case was later transferred to the EC, which repeated this advice. When the party refused to comply, the EC denied registration, arguing that the party's name was connected to the Buganda Kingdom and likely to 'confuse' the public. In July 2006 the KY brought the issue before the Constitutional Court, which decided in favour of the EC. The court argued that the name 'Kabaka Yekka' was 'likely to rekindle the old emotions of the 1960s stirring up public unrest, commotion and confusion'. While the party had proved that its membership was open to the public and had managed to obtain the necessary quota of members all over the country, its name was said to be still likely to arouse divisions:

> It is a well known fact which this Constitutional Court has to take judicial notice of that the traditional/cultural leader of Buganda Kingdom is called the Kabaka. Section 5(1) (b) of the PPOA prohibits the use of 'words' which could arouse divisions on any basis specified in para (a). Paragraph 1(a) prohibits membership based on, inter alia, ethnic origin, tribe. Since the Kabaka of Buganda is a cultural/traditional leader of the Baganda the use of the name 'Kabaka' which is a word was likely to cause divisions. I appreciate the submission by the respondents' counsel that the right thinking people were likely to assume that the Kabaka of Buganda was indulging into partisan political activities, contrary to article 246(3)(e) of the Constitution. This would cause unwarranted divisions and would be contrary to the Constitutional Principle of Unity.[50]

Summary

In sum, we see that in all three countries, incumbent governments used (party) legislation to control the opening of the political systems by regulating the registration and activities of political parties. The regulatory institutions took their tasks rather seriously and tried to enforce the existing regulations. Concerns about their impartiality were raised from time to time, and we find evidence of discriminatory practices in all countries. However, only the registrar of societies in Kenya seems to have followed a strongly 'political' registration tactic. All institutions routinely checked party constitutions for conformity with the law and also verified – within the limits of available resources – registration requirements in terms of national membership. This requirement seems to represent a considerable obstacle for political parties as shown by numerous denials of registration in Tanzania, evidence of fake names in Uganda, and the non-registration of more than

100 parties in Kenya in 2008. Court appeals by parties that were denied registration were usually not successful; therefore, almost all parties concerned disappeared afterwards. However, once a party was registered, the institutions proved hesitant to enforce the law by dissolving non-complying parties.

The effects of party regulation in East Africa

While the analysis has so far shed some light on the enforcement of particularistic party bans, the question of whether these regulations do indeed influence political parties remains open. If they are successful in fostering more national parties and preventing regional parties, we would expect a difference between parties in the three countries. While party bans and spatial distribution requirements initially influence the party programme, organization, and membership structure, ultimately, if successful, they promote parties with a national electorate. Therefore, in order to obtain a first impression of how the party regulations influence political parties, the regional distribution of party support as indicator for party nationalization will be compared.[51] According to this understanding, a nationalized party obtains a similar level of support all over the country, while a regional party receives most of its votes in only some regions.

It is possible to think of several hypotheses on how party regulation might impact on party nationalization. First, it should be easier for a party to mobilize voters nationwide if it represents itself as a party for the whole electorate through its party programme, membership and leadership. Second, parties that are able to fulfil the onerous registration requirements can be expected to have some resources and organizational capacities. This should allow them to mobilize voters more effectively. Party nationalization might however also be influenced by other factors, such as a presidential or parliamentary system, the electoral system, levels of decentralization, party funding, cleavage lines, and the degree of authoritarianism.[52] While the three countries under investigation all have a presidential system, a first-past-the-post electoral system, and a high ethnic fractionalization, the resources available to political parties have varied widely between and within these countries over time. Also, ethnicity is politically more salient in Kenya and Uganda than in Tanzania, which might cause regional strongholds to actually represent ethnic strongholds.[53] Additionally, some elections have been more heavily marred by authoritarian excesses than others (for example, Kenya in 1992). Finally, only Kenya has introduced a clause for presidential elections, which requires the presidential candidate to obtain a minimum of 25% of the valid vote cast in at least five of the eight provinces. This provision is supposed to create incentives for vote pooling and might therefore have similar effects as party regulations in Tanzania and Uganda.[54]

The analysis uses the party nationalization score (PNS), which measures how equally party support is distributed across the country, as well as the party system nationalization score (PSNS). The PNS indicates how a party's vote shares are spread over the country: a highly nationalized party has 'a relatively even share of the vote across different geographic units'.[55] In order to calculate the PNS, the Gini-Index, which represents a measure of inequalities across units, is subtracted from 1. This inverted Gini coefficient ranges from 0 to 1; the higher it is, the more equal the distribution of the vote share is. Following other applications of the PNS, the analysis relies on parliamentary election results.[56]

The PNS has the advantage of providing a clear interpretation and is comparable across cases but slightly sensitive to the number of units included.[57] In order to keep the number of units as similar as possible, the analysis relies on the eight provinces for Kenya and four regions for Uganda. Tanzania's 27 regions are grouped into seven zones according to a classification of the country's electoral commission. The discussion of the results focuses on the governing and the main opposition parties. Additionally, the PSNS is calculated. For this index, the PNS for every party is multiplied by its share of the national valid vote and the results then totalled. This measure allows for an assessment of the party system's overall level of nationalization.[58] Only parties that received at least one seat in parliament have been included in its calculation.

As Table 2 shows, in all three countries governing parties are far more nationalized than opposition parties. The most nationalized party is Tanzania's Chama cha Mapinduzi (CCM), which has also the highest vote share generally (and the largest dominance in parliament). In contrast, not only was the Kenya African National Union's (KANU) vote share significantly lower, but its support base was also more strongly regionalized. Its PNS remained widely unchanged in 2002 when the National Alliance Rainbow Coalition (NARC) won the election and ousted KANU from power. While in 2002 Kenya had two parties with a fairly national backing (one of them, though, the NARC, was a coalition of several smaller parties), the two main contenders in the 2007 elections, the Orange Democratic Movement (ODM) and the Party of National Unity (PNU), had comparatively more regionalized support bases. However, the Kenyan scores have to be treated with some caution as three out of the four major parties in 2002 and 2007 represented coalitions of smaller parties rather than parties with a fixed organizational structure. By contesting the elections under a single label, they increased their chance of winning the parliamentary and, more important, the presidential elections, including the nationwide quota. After the elections, these coalitions have however proved to be volatile.[59]

As Table 2 shows, support for the opposition parties in the three countries has been significantly more unequally distributed than support for the governing parties. Larger opposition parties, like the CUF in Tanzania, the FDC in Uganda as well as the DP in Kenya tend to have a more nationalized support base. Most of the smaller opposition parties, such as the UDP or the SDP, receive more regionalized support.[60]

In order to get a clearer picture of how the parties fare in comparison to each other, Table 3 lists the parties in the bottom and the top quarter in terms of their PNS. All parties with at least one seat in the national parliament and 3% of the national vote have been included in the analysis. While the results confirm the

Table 2. Political parties in Tanzania, Uganda and Kenya.

Tanzania		CCM	CHADEMA	CUF	NCCR	UDP	TLP	PSNS
1995	No of seats	186	3	24	16	3	0	
	% of votes	59%	6%	5%	22%	3%		0.76
	PNS	0.91	0.69	0.37	0.69	0.39		
2000	No of seats	202	4	17	1	3	4	
	% of votes	65%	4%	13%	4%	5%	9%	0.80
	PNS	0.94	0.48	0.61	0.66	0.30	0.59	
2005	No of seats	206	5	19	0	1	1	
	% of votes	70%	8%	14%		1%	3%	0.83
	PNS	0.94	0.66	0.66		0.17	0.59	

Uganda		NRM	FDC	DP	UPC			PSNS
2006	No of seats	191	37	8	9			
	% of votes	51%	16%	7%	5%			0.61
	PNS	0.86	0.80	0.36	0.42			

Kenya		KANU	Ford-A	Ford-K	DP	NDP	SDP	PSNS
1992	No of seats	100	31	31	23	-	-	
	% of votes	30%	25%	20%	22%			0.61
	PNS	0.69	0.6	0.53	0.61			
1997	No of seats	107	1	17	39	21	15	
	% of votes	39%	1%	10%	22%	11%	8%	0.57
	PNS	0.76	0.44	0.45	0.56	0.37	0.49	
		NARC	KANU	Ford-P				
2002	No of seats	125	64	14				
	% of votes	51%	28%	8%				0.71
	PNS	0.83	0.75	.62				
		PNU	ODM	ODM-K	KANU			
2007	No of seats	43	99	16	14			
	% of votes	21%	31%	7%	6%			0.52
	PNS	0.65	0.69	0.48	0.47			

Source: Author's calculations based on official election results; African Election Database, http://africanelections.tripod.com/index.html.
Note: The PNS for the Tanzania Labour Party (TLP) has not been calculated. The National Development Party (NDP) and the Social Democratic Party (SDP) were only founded in 1996 and 1997 respectively. CHADEMA: Chama cha Demokrasia na Maendeleo; CUF: Civic United Front; NCCR: National Convention for Construction and Reform; UDP: United Democratic Party; FDC: Forum for Democratic Change; DP: Democratic Party; UPC: Uganda Peoples' Congress; Ford-A: Forum for the Restoration of Democracy-Asili; Ford-K: Forum for the Restoration of Democracy-Kenya; DP: Democratic Party; Ford-P: Forum for the Restoration of Democracy for the People; ODM K: Orange Democratic Movement-Kenya.

finding that larger parties tend to have a more equal spread of the vote, they also show that Kenyan parties are not significantly less nationalized than Tanzanian or Ugandan parties: despite the fact that significantly more Kenyan parties have been included in the analysis (12 compared to four in Uganda and six from Tanzania), only two Kenyan parties figure among the six parties with the lowest score.

Table 3. Ranking the 12 most nationalized and least nationalized parties.

	Party, election year	Percent of the vote	PNS
6 parties with the lowest PNS	UDP, Tanzania 2000	4%	0.30
	DP, Uganda 2006	7%	0.36
	CUF, Tanzania 1995	5%	0.37
	NDP, Kenya 1997	11%	0.37
	UDP, Tanzania 1995	3%	0.39
	Safina, Kenya 2007	4%	0.41
6 parties with the highest PNS	FDC, Uganda 2006	16%	0.80
	NARC, Kenya 2002	51%	0.83
	NRM, Uganda 2006	51%	0.86
	CCM, Tanzania 1995	59%	0.91
	CCM, Tanzania 2000	65%	0.94
	CCM, Tanzania 2005	70%	0.94

Source: Author's compilation.

With regard to party system nationalization, Kenya displays PSNS that are comparable to the Ugandan level of 2006 (see Table 2). Only in 1997 and in 2007 the Kenyan party system exhibited a lower degree of nationalization. Tanzania, in contrast, has a strongly nationalized party system. However, this result is mainly due to the CCM's very high PNS and its large vote share.

In sum, in the three countries, results for PNS do not point to a clear effect of the party laws in favour of parties with a more national support base. Banning particularistic parties and requiring parties to have members all over the country clearly does not translate into a nationwide following for these parties. The ability of parties to reach out nationwide has varied considerably across as well as within countries. The regulations have not prevented the emergence or persistence of parties with clear regional strongholds, such as the UDP in Tanzania or the DP and the UPC in Uganda. Meanwhile, Kenya's parties have not evidenced significantly lower PNS than political parties in Tanzania and Uganda. In Uganda, the long-term ban on all party activities seems to have significantly weakened the traditional opposition parties, the DP and the UPC, and thereby furthered what this ban was allegedly intended to prevent, namely, parties without a national character.

From an international perspective, the parties in the three East African countries have comparatively low degrees of nationalization. In calculating the PNS for 17 South and North American countries, Jones and Mainwaring found that the 11 lowest party scores were at 0.7 and below.[61] Croissant and Schächter showed that nine out of 55 parties in seven Asian countries displayed scores below 0.5 for at least one election; most of the scores varied between 0.65 and 0.9.[62] In contrast, among the 39 East African parties with seats in parliament and at least 3% of the vote, 23 scored below 0.65 and 31 below 0.7. These scores are clearly below the values for other world regions. Only four opposition parties in East Africa had a score of approximately 0.7 or above, namely KANU in 2002, the CHADEMA and the NCCR in 1995, and the FDC in 2006. However, as their relative success remains singular among the opposition parties, it seems difficult to link it to the party regulations.

Almost all opposition parties in the three East African countries therefore failed to mobilize support nationwide, no matter if they fulfilled the strict representation requirements, as in Tanzania and Uganda, or if they did not, as in Kenya. General obstacles, such as a restrictive legal environment, gerrymandering, informal harassment of the opposition, insufficient coordination among opposition parties, or lacking available funding counteracted the impact of the party law.[63] The only effect we might see is the prevention of an excessive fragmentation of the party system: the fragmentation of the Kenyan party system, for example, has strongly decreased with the new Political Parties Act.

In contrast, most governing parties in Kenya, Tanzania and Uganda have tended to have a more national support base. In the case of the CCM and the NRM, however, this is clearly not a result of the registration requirements. Their nationwide institutional presence – resulting from the period of single-party rule in Tanzania and the movement system in Uganda – access to state funds and use of formal institutions and informal practices are among the factors that stabilize their rule.[64] In Kenya all major parties, except for the KANU in 1992 and 1997, represented coalitions of smaller parties, most of which have clearly identifiable ethnic strongholds. The electoral system and particularly the electoral representation requirements have constituted an incentive to vote-pooling. However, the resulting coalitions and mergers proved very fragile and even conflict-prone, as in the case of the NARC, which imploded over the constitutional referendum in 2005. It remains to be seen how the new regulations of the PPA influence this pattern.

Conclusion

This article aimed at taking a closer look at the regulation of particularistic parties in East Africa. While party bans have been the norm elsewhere in Africa, Kenya, Tanzania and Uganda have chosen three alternative ways of dealing with particularistic parties. Today, however, the respective provisions in their party laws closely resemble each other; all combine a ban on particularistic parties with spatial distribution requirements. Indeed, this convergence reflects the general tendency on the African continent: except for South Africa, all countries that have introduced legislation on political parties since 1990 have included a particularistic party ban within the regulations.

The analysis has shown that regulations of particularistic parties are at least partially enforced in all three countries under investigation. However, the enforcement is mainly restricted to the formal control of the party constitution as well as registration requirements in terms of national membership. It became clear that party regulation also represents a tool of control for the government. Particularly in the case of Kenya, the previous regulation by the Societies Act proved a flexible and easy to manipulate instrument which suited the incumbent government. While numerous parties failed to get registered, the enforced registration requirements do not necessarily guarantee that parties actually are more national in character. A comparison of party nationalization scores and levels of party system nationalization has shown that while registration requirements can help to prevent an excessive fragmentation of the party system and the mushrooming of small parties, they are less suited to ensure the emergence of aggregative parties with a national following. This result points to the importance of the broader institutional context for the effectiveness of single measures of institutional engineering: if such measures are countered by legislation with diverging incentives, their impact often remains weak.[65] By the same token, non-democratic political practices or elements of the broader political environment, such as a lack of available funds for opposition parties, can undermine efforts of institutional engineering.

Notes

1. See Moroff, 'Party Bans in Africa', this issue. There is no multiparty system in Swaziland and Eritrea.
2. For a discussion of ethnic parties and violent conflict see Chandra, *Why Ethnic Parties Succeed*; Horowitz, *Ethnic Groups in Conflict*; Rabushka and Shepsle, *Politics in Plural Societies*.
3. Bogaards, 'Electoral Systems'; Reilly, 'Political Engineering and Party Politics'.
4. For an exception see Reilly and Nordlund, *Political Parties in Conflict-Prone Societies*.
5. Chabal and Daloz, *Africa Works;* Sartori, *Parties and Party Systems*.
6. See Bogaards, Basedau, and Hartmann, 'Ethnic Party Bans in Africa', this special issue.
7. The author draws on field research conducted in March and April 2008 in all three countries.
8. For a detailed analysis of the origins of party regulation in East Africa see Moroff, 'Ethnic Party Bans in East Africa'.
9. See for example Chabal and Daloz, *Africa Works*.
10. The United Republic of Tanzania, *The Constitution of the United Republic of Tanzania*, Article 20; The United Republic of Tanzania, *The Political Parties Act*, Article 8 (1) (c). The introduction of a ban on particularistic parties was recommended by the Nyalali commission in its 1992 report.
11. The United Republic of Tanzania, The Political Parties Act, Article 10 (11) (b) (c). There are currently 26 regions in Tanzania, with three on Unguja, the main island, and two on Pemba.
12. The United Republic of Tanzania, *The Political Parties Act*.
13. List obtained at the Office of the Registrar. Fourteen parties tried to register several times.
14. Karume, 'Dilemmas of Political Transition', 94; Chege, 'Political Parties', 44; *The East African*, 9 April 2001; *The Guardian*, 2 June 2001.
15. *Daily News*, 13 September 1999; *The Guardian*, 8 March 2000; *The Guardian*, 11 February 2004. The registrar justified this with the argument that he would have to de-register all existing parties if he enforced the law strictly.
16. George Liundi, interview with the author, 8 April 2008.
17. Economist Intelligence Unit, *Country Report Tanzania*, No. 3, 1993.

18. Mtikila brought the case to court, which decided in his favour. However, when Mtikila applied anew (still without the necessary signatures in Zanzibar), his application was again rejected. Mtikila tried without success to force the registrar to register the DP, until in 2002 he finally got the necessary signatures and the DP was registered; *The Guardian*, 5 August 2000.
19. George Liundi, interview with the author, 8 April 2008.
20. In 2002 Tendwa announced that his office would control all 10 regions from then on. *The Guardian*, 18 February 2002.
21. Assistant registrar, interview with the author, 4 April 2008. According to Liundi, his office accepted applications with 1600 signatures to ease the procedure.
22. Peter, 'Determining the Pace of Change'.
23. One interviewee affirmed that he had 'bought' a large number of members and that other parties were doing the same. Another party leader claimed that he had not had the resources to do so, but that it was known that other parties had followed this strategy.
24. In June 1992 the leading Zanzibari opposition group Kamau ya Mageuz Huru (Kamahuru) merged with Chama cha Wananchi, led by opposition leader James Mapalala, to form the CUF in order to avoid its disqualification as a party because of inadequate national membership, Economist Intelligence Unit, *Country Report Tanzania*.
25. *Business Times*, 1 January 1993, Economist Intelligence Unit, *Country Report Tanzania*.
26. *Business Times*, 30 October 1992. Interviewees from different parties described the registration process as very difficult and expensive. Chairman of the National League for Democracy, interview with the author, 8 April 2008; Chairman of the Tanzania Democratic Alliance Party, interview with the author, 12 April 2008; Secretary General of the United Democratic Party, interview with the author, 2 April 2008.
27. For a similar view see Hoffman and Robinson, 'Tanzania's Missing Opposition'.
28. Republic of Kenya, *Societies Act*, Article 11.
29. Only in 1997, the omnibus statute law agreed to by the Inter-Parties Parliamentary Group specified a time limit of 120 days. See Ndegwa, 'The Incomplete Transition'.
30. Amiri, 'Kenya', 64; Registrar of societies, interview with the author, 16 April 2008.
31. *Daily Nation*, 20 June 1992; *Daily Nation*, 22 June 1992.
32. Oded, *Islam and Politics in Kenya*.
33. Peters, 'Kenya 1995'.
34. Independent Review Commission (IRC), *Report of the IRC*, 56f.
35. Republic of Kenya, *The Political Parties Act, 2007*.
36. *The Standard*, 31 October 2009.
37. Republic of Kenya, *The Political Parties Act, 2007*, Article 26 (1) (e).
38. See Museveni, *What Is Africa's Problem?* 257–61. Article 3 of the Ten-Point Program speaks about the consolidation of national unity and the necessary elimination of all forms of sectarianism.
39. Republic of Uganda, *Constitution*, Article 71.
40. The Constitutional Court of Uganda, Constitutional Petition No. 5 of 2002 (21 March 2003), *Paul Kawanga Ssemogerere and Others v. The Attorney General of Uganda*; Carbone, *No Party Democracy?*, 190.
41. Republic of Uganda, *The Political Parties and Organisation Act, 2002*, Article 5 (1) (2) (4); Republic of Uganda, *The Political Parties and Organisation Act, 2005*. In Article 7 (1) (b) the act specifies that 'region' here refers to Uganda's of 'traditional geographical regions', namely Buganda, East, North and West. Uganda currently has 77 districts.
42. Economist Intelligence Unit, *Country Report Uganda*, No. 2, 1993, 12.
43. Tibendera, *Islamic Fundamentalism*, 104f.

44. Steiner, 'Uganda 2003', 322f.
45. List obtained from the Electoral Commission of Uganda.
46. Makara, Rakner, and Svåsand, 'Turnaround'.
47. Kiiza, Svåsand, and Tabaro, 'Organising Parties', 207f.
48. Head of Legal and Public Relations Department of the Electoral Commission of Uganda, interview with the author, 21 April 2008.
49. List obtained from the Electoral Commission of Uganda.
50. The Constitutional Court of Uganda, Constitutional Petition No. 22 of 2006 (30 April 2008), *Paul Kafeero and Herman Kazibe v. The Electoral Commission and the Attorney General*. The party seems to have disappeared after the judgment.
51. Election results have to be treated with some caution as an indicator of a party's support base as electoral malpractice cannot be excluded.
52. Chhibber and Kollman, *The Formation of National Party Systems*; Croissant and Schächter, 'Die Nationalisierung politischer Parteien'.
53. See for example Cheeseman and Ford, 'Ethnicity'; Elischer, 'Ethnic Coalitions'.
54. Bogaards, 'Electoral Systems', Horowitz, *Ethnic Groups*.
55. Jones and Mainwaring, 'The Nationalization of Parties', 140.
56. According to Jones and Mainwaring, parliamentary election results are less influenced by the importance of individual presidential candidates, party coalitions and strategic voting behaviour with regard to the presidency. See ibid., 145.
57. Ibid.
58. Ibid. All PNS and regional election results are available from the author on request.
59. Elischer, 'Ethnic Coalitions'; Kagwanja and Southall, 'Introduction'.
60. For the regional election results see note 58.
61. Jones and Mainwaring, 'Nationalization'.
62. Croissant and Schächter, 'Die Nationalisierung politischer Parteien'.
63. On opposition party weaknesses in general, see Rakner and Van de Walle, 'Democratization by Elections'.
64. Hoffman and Robinson, 'Tanzania's Missing Opposition'; Makara, Rakner, and Svåsand, 'Turnaround'.
65. On the importance of 'institutional alignment' see Reynolds, 'Building Democracy After Conflict'.

Notes on contributor

Anika Moroff is a PhD candidate at the Department of Political Science at the University of Duisburg-Essen and an Associate Research Fellow at the GIGA Institute of African Affairs in Hamburg. Her research interests include political parties in Africa, ethnic conflict and institutional engineering.

Bibliography

Amiri, Jane. 'Kenya'. In *Parties and Democracy. The KAS Democracy Report 2007*, ed. KAS, 62–87. Bonn: Bouvier, 2007.
Bogaards, Matthijs. 'Electoral Systems, Party Systems, and Ethnicity in Africa'. In *Votes, Money and Violence: Political Parties and Elections in Sub-Saharan Africa*, ed. Matthias Basedau, Gero Erdmann, and Andreas Mehler, 168–93. Stockholm & Scottsville, South Africa: Nordiska Afrikainstitutet; University of KwaZulu-Natal Press, 2007.
Bogaards, Matthijs, Matthias Basedau, and Christof Hartmann. 'Ethnic Party Bans in Africa: An Introduction'. *Democratization* 17, no. 4 (2010): 599–617.

Carbone, Giovanni M. *No Party Democracy? Ugandan Politics in Comparative Perspective.* Boulder, CO & London: Lynne Rienner, 2008.

Chabal, Patrick, and Jean-Pascal Daloz. *Africa Works. The Political Instrumentalization of Disorder.* Oxford: International African Institute, 1999.

Chandra, Kanchan. *Why Ethnic Parties Succeed: Patronage and Ethnic Head Counts in India.* Cambridge & New York: Cambridge University Press, 2004.

Cheeseman, Nic, and Rob Ford. 'Ethnicity as a Political Cleavage'. Afrobarometer Working Papers No. 83, 2007.

Chege, Michael. 'Political Parties in East Africa. Diversity in Political Party Systems'. Idea: Stockholm, 2007.

Chhibber, Pradeep, and Ken Kollman. *The Formation of National Party Systems. Federalism and Party Competition in Canada, Great Britain, India and the United States.* Oxford: Oxford University Press, 2004.

The Constitutional Court of Uganda. Constitutional Petition No. 5 of 2002 (21 March 2003). *Paul Kawanga Ssemogerere and Others v. The Attorney General of Uganda.*

The Constitutional Court of Uganda. Constitutional Petition No. 22 of 2006 (30 April 2008), *Paul Kafeero and Herman Kazibe v. The Electoral Commission and the Attorney General.*

Croissant, Aurel and Teresa Schächter. 'Die Nationalisierung politischer Parteien und Parteiensysteme in asiatischen Neo-Demokratien'. *Politische Vierteljahresschrift* 49, no. 4 (2008): 641–68.

Economist Intelligence Unit, *Country Report Tanzania*, No. 3, 1993.

Economist Intelligence Unit, *Country Report Uganda*, No. 2, 1993.

Elischer, Sebastian. 'Ethnic Coalitions of Convenience and Commitment: Political Parties and Party Systems in Kenya'. GIGA Working Papers No. 68. Hamburg: GIGA German Institute of Global and Area Studies, 2008.

Hoffman, Barack, and Lindsay Robinson. 'Tanzania's Missing Opposition'. *Journal of Democracy* 20, no. 4 (2009): 123–36.

Horowitz, Donald L. *Ethnic Groups in Conflict.* Berkeley, CA: University of California Press, 2000.

Independent Review Commission. *Report of the Independent Review Commission on the General Elections held in Kenya on 27 December 2007*, 2008.

Jones, Mark P., and Scott Mainwaring. 'The Nationalization of Parties and Party Systems: An Empirical Measure and an Application to the Americas'. *Party Politics* 9, no. 2 (2003): 139–66.

Kagwanja, Peter, and Roger Southall. 'Introduction: Kenya – A Democracy in Retreat?'. *Journal of Contemporary African Studies* 27, no. 3 (2009): 259–77.

Karume, Shumbana. 'Dilemmas of Political Transition. Towards Institutionalisation of Multiparty Democracy in Tanzania'. Research Report No. 7. EISA, 2004.

Kiiza, Julius, Lars Svåsand and Robert Tabaro. 'Organising Parties for the 2006 Elections'. In *Electoral Democracy in Uganda: Understanding Institutional Processes and Outcomes of the 2006 Multiparty Elections*, ed. Julius Kiiza, Sabiti Makara and Lise Rakner, 201–30. Kampala: Fountain Publishers, 2008.

Makara, Sabiti, Lise Rakner, and Lars Svåsand. 'Turnaround: The National Resistance Movement and the Reintroduction of a Multiparty System in Uganda'. *International Political Science Review* 30, no. 2 (2009): 185–204.

Moroff, Anika. 'Party Bans in Africa – An Empirical Overview', *Democratization* 17, no. 4 (2010): 618–41.

Moroff, Anika. 'Ethnic Party Bans in East Africa from a Comparative Perspective'. GIGA Working Papers No. 129. Hamburg: GIGA German Institute of Global and Area Studies, 2010.

Museveni, Yoweri. *What Is Africa's Problem?* Minneapolis, MN: University of Minnesota Press, 2000.

Ndegwa, Stephen. 'The Incomplete Transition. The Constitutional and Electoral Context in Kenya'. *Africa Today* 45, no. 2 (1998): 193–211.

Oded, Arye. *Islam and Politics in Kenya*. Boulder, CO: Lynne Rienner, 2000.

Peter, Chris Maina. 'Determining the Pace of Change: The Law on Pluralism in Tanzania'. In *Law and the Struggle for Democracy in East Africa*, ed. Joseph Oloka-Onyango, Kivutha Kibwana, and Chris Maina Peter, 511–25. Nairobi: Claripress, 1996.

Peters, Ralph-Michael. 'Kenya 1995'. In *Afrika Jahrbuch 1995. Politik, Wirtschaft und Gesellschaft in Afrika südlich der Sahara*, ed. Institut für Afrika-Kunde, 255–63. Opladen: Leske + Budrich, 1996.

Rabushka, Alvin, and Kenneth A. Shepsle. *Politics in Plural Societies: A Theory of Democratic Instability*. Columbus, OH: Merrill, 1972.

Rakner, Lise, and Nicolas Van de Walle. 'Democratization by Elections? Opposition Weakness in Africa'. *Journal of Democracy* 20, no. 3 (2009): 108–21.

Reilly, Benjamin. 'Political Engineering and Party Politics in Conflict-Prone Societies'. *Democratization* 13, no. 5 (2006): 811–27.

Reilly, Benjamin, and Per Nordlund, eds. *Political Parties in Conflict-Prone Societies: Regulation, Engineering and Democratic Development*. Tokyo & New York: United Nations University Press, 2008.

Republic of Kenya. *Societies Act*. Nairobi: Government Printer, 1968.

Republic of Kenya. *The Political Parties Act, 2007*. Nairobi: Government Printer, 2007.

Republic of Uganda. *Constitution of the Republic of Uganda*. Entebbe: Government Printer, 1995.

Republic of Uganda. *The Political Parties and Organisation Act, 2002*. Entebbe: Government Printer, 2002.

Republic of Uganda. *The Political Parties and Organisation Act, 2005*. Entebbe: Government Printer, 2005.

Reynolds, Andrew. 'Building Democracy After Conflict. Constitutional Medicine.' *Journal of Democracy* 16, no. 1 (2005): 54–68.

Sartori, Giovanni. *Parties and Party Systems. A Framework for Analysis*. Colchester: ECPR Press, 2005.

Steiner, Susan. 'Uganda 2003'. In *Afrika Jahrbuch 2003. Politik, Wirtschaft und Gesellschaft in Afrika südlich der Sahara*, ed. Institut für Afrika-Kunde, 321–28. Wiesbaden: VS Verlag für Sozialwissenschaften, 2004.

Tibendera, Kazenga B. *Islamic Fundamentalism: The Question for the Rights of Muslims in Uganda*. Kampala: Fountain Publishers, 2006.

The United Republic of Tanzania. *The Constitution of the United Republic of Tanzania*. Dar es Salaam: Government Printer, 1977.

The United Republic of Tanzania. *The Political Parties Act*. Dar es Salaam: Government Printer, 1992.

Senegal's party system: the limits of formal regulation

Christof Hartmann

Institute of Political Science, University of Duisburg-Essen, Duisburg, Germany

Senegal has a long history of multiparty rule. In the 1970s the regime used party regulation to restrict political competition; since the 1990s and notwithstanding a steady rise of the number of political parties to around 150 at the end of 2008, there have been only a few attempts to regulate the activities of political parties. Party bans have been effective in limiting the politicization of ethnicity in the party system, but other social and political variables have contributed equally to this outcome. Formal rules have not been applied in stopping the rise of religious parties, as the electoral success of these parties remains limited. The shrinking importance of political parties in the increasingly personalist regime of President Wade makes regulation of party activities a less contested issue.

Introduction

By African standards Senegal has an excellent record as both a liberal democracy and as a peaceful country without military coups and with little civil conflict. Multiparty rule has existed continuously since 1976, and in 2000 the incumbent president was voted out of office. While in recent years concerns about the quality of the democratic process and media freedom have been raised,[1] there is still reason to inquire about the causes behind Senegal's rather singular trajectory. I will analyse to what extent Senegal's positive record is caused by the country's specific political-institutional arrangements, and the analytical focus will be on those institutions that regulate the existence and activities of political parties.

Senegal has indeed quite a long history of party regulation. Multiparty rule was re-established in 1976 by the official *octroi* of two parties besides the ruling Parti Socialiste (PS). The introduction of unrestricted multiparty rule in 1981 was accompanied by a ban on particularistic political parties and the adoption of a consciously designed electoral system. Senegal is thus an interesting case from a comparative perspective. It was one of the first African countries to introduce a party ban, and it should therefore be possible to verify the relevance of these regulations for the development of the party system in Senegal and the democratic process in general.[2] More specifically, it is assumed that the relevance of party bans is closely related to regime type, a hypothesis which is sustained by other contributions to this special issue.[3] Within the presidential systems of francophone Africa presidents rely much more on informal regulation, and rule of law lacks proper enforcement. As political parties lose their centrality in the political process, their regulation is not taken seriously by the government, but at the same time can still be used arbitrarily – as one of several instruments within a broader strategy – to influence political competition.

The article will proceed in five steps. I will first retrace the major phases of the party system starting from independence to the latest 2007 parliamentary elections. A second step consists of a detailed account of the legal instruments that the state administration used to influence the development of this party system. The main interest here is on party bans, i.e. the criteria that parties have to fulfil in order to participate in political competition and the way the state administration is applying these rules. On this basis I can then assess the relevance of party bans in shaping the party system. I will discuss in a third step the non-emergence of ethnic parties and then, fourth, look at some religious parties whose conformity with the constitutional provisions could be reasonably doubted. A final section presents the case of a prominent political party which was not registered for purely instrumental reasons before the main arguments are summed up in the conclusion.

From controlled pluralism to a dominant party system

In comparison to most other states in sub-Saharan Africa Senegal has a quite unusual political history. From 1879 the French citizens of the four municipalities Gorée, St. Louis, Rufisque, and Dakar elected a representative to the French National Assembly. The first political parties were created in the 1920s.[4] During the later phase of colonial rule the Union Populaire Sénégalaise (UPS) became the only party with a relatively dense organizational structure, and it thus emerged as a leading political force after the 1958 referendums, when Senegal decided to remain part of the French confederation.

Leopold Senghor was elected president of independent Senegal in 1960. Senegal got a new Constitution in 1963 with a purely presidential system and a plurality electoral system within one national constituency, which created a *de facto* single party system. The 1963 Constitution explicitly recognized the role of political parties in generating political will. Although the government held all 80 seats in the National Assembly and dissolved the main opposition party, the Front National Sénégalais (FNS) of Cheikh Anta Diop in 1964 without providing specific reasons,[5] there was no formal dismissal of the principle of multiparty system. The first Party Law was enacted at the end of 1964 which regulated the participation of political parties in elections. Since then, political parties have had to register with the Minister of the Interior. None of the then existing opposition parties did so, and by the end of 1966, Senegal still had only one legal political party, the ruling UPS.[6] This remained so until the mid-1970s with the UPS winning all seats in the parliamentary elections of 1968 and 1973.

Constitutional reforms in March 1976 marked a significant departure from the practice of the single-party state. In a context of growing political and social unrest the government had in 1974 legalized a second party, the newly created Parti Démocratique Sénégalais (PDS), and prepared a new Party Law in 1975 (Loi 75-68 du 9 juillet 1975 relative aux partis politiques). The constitutional reform of 1976 introduced the principle of limited party pluralism. The new Article 3 of the Constitution fixed the number of legal political parties to three, and these three parties 'have to represent different ideological perspectives'.[7] In a period when nearly all African states were ruled by one-party systems or by the military this was an unusual step.[8]

The new Constitutional Article 3 did not mention specific political parties or spell out ideological profiles, but a complementary law from April 1976 established that these three ideologies were a liberal-democratic one, represented by the PDS; a socialist-democratic one, reflected in the ideology of the party in power, the UPS (renamed Parti Socialiste in December 1976, one month after having been admitted to the Socialist International); and a Marxist–Leninist or communist ideology represented by the Party Africain de l'Idépendance (PAI).[9] The government's attempt at creating a three-party system via legal fiat was met with criticism, a low turnout in the 1978 elections, and outright opposition. Cheikh Anta Diop who had in 1976 formed a new political party, the Rassemblement National Démocratique (RND), claimed to represent the true left-radical interests instead of the PAI. The government attempted without success to convince the RND to merge with the PAI in order to be able to compete in elections.[10] The 1978 elections, however, clearly revealed the limits of such political engineering. The PS gained a large majority with 81.7% of votes (and 83% of seats), while the PDS obtained 17.9% of the votes. The third party designed by constitutional fiat, the PAI, was boycotted by the electorate, and did not gain a single seat in parliament. After the elections, the Constitution was again amended to legalize a fourth political party, the Mouvement Républicain Sénégalais (MRS) as the official representative of a nationalist-democratic ideology.[11]

Under Senghor's successor Abdou Diouf the Constitution was once again amended in April 1981 and all restrictions on the number of legal parties lifted.[12] At the end of 1983 there were 17 legally registered parties in Senegal, but most of them remained quite ephemeral. Notwithstanding this growing number of political parties, the 1983, 1988, and 1993 elections were essentially a two-party contest between the PS and PDS, with the former continuously losing its dominance. This was partly due to an ongoing reform of electoral governance that created a more level playing field for all competitors.[13]

The decisive change in the Senegalese party system had, however, less to do with the changing institutional framework or the demonstration effects in francophone Africa. Rather, it had to do with President Abdou Diouf who lost control of his own party. Within the Parti Socialiste, factional battles led to open defection.

In the 1998 parliamentary elections, a breakaway party from the PS, the Union pour le Renouveau (URD) of Djibo Kâ, gained 11% of the votes, and the PS was reduced to 50.2% of the votes (although the majoritarian component of the electoral system manufactured a stronger majority of 93 seats out of 140). In 1999, a second PS heavy-weight, former prime minister Moustapha Niasse, formed his own party, the Alliance des Forces de Progrès (AFP). In the 2000 presidential elections, Diouf was thus defeated in the run-off, when both Niasse and Kâ shifted their support to opposition leader Abdoulaye Wade from the PDS.[14]

The newly elected President Wade dissolved the National Assembly, which was still dominated by the PS, and early elections were held in April 2001. The elections did mark not only the definitive defeat of the Parti Socialiste but also a more profound change in the party system. The former ruling party fell apart with other former key PS politicians forming their own parties such as Abdourahim Agne (Parti de la Réforme, PR), Abdoulaye Makthar Diop (Socialistes unis pour la Renaissance, SUR), or Robert Sagna (see below). The newly elected president also started to create what is usually called a *mouvance présidentielle* in francophone Africa, i.e. a loose coalition of a multitude of smaller parties around his own party PDS.[15] Rightly fearing that the PDS alone could not win an outright majority in parliament, the formation of the SOPI coalition (meaning 'change' in Wolof) with nearly 40 parties allowed the president to win 49.6% of the votes, and with a little help from the electoral system, to get 89 out of 120 seats.

Fresh parliamentary elections to be held in 2006 were postponed by President Wade to February 2007 (the date of the presidential elections) amidst criticism by the opposition parties. In April 2007 most opposition parties decided to boycott these elections, as a protest against alleged electoral malpractices and the use of an outdated electoral register during that year's presidential elections, when 81-year-old Wade had won a new mandate. In the June 2007 parliamentary elections the SOPI coalition won 131 of 150 seats with a historically low turnout of 34%.

The victory of the opposition in 2000–2001 thus led to a major restructuring of Senegal's party system. It has become more like the francophone African average model of a poorly institutionalized dominant party with a myriad of smaller political parties crossing the floor at times and few genuine opposition forces whose main strategy is (to threaten) to boycott elections.[16] The *alternance* in 2000 led to a sharp increase in the number of political parties from 26, at the end of 1997, to 57 (at the end of 2000), 94 (at the end of 2006), and then 145 (at the end of 2008). It is particularly noteworthy that President Wade has apparently no interest in strengthening his own party, the PDS, but prefers to rely on many small parties that are easier to manipulate and that to a certain extent have been deliberately created and funded by the government.[17]

Party bans and other instruments of regulation

The cursory overview on the evolution of Senegal's party system has already emphasized the heavy influence of state regulation. I will now take a closer look at particular strategies of state regulation of political parties which have changed over the years. The introduction and enforcement of party bans has thus to be understood as part of a broader institutional arrangement aiming at structuring and controlling political competition.

The first 15 years of independence were marked by a *de facto* single party rule of the UPS, even though the Independence Constitution attributed a central role to political parties. With the 1975 Party Law, for the first time the regime brought formal rules in line with actual practice. Senegal's 1976 constitutional reform remains a very original (but inefficient) model of institutional engineering. It is important to stress that this attempt to manufacture an ideology-based party system (ignoring the lack of respective social cleavages) was accompanied by the banning of other potential socio-political cleavages within the party system. The 1978 constitutional amendment in fact included for the first time a provision according to which the three respective constitutional parties should have a national vocation and not be allowed to refer to racial, ethnic, religious, linguistic, gender or regional identities. The preamble to the law clarified that these amendments were necessary to save national unity.[18] This artificial creation of an ideological party system sparked a lively debate among Senegalese constitutional lawyers and political observers, while the exclusion of ethnic, religious or other particularistic parties did not.[19] As Senghor himself remained silent about this constitutional provision and the only clandestine parties at that time were various Marxist-Leninist groups and no obviously particularistic party had emerged,[20] one can only speculate whether Senghor reacted to the rise of particularistic parties in neighbouring countries and/or whether these clauses reflected his republican-nationalist personal convictions. It is, however, clear that the introduction of party bans was directly linked to the establishment of an ideology-based party system and was thus intended to pre-empt a politicization of other particularistic social cleavages.

After 1981 and Diouf's adoption of *multipartisme intégral*, the strategy of the president and the ruling party changed. State regulation was from then on less used to limit political party competition but, on the contrary, to fragment and weaken the opposition. A rigid policy of restricting the number of political parties was, thus, against all contrary policy statements, not in the interest of the ruling party. The main instruments of controlling the party system were both the electoral system and the rules of electoral governance, heavily tilted in favour of the ruling party. For the 1983 elections, the Diouf government introduced a segmented (or parallel) system with half of the 120 seats elected by plurality at the departmental level (via party lists in small constituencies of different size) and the remaining 60 seats distributed to party lists at the national level via proportional representation. This system favoured the party with the most thorough territorial penetration, i.e. the Parti Socialiste, and as voters had a single vote for both segments of the electoral system, coordination of opposition parties was made impossible.[21] In 1983 the PS won all departments and got 92.5% of the seats (with 79.9% of the votes won); in 1993 and 1998 the electoral system transformed narrow absolute majorities of

56.6% and 50.2% respectively of the votes into relative comfortable seat majorities in the National Assembly (70.0% and 66.4% respectively).

If the growth of political parties was in the government's interest, this strategy thus paid off. At a practical level, this meant to create low entry thresholds which made a strict enforcement of party bans unlikely. Although a Party Law[22] does exist, the creation of political parties in Senegal has been regulated on the basis of the law on associations (Art. 812-814 of the *Code des Obligations Civiles et Commerciales*), which means that there is, in principle, only an exam of the procedural conditions on completion of which the Ministry is supposed to deliver a receipt (*récépissé de declaration*) which gives the party or association a legal status. According to the law, the application has to be addressed to the local administration (*prefecture*) where the headquarters of the party is located. At prefecture level the application is formally evaluated (lists of party members, postal address of headquarters, copies of identity card, minutes of formative session, party programme and so on) and transferred to the Ministry of Interior, where the application is assessed against the material principles as mentioned in Constitution Art. 3 and Art. 2 of the Party Law.

When case errors are discovered or there is a discrepancy of registration dossier during the examination by the Ministry of Interior, then the application is sent back to the prefecture. During the last two decades some registration procedures were delayed due to such problems, in some cases also because the name of the party was already taken. My interviews in the Department of the Ministry of the Interior made very clear that the Ministry sees the legal exam as a procedural question. If a party writes in its programme that it intends to promote the interests of a specific region, the Ministry asks it to correct the formulation so as not to violate the letter of the law. It does not come as a surprise then, that there are very few cases of failed registration, all of which concern religious parties that refused to water down their programmes or parties formed by personal rivals of the President of the Republic, as discussed in more detail below.[23]

While there are few obstacles to creating a political party, it is much more difficult to dissolve one. The Party Law provides for the dissolution of parties in a number of instances, and particularly so where a party, 'through its general activities and public statements has severely violated the obligations of Constitutional Article 3'.[24] The Party Law further stipulates that parties might be dissolved by a decree at the request of the Minister of Interior, but it fails to mention a specific procedure in a case when a political party after having been registered does no longer fulfil the conditions of Constitution Article 3.[25] In practice, the Ministry is restricting itself to a formal review of the party statutes upon registering a party. Whether this party then adheres to the general principles in practice or has a hidden agenda is not observed or monitored. The Party Law also requires political parties to prepare annual reports on their financial situation and to give an update on the addresses and membership of the current board (Article 3). According to Ministry staff, none of the more than 100 parties, including the ruling party, fulfilled these conditions and yet no sanction was enacted. From a purely legal perspective the Ministry should thus dissolve all political parties currently operating in Senegal.[26] The formal regulations for initiating a ban of an existing party are not detailed enough and the government apparently never saw a need to formalize it.

No particularistic political parties were thus ever dissolved in the history of Senegal.[27] Does this allow us to conclude that the constitutional provisions effectively blocked the articulation of ethnicity and religion within the party system, i.e. potential party-founders were convinced that there was no legitimate expression of these cleavages within the party system? The fact that there has not been an outright party ban still leaves us with another scenario: ethnic or religious parties are allowed to participate in the political competition (against the constitutional provisions) provided that the government does not perceive them to be dangerous to regime survival, as long as these particularistic parties might be useful allies in the political process, or simply because the regime might use other – informal – ways to limit the political relevance of these parties.

I now turn to a more detailed analysis of particularistic parties, some of which apparently did not fulfil the constitutional criteria of not having a racist, sexist, ethnic, regional, linguistic or religious orientation.

The lack of ethnic parties

Like nearly all other African states, Senegal is an ethnically heterogeneous country. The ethnic group of Wolof is the largest group, and since colonial times, has dominated economic and political life. Wolof has thus become the lingua franca in the country. Ethnic relationships within the strongly urbanized Senegalese population have been peaceful since independence.

During the early 1980s, however, a violent conflict erupted in the Southern province of Casamance, virtually cut from the rest of Senegal by the enclave of the Gambia. The mostly Dioula and Christian population resented a growing economic and social marginalization and a large influx of 'Northerners' within the administration and business elites of the Casamance. The local populations eventually started to give widespread support to a rebel movement (Mouvement des Forces Democratiques de Casamance, MFDC) fighting for the separation of Casamance from Senegal. Large-scale violence was brought to an end in the early 1990s, but violence has persistently erupted and no sustainable political solution has been found yet.[28] Many Senegalese deny that the conflict in Casamance is really about ethnicity or religion as not all of the Casamançais are Dioula and there are numerous non-Christian among them.

As surprising as it might sound, among the 145 Senegalese parties there are indeed no openly ethnic or regional parties, irrespective of whether we define an ethnic party on the basis of its programme and behaviour or its voter support. We certainly lack any systematic assessment of the party programme and behaviour of all parties, but students of Senegalese party politics, local political analysts and journalists agree that within the 'visible' part of the party spectrum there are no parties with an ethnic or regionalist programme or rhetoric.[29] While some parties exist only on paper, the large majority are based in the capital city Dakar and have never reached out to the rural population. Many of the new parties are clearly the result of economic reforms since the late 1980s, in so far as the party leaders are former teachers or employees of the public sector who lost their jobs in the various civil service reform programmes.

Even more interesting is the fact that among the 145 parties there is not one single political party of the Casamançais. During peace negotiations, the MFDC was offered the opportunity to participate in politics and to transform into a political party (although with a different name). So far, it has declined.[30] During the latest presidential elections in 2007, Robert Sagna, a popular (Christian) mayor of Ziguinchor (capital city of Casamance) between 1984 and 2009, ran a clearly regionalist electoral campaign and obtained 2.58% of the national vote. Sagna, formerly a cabinet minister with the PS for many years, decided to stand in the presidential elections as independent candidate, and subsequently, in October 2007, created his own party, the Rassemblement pour le Socialisme et al Démocratie (RSD). This RSD, however, soon joined the national oppositional party coalition, Takku Défaraat Sénégal, and is therefore, an unlikely candidate for an ethnic party. In the municipal elections of 2009 Sagna's party fielded again common candidates with other opposition parties, particularly the Parti Socialiste.

Do we find political parties that receive electoral support exclusively or mostly from one ethnic group in Senegal? This is clearly not the case for the two traditional strongest parties of the country, the PS and the PDS.[31] The smaller the electoral support of the political party, the more likely it is that it will get significantly more votes in the home province of its party leaders. Some few parties have thus a strong support from specific towns where their leaders originate from, such as the URD of Djibo Kâ among the Peulhs populations, or the smaller parties Parti pour la Démocratie et la Citoyenneté (PDC) in Rufisque, and the Action patriotique de Liberation (APL) in Kaolack, but they do not openly promote the interests of these regions nor do they field candidates exclusively in these districts. The URD is also not an ethnic party in the sense that the Peulhs comprise up to 30% of the national population and are settled throughout the national territory in many regions where the URD does not get any votes.[32] It is quite telling in this regard, that demands for regulations that require parties to prove their national character through party offices nationwide or by membership in all regions of the country (such representation requirements aiming at the prevention of regional parties exist in many other African countries[33]) have been totally absent in Senegal.

Should we infer from this that ethnic party bans have been a particular powerful instrument in de-politicizing ethnic identity and blocking the emergence of ethnic parties? The astonishing lack of ethnic parties is certainly as much reflecting the structural contexts as it is resulting from party regulation.

The often ridiculed idea of manufacturing an ideological party system in an African country might still have created an institutional legacy that strongly benefited the two large parties. Until very recently the party system was still largely dominated by the two traditional parties, the PS and PDS, and their various breakaways, all of which are strongly committed to a centralist and republican state. The particularistic party-ban provisions may have had a role in strengthening this already existing consensus among the party elites. At the same time, these party-ban provisions reflected underlying political culture, the existing strong social integration (*cousinage à plaisanterie*) and the common membership in religious communities as cross-cutting issues.[34]

Party bans and the rise of religious parties

In contrast to ethnic parties, there is no lack of religious parties in Senegal, with several of them clearly pursuing religious or sectarian objectives. Over the years there have been three cases of denied registration. In 1979 El Hadji Ahmed Khalifa Niasse, a marabout from the brotherhood of the Tijanes, left the Parti Socialiste and wanted to register a party with the name Hisbollah. We have to remember that this was still the time of the constitutionally mandated four-party system, and the Constitution had clearly not provided for an Islamic party. Inspired by the Iranian Revolution, the 'Ayatollah from Kaolack' publicly denounced President Senghor and asked for the mobilization of several hundred thousand *talibés* and the introduction of the *sharia* in Senegal. The government not only refused to register the party, but started to act against Ahmed Khalifa Niasse because he was recruiting armed men for the so-called Islamic Legion of Libyan leader, Muammar Qadaffi. When he was denied political asylum in France he fled to Libya, and Senegal broke relations with Libya over this issue in 1980. Niasse was later arrested in Niger and detained in Senegal until 1982, when Abdou Diouf pardoned him.[35] Clearly, this episode was about much more than restricting party competition.

There were two further cases of denied registrations, but both of them are scarcely documented. In 1981 a party called Rassemblement pour le salut national applied for registration, but its application was refused due to its religious objectives.[36] In 1991 the Ministry of Interior denied registration to the Parti pour la Libération et la Démocratie Islamique.[37] Since the Ministry does not have a proper archive, it proved impossible to check the background of these two cases.

The character of the relationship between religion and politics has undergone a slow but steady change over the last three decades.[38] In Senegal the boundaries between a religious and a civic sphere were always blurred. Since colonial times the Islamic brotherhoods (the two important ones being the Murides and the Tijanes) were deeply involved in economic and political issues. During the period of Senghor's rule and the first decade of Abdou Diouf's rule there was a clear alliance between the brotherhoods and the Parti Socialiste. The secular Senegalese state, indeed, promoted the local interests of the religious leaders (*marabouts*), while these religious leaders asked their followers to vote for the PS. These direct orders to vote (*ndigël*) became more contested since the early

1990s, as the brotherhoods gained more autonomy from the political leadership, and it became more risky to fully align with one political party.[39]

Under President Diouf the Tijanes had grown more important, but President Wade clearly shifted the loyalty of the new government in a very explicit way towards the Murides.[40] In unprecedented way the current president is instrumentalizing and politicizing allegiance to Islamic brotherhoods, which has created resentment among other such groups and the Christian minority, and puts at risk the secular character of the Senegalese state.[41] As a reaction to this growing politicization there is also a growing pluralization of religious groups and beliefs with intergenerational conflicts within the brotherhoods and a growing social and economic influence of more radical Arab versions of Islam.[42]

There are five religious parties currently active in Senegal, all of which are officially registered by the Ministry of Interior.[43] There are obviously no disaggregated voter data for religious groups; I therefore classify a party as religious based on the composition of its leadership and its actual party programme and rhetoric. There are two political parties 'representing' the Murides. One is the Mouvement des Citoyens pour une Démocratie de Developpement (MDC) of Serigne Fall, created in March 2000. The MDC participated in the 2001 elections and failed to win a seat (0.47% of votes in 2001). Serigne Fall had also run as candidate in the 2000 presidential elections for another party (PRS) because the MDC had not obtained registration from the Ministry in time. In 2007 the MDC became part of Wade's SOPI coalition, but still did not get elected. While Serigne Fall's religious discourse is moderate, this is not necessarily the case for the second Muride party: the Parti de la Vérité pour le Developpement (PVD), headed by Marabou Serigne Modou Kara Mbacké, a nephew of the current Caliph of the Murides. After his movement had operated as a religious association, Mbacke transformed it into a political party in 2004. The PVD participated in the 2007 elections, also as part of the SOPI coalition, without any seat being won by PVD candidates. Although electorally insignificant, the PVD is important because of the religious stature of its leadership; these are, in fact, religious leaders who count much more on having *talibés* than on having party members or a regular party organization. The PVD leadership at times uses an Islamist discourse, but refrains from acting publicly in a way that would challenge the president's policies.[44] President Wade appointed Mbacké's wife Sokhna Dieng Mbacké to the newly created Senate, and the PVD can hardly be seen as a political-religious threat to a civilian-republican regime.

There also exist two parties led by religious leaders from the Tijanes brotherhood. The Rassemblement pour le Peuple (RP) headed by the Marabou Mamoune Niasse was created in 2004. It participated as one of few opposition parties in the 2007 elections and won two seats in the parliament (4.25% of votes). In fact after the elections Niasse declared himself 'leader of the opposition'.[45] During the electoral campaign for the local elections in March 2009 he made a spectacular turn-around and asked (as official representative of the

Caliph Mouhamed Dame Ibrahima Niasse) the local *talibés* to support President Wade and his government, a declaration which created a lot of protests.[46]

The Front pour le Socialisme et la Démocratie/Benno Jubël (FSD/BJ), on the contrary, has a longer history. It was created by Cheikh Abdoulaye Dieye in April 1996 and has a strong territorial base in the northern city of St. Louis. It gained one seat in the 1998 elections (1.33% of the national vote), but failed to earn any in the 2001 elections (0.42%). Cheikh Bamba Dieye, the son of the party leader, got elected in the 2007 elections (2.18%). In the presidential election of February 2007, he ended up in the ninth place after managing only 0.5% of the valid votes. As the party's more radical religious rhetoric used by Cheikh Abdoulaye Dieye (such as collective prayers during the electoral campaign, strict demands for a change of the *code de la famille*, defence of female circumcision, introduction of obligatory HIV testing for young men before marriage) was not honoured by the voters in 2001, and he was officially reprimanded by the Haut Conseil de l'audio-visuel (HCA), his son softened the party's religious character in the 2007 elections.[47]

All four parties discussed so far are controlled by religious leaders from one of the two main brotherhoods. This is not the case for the Mouvement de la réforme pour le développement social (MRDS). This movement is directed by Imam Mbaye Niang and represents the still minority strand of radical Wahhabism in Senegal. The MRDS was registered in October 2000 and participated with minimal success in the 2001 (0.55%) and 2007 elections (1.12%, one seat for party leader Imam Mbaye Niang). The MRSD has promoted a different type of Islamic discourse with a more serious commitment to Islamic values in daily life, which has failed to attract a larger number of the electorate but seems to have gained popularity among the urban youth in the suburbs of Dakar. Its relevance seems to have increased over the last years as evidenced by their financial support from the diaspora and Arab donors. In 2007 the MRSD was behind several public protests against gay people, and has publicly demanded the introduction of *sharia* in Senegal. The MRSD is clearly an opposition force, and should it gain political importance, both the government and the brotherhoods will try to act against them. According to many observers, the pure form of Islam advocated by MRSD is, however, facing many challenges in a society which has a long history of syncretist beliefs and a tradition of electing Presidents of the Republic with Christian wives (Senghor himself was also a Christian).

What remains to be seen is whether the rise of religious parties really marks a new phase in the evolution of the Senegalese party system. It certainly marks a transformation of the religious actors and their relationship with the political system.[48] The ideological position of the religious parties in the Wade or opposition camp seems rather unclear. The Islamization of parts of the public life is less visible in the elections but is reflected in different forms of resistance against a political system with 'corrupt politicians' (and allied brotherhood leaders), which are sometimes radical and violent. Viewed from this perspective, political parties such as PVD, FSD/BJ or PR are neither an electoral threat for the government nor indeed an obvious attempt to question the existing mode of governance with a President of the Republic spending a considerable part of his time going to pray at Touba. Their growing importance is an indicator of the government's minimal resistance against the politicization of religion. Electoral results show so far that the population is not inclined to support this trend. The assessment of MRSD is different. From a purely constitutional perspective, the Ministry of the Interior is bound to dissolve political parties which do not respect the secular and republican character of the state, and henceforth, the government ought to have banned the MRSD. As long as the MRSD commands some electoral support, a formal ban against a religious party creates unnecessary problems for the government, because it would raise many questions concerning other religious parties and the many links between political and religious actors. In a context of growing social and economic crisis toleration of radical strands of Islam might, however, backfire against a government which has at various times publicly questioned the secular character of the country.[49]

The Rewmi saga

The possibility of a manipulative use of the party-ban provisions in structuring political competition might be finally demonstrated by the recent emergence of a party led by the former Prime Minister Idrissa Seck (2002–2004). Seck fell out with the President of the Republic, was sacked, and accused of financial malpractices. One of Seck's lieutenants, Yankhoba Diattara created the FIDEL (Forces Integrées pour la Démocratie et la Liberté) party, which was never registered. Diattara was arrested in November 2005 after he had publicly announced on a popular radio station that he wished his comrades to 'welcome' President Wade to Thies, the stronghold of Idrissa Seck. During the visit violent clashes occurred. Diattara was sentenced to six months' imprisonment, and was later pardoned by President Wade after serving three months.

Seck eventually became leader of another newly created political party, six months ahead of the presidential elections in February 2007. The party, named Rewmi (Wolof for 'the country'), had been created by Insa Sankharé, and FIDEL was merged into the new party. Rewmi applied for official registration with the Ministry of the Interior, but the Ministry simply did not respond, and consequently the party was never legalized.[50] Idrissa Seck nevertheless participated quite successfully as independent candidate in the presidential elections and then announced the boycott of his would-be party in the June 2007 parliamentary elections. Even without having registered his party, he participated in the municipal elections on a common opposition list. Senegalese observers have very different interpretations about the creation and mixed success of Rewmi. According to some observers, Seck never intended to turn his back on Wade and hoped to return as soon as possible into the fold of the PDS. Wade, who is attempting to promote his son Karim as his successor, would like to keep Seck as a second-best choice in case his not-so-popular son does not succeed in becoming president.[51] Thus, neither Wade nor Seck were particularly interested in formaliz-ing the creation of a separate party, and Rewmi could be considered rather as an autonomous *courant* within the PDS. Indeed, by early 2010 Seck and his followers formally rejoined the PDS.

Officials from the Ministry of the Interior made it very clear that the President of the Republic had communicated to Sankharé and Seck that he had never allowed the registration of a party called 'the country' because the name of the party and its implicit message of making Senegal a Wolof country violated the constitutional principles of Art.3. Rewmi actually had no regionalist or ethnic bias, and was 'banned' for the only reason that Seck would have always been introduced as the 'President of Rewmi' which is for all Wolof-speaking, i.e. the vast majority of Senegalese, the 'President of the country'. President Wade has added to the legal uncertainty by publicly announcing several times that in the perspective of the parliamentary and then local elections 'members of the two parties' (i.e. PDS and Rewmi) should discuss their co-operation and presentation of common lists.[52]

From a legal point of view a party which is refused registration by the Ministry could apply to the *Conseil d'Etat*. The Ministry's apparent strategy in the cases of FIDEL and Rewmi was simply not to react, because there were no legal arguments to deny the receipt. They knew Sankharé, Diattara or Seck already understood that the *Conseil d'Etat* was not going to officially act against the President in such a politically delicate issue.

Conclusion

Formal party regulation was introduced in Senegal in 1976 from the perspective of a liberalizing regime which wanted to control the degree of political competition. After the introduction of a fully fledged multiparty system, the regime strategy was more directed at using the electoral system and rules of electoral governance to secure control of the political process. The specific constitutional qualifications of Article 3 were introduced in a pre-emptive sense, i.e. there was no actual parti-cularistic party which threatened the republican character of the political system. Although there has been considerable change within the party system, no ethnic parties have emerged over the last 30 years.[53] It has been argued that the interaction of social and institutional factors best explains this rather unusual development and has thus also contributed to democratic stability.

The Senegalese case, however, also illustrates the relevance of broader features of the political system for the use of party bans. The growing presidential character of the government system since the accession of President Wade has produced both an enormous rise in the number of parties and a concomitant loss of influence of parties within the political system and for making policy decisions. President Wade shows no interest of building up a strong government party but rather relies on *ad hoc* party coalitions or informal networks and good contacts with Islamic leaders, and it does not come as a surprise if he has ignored the certainly still limited but growing role of Islamic parties in political competition. Formal rules were used, on the contrary, to prohibit the formation of a political party, when the personal interests of the President were concerned.

All this warns us against being overly enthusiastic about formal party regulation and its beneficial effects in managing state-society relations in Senegal. Enforcement of formal rules needs both administrative capacities and respect for the rule of law, both of which have been on the wane in Senegal over the last decade.[54] There remains a solid tradition of less formalized ways of solving conflicts, especially when it comes to sensitive issues such as Casamance or the relationship with the Marabouts, and a huge majority of the population which still does not favour voting instructions from religious leaders or the ethnicization of party politics.[55]

Acknowledgements

The article is based on a research stay in Dakar, Senegal in February–March 2008. The author thanks the Fritz-Thyssen Foundation for financing the research project 'Ethnic Party Bans in Africa'. He is also particularly thankful to various (in this article unnamed) officials in the Ministry of the Interior for their willingness to share their knowledge on party regulation in Senegal as well as to a number of journalists, party leaders and academics for helping me to get a better understanding of the development of party politics in Senegal. Many thanks also to Anika Moroff, the journal editors, and the two reviewers for their insightful comments. The usual disclaimers apply.

Notes

1. Mbow, 'Senegal: The Return of Personalism'.
2. The article thus applies an institutionalist approach, and considers party bans as formal institutions that restrict the menu of options available to political actors.
3. Hartmann and Kemmerzell, 'Understanding the Variations in Party Bans', and Moroff and Basedau, 'An Effective Measure of Institutional Engineering?', this special issue.
4. Coulon, 'La tradition démocratique au Sénégal'.
5. Ziemer 'Senegal', 1839–40.
6. Several smaller parties, such as the PRA-Sénégal were co-opted by the UPS and thus disappeared; cf. Tine, 'Du multiple à l'un et vice versa?', 67–8.
7. In the original French version, the political parties 'doivent représenter des courants de pensée différents'. The new Article 3 also complemented the existing provision by saying that the party law did determine the conditions under which the parties were created and existed, and now for the first time also under which parties 'ceased to exist'.
8. For different interpretations see Fatton, *The Making of a Liberal Democracy,* and Coulon, 'Senegal', as well as Young and Kanté, 'Governance, Democracy and the 1988 Senegalese Election'.
9. Fall, *Evolution constitutionnelle du Sénégal,* 68–9.
10. Wiseman, *Democracy in Black Africa,* 170.
11. All information on electoral data within this article are based on Bendel, 'Senegal' and Kamara, *Les élections au Sénégal.*
12. A new party law (Loi 81-17 du 6 Mai 1981) also came into force.

13. Diouf, 'L'échec du modèle démocratique au Sénégal', and Back, 'Senegal's patrimonial democrats'.
14. Diop, Diouf and Diaw, 'Le Baobab a été déraciné. L'alternance au Sénégal'.
15. President Wade's victory also allowed the PDS to re-integrate parties that had left the PDS long ago, such as the PDS/R of Serigne Diop (after 15 years of separate existence).
16. For critical assessments of Senegalese authors cf. Dia, *Sénégal: Radioscopie d'une alternance avortée*; Coulibaly, *Une démocratie prise en otage par ses elites*; Diop, 'La Sénégal à la croisée des chemins'.
17. This seems to be the case for the Waar-Wi coalition directed by Wade's former environmental minister; see Mbow, 'Senegal: The Return of Personalism', 159.
18. For the new 1978 text of Art. 2 (3) cf. Fall, *Textes constitutionnels du Sénégal de 1959 à 2007*, 99.
19. Ismaila M. Fall rather typically commented: 'cette réforme constitutionnelle apporte des restrictions salutaires et irréversiblement gravées dans la pierre constitutionnelle sénégalaise'. Fall, *Evolution constitutionnelle du Sénégal*, 70.
20. The separatist conflict in the Casamance broke out fully only in late 1983.
21. In order to win in the small multi-member constituencies they needed to build coalitions, but this minimized their chances of winning seats in the PR segment (national list). For an insightful and more comprehensive analysis of the electoral system change (including changes in electoral governance and lowering voting age in 1993) see Mozaffar and Vengroff, 'A "Whole System" Approach to the Choice of Electoral Rules in Democratizing Countries'.
22. The relevant legal documents are *Loi 81-17 du 24 Janvier 1981* and its successor laws, *Loi 89-36 du 12 Octobre 1989*, and *Loi 92-57 du 3 Septembre 1992*.
23. There seems to have existed one case of a failed registration of a party called Parti des Jeunes du Senegal in 1993, because it intended to promote the interests of young people, and this was considered as a violation of the constitutional principles of Art. 3. The party was later registered as Parti de l'Unité et de Rassemblement (PUR) in 1996 without reference to the particular promotion of young people's interests. No official documentation could be obtained. I refer here to the remarks of PUR leader Khalifa Aboubacar Diouf as quoted in Moegenburg, *Die Parteienlandschaft im Senegal*, 250.
24. Article 4, Party Law (1989) explicitly mentions the respect for a republican, secular and democratic state, the republican institutions, national independence, territorial integrity and national unity as well as public order and public liberties.
25. The Party Law also does not mention the possibility of suspension.
26. Parties which merge with others do not necessarily report to the Ministry, and the Ministry's list is thus not very reliable with regard to the exact number of legal and actually operational parties.
27. As previously mentioned, some parties were not registered, and the FNS of Cheikh Anta Diop was dissolved in 1964, but the FNS was not a particularistic party.
28. Foucher, 'Pas d'alternance en Casamance?'; Englebert, 'Compliance and Defiance to National Integration in Barotseland and Casamance'.
29. Cf. Tine, 'Du multiple à l'un et vice versa?'; Hesseling, *Histoire politique du Sénégal*; Moegenburg, *Die Parteienlandschaft im Senegal*; Osei, *Party-Voter Linkage in Ghana and Senegal*; Dahou and Foucher, 'Le Sénégal, entre changement politique et révolution passive'; Fall, *Evolution constitutionnelle du Sénégal*; Dia, *Sénégal: Radioscopie d'une alternance avortée*; Coulibaly, *Une démocratie prise en otage par ses élites*.
30. Interviews with officials in the Ministry of the Interior.

31. As the opposition boycotted the 2007 elections, no recent data for regional voting behaviour is available. Data for the 2001 parliamentary election show a range of 33.2% to 70.1% for the PDS and between 9.4% and 28.8% for the PS. The third party in the 2001 elections, AFP, got a minimum of 6.7% in each province, but only 32.8% in party leaders Niasse's home province Kaolack. Data from Osei, *Party-Voter Linkage in Ghana and Senegal*.

32. Interview with Ibrahima Fall, 28 February 2008, Dakar.

33. Moroff, 'Party Bans in Africa', this issue

34. *Cousinage à plaisanterie* refers to social norms widely accepted in West African societies which allow joking relationships between members of different communities, for an introduction to the socio-cultural context of Senegalese politcs cf. Schaffer, *Democracy in Translation*.

35. Magassouba, *L'Islam au Sénégal*, 130–6.

36. Ibid., 137.

37. *Sud Quotidien*, 10 May 2000.

38. Villalón, *Islamic Society and State Power in Senegal*.

39. In 1993 the Tijane Marabout Moustapha Sy heavily criticized Abdou Diouf, but his family distanced itself from him and a spokesperson of the Tijanes affirmed 1993 in television 'ceux qui refusent de voter pour Abdou Diouf sont des imbéciles'. Interview with Soro Diop, *Le Quotidien*, Dakar, 6 March 2008.

40. In what was a hotly contested gesture Wade went directly after his election in 2000 to Touba, the capital city of the Murides, and kneeled in front of the Caliph. The scene was broadcast on national television.

41. According to some of the author's interviewees the main purpose of the president's religious zeal – besides its political usefulness – is to hide his non-Islamic beliefs and way of life: Wade also has a Christian wife. The brotherhoods also remain important economic players, less because they control groundnut production but because their religious networks are the main channels for the transfer of the many remittances that represent a growing part of Senegal's national income.

42. Villalon, 'Generational Changes, Political Stagnation'; Dahou and Foucher, 'Le Sénégal, entre changement politique et révolution passive'.

43. All Senegalese interviewees agreed about these parties being religious, although some did not consider them serious actors on the national political scene.

44. Audrain, 'Du "Ndigël" avorté au Parti de la Verité'.

45. *Sud Quotidien*, 16 June 2007.

46. *Sud Quotidien*, 11 March 2009.

47. Interview with I. M. Fall, Dakar, 28 February 2008. It might be, however, questioned, whether the party would have won a single mandate without the boycott of the major opposition parties. The HCA has the task to monitor the behaviour of candidates during the electoral campaigns. During the debate about the constitutional revision in 2001 the FSD/BJ advocated a deletion of the attribute 'secular' in Article 1 of the Senegalese Constitution. *Sud Quotidien*, 24 November 2000.

48. Religious actors keep their role as mediators in many instances, such as the Christian bishops in the Casamance, or the *marabouts* in several conflicts between the president and his prime minister. Interview with Abdou Latif Coulibaly, Dakar, 4 March 2008.

49. In the end, President Wade's attempt at minor modifications of the Constitution, for example, in the field of family law, failed after civil society protests.

50. The evidence presented here is based on interviews with staff members of the Ministry of Interior. During the interviews they insisted that the Rewmi case was never handled by the competent department within the Ministry but directly by the Minister.

51. This is the theory of Abdou Latif Coulibaly, among others. Interview, Dakar, 4 March 2008.

52. Interview with Antoine Diouf (Redacteur en Chef, RJN), Dakar, 26 February 2008.
53. It could be argued that a heavy military presence and rebel activities hindered true regional parties from emerging in Casamance.
54. cf. Thiam, 'Une constitution ça se révise.'
55. At least if we believe in the results of the Afrobarometer Survey, cf. Wantchekon, *Support for Competitive Politics and Government Performance.*

Notes on contributor

Christof Hartmann is Professor of Political Science at the University of Duisburg-Essen (Germany). His research focuses on democratization, democratic institutions, and institutional change, with particular emphasis on sub-Saharan Africa.

Bibliography

Audrain, Xavier. 'Du "Ndigël" avorté au Parti de la Verité. Evolution du Rapport Religion/Politique à travers le Parcours de Cheikh Modou Kara (1999–2004).' *Politique Africaine* 96 (2004): 99–117.

Beck, Linda J. 'Senegal's Patrimonial Democrats. Incremental Reform and the Obstacles to the Consolidation of Democracy'. *Canadian Journal of African Studies* 31 (1997): 1–31.

Bendel, Petra. 'Senegal'. In *Elections in Africa. A Data Handbook*, ed. Dieter Nohlen, Michael Krennerich and Bernhard Thibaut, 755–74, Oxford: Oxford UP, 1999.

Coulibaly, Abdou Latif. *Une démocratie prise en otage par ses élites. Essai politique sur la pratique de la démocratie au Sénégal.* Dakar: Editions Sentinelles, 2006.

Coulon, Christian. 'Senegal. The Development and Fragility of Semi-Democracy'. In *Democracy in Developing Countries, Vol. II Africa*, ed. Larry Diamond, Juan Linz, and Seymour M. Lipset, 140–78, Boulder, CO: Lynne Rienner, 1988.

Coulon, Christian. 'La tradition démocratique au Sénégal. Histoire d'un mythe'. In *Démocraties d'ailleurs: démocratie et démocratisation hors d'Occident*, ed. Christophe Jaffrelot, 67–92, Paris: Karthala, 2000.

Dahou, Tarik, and Vincent Foucher. 'Le Sénégal, entre changement politique et révolution passive'. *Politique Africaine* 96 (2004): 5–21.

Dia, Mamadou. *Sénégal: Radioscopie d'une alternance avortée.* Paris: L'Harmattan, 2005.

Diop, Momar-Coumba, Mamadou Diouf, and Aminata Diaw. 'Le Baobab a été déraciné. L'alternance au Sénégal'. *Politique Africaine* 78 (2000): 157–79.

Diop, Momar-Coumba. 'La Sénégal à la croisée des chemins', *Politique Africaine* 104 (2006): 103–26.

Diouf, Mamadou. 'L'échec du modèle démocratique du Sénégal, 1981–1993'. *Afrika-Spectrum* 29 (1994): 47–64.

Englebert, Pierre. 'Compliance and Defiance to National Integration in Barotseland and Casamance'. *Afrika Spectrum* 40 (2005): 29–59.

Fall, Ismaila Madior. *Evolution constitutionnelle du Sénégal de la veille de l'Indépendance aux élections de 2007.* Dakar: CREDILA 2007.

Fall, Ismaila Madior, ed. *Textes Constitutionnels du Sénégal du 24 janvier 1959 au 15 mai 2007.* Dakar: CREDILA, 2007.

Fatton, Robert. *The Making of a Liberal Democracy. Senegal's Passive Revolution, 1975–1985.* Boulder, CO: Lynne Rienner, 1987.

Foucher, Vincent. 'Pas d'alternance en Casamance? Le nouveau pouvoir sénégalais face à la revendication séparatiste casamançaise'. *Politique Africaine* 91 (2003): 101–19.

Hartmann, Christof, and Jörg Kemmerzell. 'Understanding Variations in Party Bans in Africa'. *Democratization* 17, no. 4 (2010): 642–65.

Hesseling, Gerti. *Histoire politique du Sénégal: institutions, droit et société*. Paris: Karthala, 1985.

Kamara, Mamadou. *Les élections au Sénégal. Rôle, place et responsabilités des différents acteurs*. Dakar: Les Presses de la Sénégalaise, 2007.

Magassouba, Moriba. *L'Islam au Sénégal. Demain les mollahs? La question musulmane et les partis politiques au Sénégal de 1946 à nos jours*. Paris: Karthala, 1985.

Mbow, Penda. 'Senegal: The Return of Personalism', *Journal of Democracy* 19 (2008): 156–69.

Mögenburg, Ilka. *Die Parteienlandschaft im Senegal – tragfähige Grundlage der Demokratisierung?* Münster/ Hamburg: Lit, 2002.

Moroff, Anika. 'Party Bans in Africa – An Empirical Overview'. *Democratization* 17, no. 4 (2010): 618–41.

Moroff, Anika, and Matthias Basedau. 'An Effective Measure of Institutional Engineering? Ethnic Party Bans in Africa'. *Democratization* 17, no. 4 (2010): 666–86.

Mozaffar, Shaheen, and Richard Vengroff. 'A 'Whole System' Approach to the Choice of Electoral Rules in Democratizing Countries: Senegal in Comparative Perspective'. *Electoral Studies* 21 (2002): 601–16.

Osei, Anja. *Party-Voter Linkage in Ghana and Senegal*. Unpublished PhD thesis, Leipzig, 2010.

Schaffer, Frederick C. *Democracy in Translation. Understanding Politics in an Unfamiliar Culture*. Cornell: Cornell UP, 2000.

Thiam, Assane. 'Une constitution ça se révise. Relativisme constitutionnel et état de droit au Sénégal', *Politique Africaine* 108 (2007): 145–53.

Tiné, Alioune. 'Du multiple à l'un et vice versa? Essai sur le multipartisme au Sénégal (1974-1996)'. *Polis. Revue Camerounaise de Science Politique* 3 (1997): 61–102.

Villalón, Leonardo A. *Islamic Society and State Power in Senegal: Disciples and Citizens in Fatick*, Cambridge: Cambridge UP, 1995.

Villalón, Leonardo A. 'Generational Changes, Political Stagnation and the Evolving Dynamics of Religion and Politics in Senegal'. *Africa Today* 46 (1999): 129–47.

Wantchekon, Leonard et al. *Support for Competitive Politics and Government Performance: Public Perceptions of Democracy in Senegal*. Afrobarometer Working Paper No. 77, 2007.

Wiseman, John A. *Democracy in Black Africa: Survival and Revival*. New York: Paragon House, 1990.

Young, Crawford, and Babacar Kanté. 'Governance, Democracy and the 1988 Senegalese Election', in *Governance and Politics in Africa*, ed. Goran Hyden and Michael Bratton, 63–70. Boulder, CO: Lynne Rienner, 1992.

Ziemer, Klaus. 'Senegal' in *Politische Organisation und Repräsentation in Afrika*, ed. Franz Nuscheler and Klaus Ziemer, 1809–1870. Berlin: de Gruyter, 1978.

Index

For Product Safety Concerns and Information please contact our EU
representative GPSR@taylorandfrancis.com
Taylor & Francis Verlag GmbH, Kaufingerstraße 24, 80331 München, Germany

9 781138 946491